THE REAL WORLD ORDER

THE REAL WORLD ORDER

Zones of Peace / Zones of Turmoil

REVISED EDITION

MAX SINGER

AND

AARON WILDAVSKY

Chatham House Publishers
Chatham, New Jersey

THE REAL WORLD ORDER
Zones of Peace / Zones of Turmoil
REVISED EDITION

Chatham House Publishers, Inc.
Box One, Chatham, New Jersey 07928

PUBLISHER: Edward Artinian
PRODUCTION SUPERVISOR: Katharine Miller
COVER DESIGN: Lawrence Ratzkin
COMPOSITION: Bang, Motley, Olufsen
PRINTING AND BINDING: R.R. Donnelley & Sons Company

LIBRARY OF CONGRESS CATALOGING-IN-PUBLICATION DATA

Singer, Max, 1931–
    The real world order : zones of peace, zones of turmoil /
Max Singer and Aaron Wildavsky. — Rev. ed.
        p.   cm.
    Includes bibliographical references and index.
    ISBN 1-56643-031-3
        1. Peaceful change (International relations)   2. Cold War.
3. World politics—1989–   I. Wildavsky, Aaron B.   II. Title.
JX1952.S6795   1996
327.1'72—dc20   95-33627
                                                          CIP

Manufactured in the United States of America
        10 9 8 7 6 5 4 3 2 1

*To the memory of Herman Kahn,
from whom the authors learned about
optimism and many other things;
he would have gloried in the world's
brilliant prospects.*

CONTENTS

Part II: New Policy Thinking for the Real World Order

TABLES

ACKNOWLEDGMENTS

This book began for me when I became unhappy with the interpretation of foreign policy news in the media and among my colleagues in academia. Apparently, if bad things happened in the world, that meant there was no new world order. That the great changes were not to be found in Somalia or Bosnia but in the democracies seemed absent from everyone's consciousness. I thought there was growing good amid the bad, that what was true of one part of the world was not true of all. So I dropped a note to my long-time sometime collaborator, Max Singer, expressing my disagreement with what continues to be current wisdom, thinking that among those I know he was most likely to remain unaffected by the climate of opinion. He responded with a deluge of papers. Thanks, Max.

— Aaron Wildavsky

When Aaron wrote to me in the spring of 1991, I sent him something I had written about how "the next world order" could be understood only if two parts of the world were considered separately. The piece I sent him was too much for an article and too little for a book, and I asked Aaron what he thought I should do with it. He said, "Let's do a book together"; this is the result. Thanks, Aaron.

Former colleagues at the Hudson Institute provided invaluable help in writing this book—in addition to the education they provided when I worked at Hudson. I thank Francis Armbruster, Raymond Gastil, Martin Zlotnick, and Andrew Caranfil. I also appreciate the willingness of Louis Sohn, Richard Pipes, and Allan Gerson to comment on drafts of individual chapters. Conversations with Eugene Rostow, Constantine Menges, and Joseph Churba were also helpful (although our talk was mostly about our disagreements). Jane Jacobs's valuable comments on an earlier expression of the idea of competitive subnational units of government are reflected in chapter 6. Michael Ledeen first convinced me that the fall of communism had actually begun and taught me other things as well.

My wife, Suzanne, is not only a wise influence on my perspective but also a professional editor; our marriage has flourished despite the valuable improvements her work has made in this book. My son Saul, who is my favorite student, has recently become a gentle critic for whose help I am grateful.

— Max Singer

The main lines of the book were agreed on by the fall of 1991. Since then we have added illustrations and policy suggestions, but we have not changed our description of the nature of the world order. In particular, the judgment that the Soviet/Russian situation was out of control and that when it stabilized Russia would be weak was our view from the beginning. Although we have been pleasantly surprised by how relatively peaceful and benign things have been so far in the former Soviet Union, our view that the fundamental stresses and weaknesses we discuss in chapter 5 are likely to lead eventually to breakdown has not changed.

1 June 1993   — Max Singer and Aaron Wildavsky

Aaron is not here to work with me on these revisions, and I miss him. He died after a summer of cancer while the first edition was in press. It was a sad day, not only for his family, friends, and me, but also for his profession and the world.

Aaron is still the coauthor because the book is essentially as we wrote it. I know him well enough to be confident that he would have agreed with the revisions.

This edition adds a new idea to the previous volume about how the democracies should respond to the challenge of events in the former Yugo-slavia, and it clarifies and corrects some minor or peripheral errors in the original text without altering our basic vision of the shape of the world.

The expert discussion in the two years since we finished the first edition increases my confidence that this vision is the correct way to begin to understand international affairs in this generation (and perhaps the next). But I have come to appreciate how difficult it is—especially for experts—to adjust one's thinking to respond to a profoundly changed world.

1 December 1995   — Max Singer

INTRODUCTION

Whether this book is optimistic or pessimistic depends on whether a century is a short time or a long time.

It is impossible to prevent most of the world from being subject to violence, injustice, poverty, and disorder for at least several more generations. But we believe that a process is well started that will make most of the world peaceful, democratic, and wealthy by historical standards by about a century from now, or perhaps two.

Since human society has been dominated by poverty, tyranny, and war for thousands of years, it is easy to argue that our vision of the spread of wealth, democracy, and peace in "only" another century or so is too optimistic. (And we are not at all free from doubt about it.) But since people's lives are shorter than a century, our view of the world also says that billions of human beings are doomed to have their lives cut short or mutilated by poverty, tyranny, and violence. Some may see this view as pessimistic, because a century is such a long time.

We care less about labels such as "optimist" or "pessimist" than about the implications for action. The specter of suffering, injustice, and unnecessary death in the zones of turmoil is a goad to action, even though they are mostly temporary and partly unavoidable evils. The tasks of speeding the spread of wealth, democracy, and peace and limiting the damage from the turmoil of transition are urgent challenges for individuals and for the United States and the other democracies. If we can be wise and energetic in reinforcing the current trends, we can enable millions and millions of people to have more decent lives.

The inference we draw from our "optimistic" view, that our part of the world is now richer and safer, is that we can afford, and have a responsibility, to speed the day when more of the world will be richer and safer.

This book presents a perspective that makes it possible not only to balance "the best of times and the worst of times" but to understand how our current world order will work. There is always some kind of world order, although usually it is not very orderly. The world order may be more or less stable, lawful, decent, or violent, but there is always some pattern of forces and relationships that determines how the critical decisions are made in the world. The opposite of "orderly" in this sense is not "anarchic" but "random" or "unpredictable."

The term "world order" as we use it signifies an analytic structure that makes possible understanding and prediction, hence policy and diplomacy. Like the old order, the current world order (or the "new world disorder," as some are complaining recently) will be based on the system of states, although forces and arrangements that are international or subnational will have increasing importance. But, within the broad structure, new patterns, not based on military power, will be increasingly important.

Now, as in the past, quality is more important than quantity, for both military and economic success. A high-quality military force from an advanced society can defeat a larger military force from a more primitive society. The exact ratio depends on particulars, but now, as in the past, the ratio can in some circumstances be very high (even 10 to 1). Military power depends, in addition to equipment, on the training, discipline, organization, and strategy of the troops and officers and on the intelligence, initiative, and motivation of all personnel. The highest military performance demands the same human and social qualities required for building a productive economy. So a society that cannot operate the highest-quality economy cannot operate the highest-quality fighting force.

What can we mean by suggesting that there has been a "qualitative revolution" that makes the world different? In addition to the ages-long advantage of quality over quantity, modern technology confers more decisive advantages. Figuratively, those nations that cannot produce and program missiles to fly around buildings on their way to hitting their precise targets are no longer serious military competitors against those who can. The quality/quantity gap is now more absolute, making it very difficult, if not impossible, for quantity to overcome quality and will. Although quality can become so complacent that it becomes vulnerable to being outwitted, it now enjoys a decisive advantage.

Why do we believe that this world order will be different than any of those that have preceded it? For one thing, the world's major democracies (if not exactly "the good guys," at least "the less-worse guys") have a near monopoly on the most effective military force. Not even a wholly unlikely alliance of all the world's dictatorships would be strong enough to defeat the United States, let alone the world's democracies.

Modern technology and productivity make a drastic difference in how defeat and victory are counted. Whereas, in the past, a country became victorious by conquering more people or more resources, now such victories are self-defeating. Only countries with high-quality populations and institutions are worth taking, precisely those nations—for example, Taiwan,

Switzerland, Japan—that are the least likely targets for successful military aggression.

The two propositions together—the overall qualitative revolution and the military dominance of democracies—explain why we believe that the United States will follow what might be called the "reverse domino theory," namely, it will multilateralize its military and economic intervention in the rest of the world. It will seek to moderate the behavior of feckless countries by filtering its activities through a variety of multilateral agencies and groups. In short, what some opponents of American military intervention have long wanted has, with the end of the cold war, become a reality. The words are not there yet, but the multilateral music is playing for all to hear.

The first part of the book describes the real world order, beginning with the division of the world into zones of peace and democracy and zones of turmoil and development. The second part discusses policies for this world order and makes a number of suggestions.

Because the current world order will be different than the one with which we are familiar, "old thinking" using outdated assumptions will produce poor policy and will miss opportunities. Part II puts on the table our efforts to apply "new thinking" that is responsive to the real world order. We assume that once they appreciate the nature of the current world order as we describe it, others can do "new thinking" at least as well as we can, but we believe that the fundamental features of the current world order described in part I are as inevitable for those who may disagree with our views on policy as for those who share them. *The Real World Order*'s special contribution is to provide common ground for a new debate about foreign policy, suitable for the new world in which we now live.

PART ONE

The Real World Order

CHAPTER 1

A TALE OF TWO WORLDS

The key to understanding the real world order is to separate the world into two parts. One part is zones of peace, wealth, and democracy. The other part is zones of turmoil, war, and development. There are useful things to say about the zones of peace; and there are useful things to say about the zones of turmoil; but if you try to talk about the world as a whole all you can get is falsehoods or platitudes.[1]

The zones of peace and democracy include Western Europe, the United States and Canada, Japan, and the Antipodes, which together have about 15 percent of the world's population. The rest of the world, including Eastern and Southeastern Europe, the territory of the former Soviet Union, and most of Africa, Asia, and Latin America, is composed, for now, of zones of turmoil and development.

The countries in the zones of peace and democracy will not be divided into competing military blocs seeking to balance each other's power. Their political relationships with each other will not be substantially influenced by how the military power of one compares with that of another—except for differences of scale, such as between the United States and the European democracies.

There probably will be plenty of national and other conflict in the zones of peace, but the decisive special characteristic of this conflict is that no one will believe that it can lead to war. Moreover, the countries in the zones of peace and democracy will have most of the power in the world, so they will not face a serious threat to their national survival or freedom, regardless of the outcome of conflicts in the other zones.

The fact that today England, France, Germany, Japan, Italy, and the United States cannot imagine going to war with each other again does not mean that they never will. But it does mean that in these countries there will not be political support for any major program that depends on the possibility of war with one of the other members of the "big six." This practical political conclusion—with which few people would disagree—

3

would have major implications even if the circumstances were just a temporary phase, and we will argue that it is much more.

Some security experts believe that the current absence of the danger of war within the "big six" is a short-term phenomenon and that prudent national security planning requires each country to take into account the possibility of war with any other major power. Of course one or more of the big-six democracies could change character and become a security threat to the others, or perhaps go to war with another without having changed character. But the likelihood of such a war is too remote to influence policy. It would be false prudence for any of the big six to build policy on the basis of the possibility of war with another member of the group.

Since the United States and the other great democracies will benefit significantly by recognizing the new reality that not every power is a potential enemy, they should put aside the classic military principle of paying attention to "capabilities, not intentions." Even the most cautious protector of national security in the big six should make policy on the assumption that there is no longer a need to consider the possibility of war with another member of that group. If the need arises later, there will be enough time to change policy.

The bottom line is this: *Since the countries in the zones of peace will no longer take seriously the possibility of going to war with one another, the current world order is different from all previous ones.*

A key reason why the zones of peace can be expected to have internal peace is that all the countries in these zones are modern democracies. A central pillar of this world order is that the modern democracies will not go to war with one another. Chapter 2 argues that the reason they will not is that they are are all democracies and considers the limits and doubts about this critical proposition.[2]

We stress, however, that the *reason* why the big six will not war with one another again is secondary; the main point is that they will not. International politics will be shaped by the political reality that *something* about the countries in the zones of peace prevents them from taking seriously the possibility of going to war with one another—and will continue to do so for many years. This reality is not ephemeral; it is a deep reflection of the fundamental condition of the societies and their histories.

Our major thesis is not about the *cause* of the peacefulness of the zones of peace but rather the *effect* of this reality on international politics. The fundamental differences between the areas of the world where the major democracies are and the rest of the world do not depend on why they and their neighbors are no longer a threat to each other.

Although terms like "great democracies" are frequently used in this book, someone who does not accept our view of the importance of democracy can treat such phrases simply as labels for the specific countries to which they refer. Most of what we say is just as true if you substitute "big six" where we have written "great democracies." Our phrase does not require accepting the notion of peace being based on democracy.

The undoubted fact is that for the first time in history a small number of modern democracies will have most of the world's power.[3] One of the important reasons is the gradual change in the technical basis of power, the continuing triumph of quality over quantity, brainpower over muscle power, of mind and imagination over physical resources, of the uncontrolled order of freedom over the rigid order of central control and planning.[4]

The real world order in the democratic part of the world will be fundamentally different from any past world order. Never in history have there been large diverse areas, containing most of the world's power, in which no country faced substantial military danger to its independence or survival.

Since the fundamental facts underlying international relations in the zones of peace and democracy have never existed before, the nature of the international order in these zones will be new. In thinking about the future of conflict in the zones of peace we are all amateurs; no one has relevant experience. The lessons of history all need adjustment because they all come from fundamentally different worlds.

Human nature will not be different. Domestic politics will work basically in familiar ways and will influence foreign policies much as it has in the past. There will be ample sources of conflict between countries, although most of the conflict will not be about issues of national life or death, or even basic national welfare (which was also often true in the past). The prediction of peace in these zones is not a prediction of amity and good feeling. We do not know whether the democracies will continue to avoid serious conflict among themselves.

In the past, one of two factors ultimately dominated the conflicts between nations. The normal situation was that the contending nations might eventually go to war with one another, so they had to resolve their conflict in a way that reflected their willingness to fight and their expectations about what the results of fighting would be. This is not to say that the strong always took what they wanted from the weak. There have always been many considerations leading the strong to act "reasonably" with other nations. But serious conflict always was influenced in some way by the shadow of military power.

The recent situation was that conflict among the democracies was less important than their common danger from the Soviet Union. The question of whether shared democracy prevented fighting was not reached because the democracies were prevented from fighting—or expecting to fight— among themselves by their joint interests in containing the Soviet Union. The danger from the Soviet Union was more important than issues that divided the democracies.

The fundamental change that will challenge the historian's ability to understand the future is that conflict in the zones of peace will not be settled on the basis of perceptions of fundamental national security requirements and dangers. In the past, even when statesmen spoke about ideology, economics, international law, world opinion, and the like, most people and most national leaders understood deep in their bones that their nation's safety was ultimately protected only by the strength of their national army. They believed that someday the nation could expect to survive only if it had or could produce an army—or allies—strong enough to protect it.

While there was elegant talk of subtle issues, at bottom governments always asked themselves what they had to do to make sure that their country would survive. All other problems had to give way before the need to do what was necessary for survival. Prudent leaders could follow other diplomatic interests only after they had satisfied the requirements of their theory of national survival.

Practically everyone believed that if a nation was (much) more powerful than its neighbors, it would use its power to control or conquer them.[5] This traditional understanding of the ways of the world, which will continue to have substantial validity in the zones of turmoil, will not disappear quickly in the zones of peace, even though it has become largely anachronistic. But gradually public and leaders' perceptions will change. Concern about military threats to national survival will slowly lose importance. The result will be a different set of feelings about the military and about the relations among countries. This is such a deep change that it is very difficult to understand its timing or the nature of its effect.

It is hard for people to give up old ways of thinking. All of the recent discussion concerning policy within the zones of peace is deeply anachronistic. Most academics and diplomats have so far failed to grasp how different the foreseeable future in the zones of peace will be from the world with which they are familiar. The most basic foundations have changed, and it is not yet possible to grasp all the effects the changes will have. Thoughtful commentators on the post-cold-war world cannot bring themselves to give up traditional concerns—the German danger, the Japanese danger, the Russian danger, Central European backsliding, and so forth.

They recognize how remote these dangers are, but they muffle that recognition by using vague warnings about things like "confrontations which threaten our stability in subtle and indirect ways."[6] They talk about the biggest problems that will exist with open-ended phrases. But in our view they miss the fundamental distinction between past national security concerns and future ones in the zones of peace; in the past there were national life-and-death military issues, in the future there probably will not be, at least for a generation.

While it is possible to talk about how democracies may get into conflicts in the Third World, the decisive point is that the World War I model —of small disputes outside the main arena leading to big wars between the central powers—is unlikely to apply in the future. Conflict between England and Germany in their former colonial areas will not lead England and Germany to go to war, any more than bitter conflict between their soccer teams will. In the zones of democracy there will not be competitive military power blocs worrying that the outcome of some dispute in the zones of turmoil might change the balance between them. Strategist Colin Gray is wrong when he says, "it is a certainty that balance-of-power problems on a large scale will return."[7]

Of course there are always problems, dangers, needs for military force, uncertainties, and grounds for concern. It is right to draw attention to such matters, to consider how to respond to them, to recognize that the millennium has not arrived, that the end of the cold war has not solved everything. But to talk about these problems—the worst that we will be facing—without stressing that they are fundamentally different from the national life-and-death issues we are used to, is a triumph of the taste for continuity over the ability to recognize the decisive.

Part of the reason people have failed to recognize how fundamentally different things will be in the zones of peace is that most people ask themselves "Is the world basically different than it used to be?" and answer "No" because they see familiar patterns in places like the former Yugoslavia. Trying to answer for the whole world forces you to miss what is new. The correct answer is, "No, the world isn't fundamentally different, but part of it is." You can only appreciate the difference when you think about the world in two parts.

Unfortunately, only 15 percent of the world's population now lives in zones of peace and democracy. Most people now live in zones of turmoil and development where poverty, war, tyranny, and anarchy will continue to devastate lives.

The basic description of the international order in the zones of turmoil is that it will be traditional, with the nineteenth century probably as good a model as any (except for colonialism). Past experience will be much more of a guide to how things will work in the zones of turmoil than it will be to developments in the zones of peace. A lot of old-fashioned history will still be seen in the zones of turmoil. Looking back fifty years from now, the recent horrors in Bosnia and Somalia will not seem unusual.

But these zones can expect not only violent and deadly turbulence but also the difficult processes of economic and political development, which will cause wealth, democracy, and peace gradually to spread through these zones. (This would be an optimistic claim if we said that it would happen quickly or painlessly. It would be pessimistic if we said that it would take longer than a millennium. As it is, it is dramatically neutral.) The people in the zones of turmoil are not worse than those who have succeeded else-where—and ultimately it is the people who count. And each new example of success makes it easier for others to follow.

Of course, it is a great oversimplification to say that the world is di-vided into only two parts, suggesting that each part is uniform. The zones of turmoil and development are especially diverse, since they cover most of the world. What we are really saying is that the fundamentals of interna-tional relations in one part of the world, the zones of peace, are different than they were in the past. Zones of turmoil is just a name for "the rest of the world" outside of the zones of peace. The main generalization about these zones is that they are not like the zones of peace; they are more like past experience. And within them there is great variety.

There are many ways to divide the non–zones of peace into different subunits. But this book focuses on one fundamental point: all the world outside the zones of peace is different from the zones of peace. The first thing to grasp, then, is that there are two parts of the world. Then we can also learn that the second part is not all the same, but actually three or thir-teen different parts. The more distinctions you make, the better you under-stand; but sometimes a single elementary distinction is crucial and is lost when it is included with others.

A large part of the area of the zones of turmoil is already peaceful most or all of the time, and there are a number of democracies in these zones. And most of the countries have moved a good share of the way along the path from traditional poverty to the threshold of modern wealth. Outside the zones of peace, however, there is not yet any geographic area where peace and democracy are as well established as they are in, for ex-ample, Western Europe or North America.

There is no policy that the United States and the other democracies can follow that will prevent the zones of turmoil and development from having coups and revolutions, civil and international wars, and internal massacres and bloody repression—that is, at least mild forms of the kinds of experience that the zones of peace had until recently. For the zones of turmoil as a whole, stability is at best a meaningless goal. Chapter 3 considers the prospects for these zones in greater depth, and chapters 7 and 8 discuss how U.S. policy should respond. The challenge for those who want to help is to accelerate development in the zones of turmoil so that it is largely completed in one century, rather than two or three.

Chapter 4 tells why we have not said more about nuclear war and weapons in this summary of the prospects for the next century. It also contains suggestions for reducing the dangers from nuclear weapons in both the short and the long run.

Because the democracies of the zones of peace have such a predominance of economic and military power—plus the psychological advantage of having already come through the painful development processes with which the countries of the zones of turmoil are still wrestling—nothing that happens in the zones of turmoil will threaten the existence or freedom of the countries of the zones of peace. (But see the discussion beginning on page 171 of the need to prevent a series of "Yugoslavias" in Southeastern Europe.)

One near exception might be political manipulation of the oil of the Persian Gulf if it all came into the hands of a single power. But the probability of that is low. The enmities and differences among the people and countries there are so great that they are unlikely to be united peacefully, and Desert Storm demonstrated that they cannot be united militarily against democratic resistance.

Although it will be physically possible for countries in the developing world to use long-range (or covert) delivery of weapons of mass destruction to kill large numbers of people in the zones of peace, this will not be a politically realistic threat, particularly if the United States or Western Europe deploys missile defense systems. In any event, it will not be a threat to national survival or independence.

Why We Will Be Better Off

The end of the cold war has brought a flood of glum views of the future. The tone of the Op Ed pages has ranged from pale gray to nearly coal black discussing the replacement of the Soviet Union by four new nuclear powers, the bloodbath in the former Yugoslavia, the grim future of democracy in Russia, the Iraqi demonstration that neither the United States nor the United Nations is qualified to prevent fearsome slaughters in the Third World, and the specter of nuclear or chemical war coming closer and closer.

We believe this pattern of opinion is a classic example of low morale, an emotional malady evidenced by a strong tendency to use whatever standards of judgment are too high to pass. With reasonable standards of judgment, the world's future is remarkably bright and is sharply improved from the recent past, although there are indeed plenty of problems to work on and many to come.

Our biggest gain is that the United States no longer faces any danger of defeat. While the Soviet Union was alive, there was at least a slight danger that the United States could lose its freedom or be defeated in a war. Nor is there any longer a powerful country spending billions of dollars as part of a political strategy to weaken the West wherever any opportunity could be found.

There was an enemy with whom the United States could fight a war that could cost 50 or 100 million American lives. Such an enemy no longer exists, nor does it seem plausible that there will be such an enemy during the next generation. No threat now existing or on the horizon remotely approaches the size of the threat that the West lived with for decades and that has suddenly been lifted from us. We have been given a Cadillac and are drowning in moans about the fullness of the ashtray and the need to buy gas.

A happy by-product of the disappearance of the Soviet Union is that the world is relieved from having to pretend to believe in the moral equivalence of superpowers; we can again understand that democracies are morally better and militarily less threatening.

There is every kind of foreboding and hand wringing about growing conflict among the United States, Japan, and a united Europe, and much alarm about renewed German dominance. But no one claims to be able to imagine that the United States will have a war with Japan or Germany or Europe, or that there will be a war between France and Germany, much less between England and France. And when one gets realistic, it is apparent that none of these countries will have a war with Russia either, even in the likely event that Russian democracy is soon replaced by a new dictatorship which brings many old communists back.

How much tragic history would be wiped out if the wars among those countries had disappeared two centuries ago instead of in our own generation! Why is there no joy that for the first time there is no prospect of war among the leading powers of the world? It is true that there is still a slight possibility of war with Russia or China, but it is very slight, they are only marginally leading powers, and they are very likely to become even less dangerous during the next few years. And it is not this danger that makes people so grim.

There is distressing disorder in the six-sevenths of the world that is not yet wealthy and democratic. Millions of people will die unnecessarily in the next century—from starvation and disease, from war, and from government murder—and we cannot stop these horrors from happening. Most of the world is going to be more or less like the world has always been.

But it is not usually regarded as a tragedy if things stay the same, especially when the world also has the blessing of the end of communism. More important, while it is true that we in the democracies cannot make things right, there is every reason to expect that there will be much less of some of the worst things in the next century than there was in this.

Although there will be roughly twice as many people, the authors have good reason to think (although we cannot be sure) that wars will not kill 40 million people in the next century, as they did in this. We have better reason to think (although, again, we cannot be sure) that governments will not kill well over 100 million people in the next century, as they did in this. And probably less than half as many people will die of starvation and malnutrition in the next century as did in this.

On the positive side, in the next century billions more people will live long enough to know their grandchildren. A much larger percentage of people will live in countries where the government is chosen by reasonably free elections. More than ten times as many people will be able to read and will have high school educations, with all that means about being able to be in touch with the wide world. None of this amounts to heaven, but since when do we expect heaven on earth? If fundamental evils are reduced in each century, should gloom really be our predominant feeling?

It is true that the international order in much of the world is basically what it has always been. But two other powerful facts stand out: For the first time, the scourge of war has been lifted from at least one-seventh of the world. Not only that. The one-seventh of the world that will be different in the future is the part we live in. And it has such a big share of the world's power that we do not have to be afraid of the rest of the world, and can hope to be a favorable influence on it. Also, the powerful forces of economic and political development are spreading through the other six-sevenths of the world. And all over the world people are racing to discard the statist delusions that have been one of the biggest obstacles to economic advance in most countries.[8]

While all these statements are made boldly here (the necessary qualifications and justification are provided later) the reason they will strike many as surprising is not that most writers have disagreed with them. There is relatively little in the current discussion that would challenge the center of these propositions. They answer questions that people do not ask. The gloom comes, not from disagreement with these happy estimates, but from choosing to ignore the good news, focusing on things that need to be complained about, and finding standards of judgment that will not be met. That may be the right way to look for an agenda for action. It is dead wrong when looking for perspective, or when setting the mood.

We are not in the business of countering unnecessary gloom or making people happy, nor do we believe that progress is inevitable. This book reports good news and bad news. We do not argue that the world is getting better in every way, or that people will be happier in the future. We do not know about that. What this book aims to do is to make it easier to understand what is happening in the world—how it is different from, and how it is like, our experience in the past.

A different approach from ours, one frequently used to induce the United States to do more for the world, is to reject "optimistic" reports and charge that because Americans have been evil and selfish the world is not improving and is in crisis ("the rich are getting richer and the poor, poorer" and "we are destroying our habitat"). This approach is not intellectually sound or idealistic or effective. Even worse, preaching guilt and doom to get support for remedies has often produced remedies that kill instead of cure.

The best way to get popular American support for efforts to help others is an accurate understanding of how good the long-term prospects are for us and for the world, how much success we have already produced, and why our system works as well as it does. The correct "optimistic" description of the prospects for the future can help the democracies to have the pride and self-confidence they need to be effective. The democracies' ability to help others depends on their having a strong belief in and understanding of what they have been doing: democracy, market economies, and ethical and social values.[9]

Such a belief in ourselves does not imply that we in the democracies can impose our ways on others. Each society has to have its own forms, and each has to learn for itself the truths it will live by. Moreover, because the democracies learned those lessons only slowly and at great cost, and because we still do not understand our own systems well and continue to make costly mistakes, and may fall away from democracy ourselves, our confidence needs to be combined with humility before societies that have not yet learned.

Feelings of American guilt and failure, perceptions of crisis and impending disaster, are such misunderstandings of the world that they stand in the way of effective programs to make the world better. Since there is good reason to believe that current trends will bring wealth, peace, and democracy within a century or two, there is a lot to lose. We need to understand the process now working, to make sure that we do not make radical changes that interrupt it.

Unfortunately, radical change and slow progress are often enemies. If things are mostly going in the right direction, people are usually reluctant to adopt radical new measures that might jeopardize the progress that is taking place. Therefore those who seek radical change insist that things are getting worse and deny that there will be any progress at all unless their radical remedies are used. But those who deny the forces that are now slowly spreading wealth, democracy, and peace around the world will have difficulty making sure that their radical proposals do not interfere with what is working now.

We have no quarrel with anyone who recognizes the process of spreading wealth, democracy, and peace, who tries to understand that process with some respect, and who promotes radical change to make it go faster. But it is prudent to beware of those who deny the virtues and prospects of the systems that have brought wealth, democracy, and peace to our one-seventh of the world and that seem likely to bring those blessings to much more of the world in the next century. Approaches that reject the successful democratic systems and their underlying values (as communism did) risk going in the wrong direction. For thousands of years almost all efforts to solve the problem of relations among nations failed, which suggests that it may be easier to find wrong answers than right ones.

In summary, the dominating new features of the international order in the zones of peace are that the countries there are modern, wealthy democracies that will not go to war with one another and that each country's safety and bargaining power will not depend on its military forces or its position in a delicate balance of power. Traditional political and diplomatic behavior will govern, except as it is changed by these new facts, which will have pervasive significance.

The dominating features of the new international order in the zones of turmoil and development will be traditional and familiar conflicts and imperatives. But the traditional pattern will be significantly modified by new factors. These include the changing nature of wealth, which makes land and asset grabbing much less attractive than it used to be, and less attractive than improving a nation's social and intellectual quality; the example provided by the zones of peace and democracy; the requirements and results of changing to become more productive; and the responses of the democracies to conflict in the zones of turmoil.

Thus the international order in the zones of peace and democracy will be new and different—but with important familiar elements; and the international order in the zones of turmoil and development will be basically traditional—but with important new elements growing in importance.

If we are looking for a world as it should be, the next world order will fail us. We must expect violence and poverty to take many millions of human lives. But if we feel that vast improvement over the performance of this century should be called "success," then we have good reason to look forward to the current world order with confidence that it will be better than any that preceded it.

Notes

1. Gaddis's useful discussion of forces of integration and forces of fragmentation in the world would have been much more powerful if he had talked about the very different ways these forces will work in the two parts of the world, the great difference between their significance in the zones of peace as contrasted with their significance in the zones of turbulence. See John Lewis Gaddis, *The United States and the End of the Cold War: Implications, Reconsiderations, Provocations* (New York: Oxford University Press, 1992).

2. Analysis of the proposition that democracies do not go to war with one another, the evidence for it, and the reason it has been so generally overlooked in this century can be found, among other places, in R.J. Rummel's *Understanding Conflict and War* (Beverly Hills, Calif.: Sage, 1975–81), vols. 1–5, and *The Conflict Helix: Principles and Practices of Interpersonal, Social, and International Conflict and Cooperation* (New Brunswick, N.J.: Transaction, 1991). The extensive recent literature on this issue until 1993 is reviewed and analyzed in "Democracy and Proclivity to War," a paper by Kerry G. Herron of the University of New Mexico, delivered at the annual meeting of the Western Political Science Association, Pasadena, California, March 1993. Herron reports a "convergence" on this point in the work of twenty scholars who disagree on other related questions, mostly in the last twelve years.

3. While the big six produce "only" about 20 percent of the Gross World Product, the remainder is so dispersed that the phrase "most of the power" is justified. (And the great democracies also have other elements of power beyond that represented by the GNP.)

4. George Gilder has eloquently presented the reasons why modern technology strengthens freedom and works against rigid and centralized command systems. See, for example, his *Microcosm* (New York: Simon and Schuster, 1989). Friedrich Hayek has done most to celebrate the virtues of the "spontaneous order." See his *The Constitution of Liberty* (Chicago: University of Chicago Press, 1960).

5. This view is codified in the academic doctrine of neorealism, which locates the causes of countries' international behavior in their relative power in international systems, and it now has to explain why the United States will not follow this time-worn path. Kenneth Waltz, *Theory of International Politics* (New York: Random House: 1979).

6. Sir Michael Howard, *London Times,* 31 December 1991.

7. Colin Gray, "Strategic Sense: Strategic Nonsense," *The National Interest,* Fall 1992, 11–19.

8. In the first edition Aaron convinced me that we should not mention another point on which we agreed: neither population growth, potential shortages of natural resources, nor dangers to the environment give us any reason to temper our positive view of the state of the world as we enter the twenty-first century. He felt that challenging orthodoxy on this point would turn many readers away, and that it would be a mistake to bring in an emotional controversy largely unrelated to our book.

But since our first edition the united front of environmental doomsaying has been broken, most notably by Gregg Easterbrook's recent book, *A Moment on the Earth* (New York: Viking). Most of its 700 pages is a deeply felt and rationally argued plea to fellow environmentalists to abandon their insistence that the world's environment is worsening, as well as their exaggeration of almost every danger and denial or downplaying of all good news about it.

While the same facts have been presented by other people for a number of years (see my *Passage to a Human World* [Indianapolis, Ind.: Hudson Institute, 1987] and Aaron Wildavsky, *Searching for Safety* [New Brunswick, N.J.: Transaction, 1987]), I think Easterbrook's book—and some other recent voices—are signs of a turning point. Easterbrook is a liberal and a good writer. The *New Yorker* published a long excerpt from his book in its 10 April 1995 issue, almost exactly thirty years after it published an excerpt from Rachel Carson's *Silent Spring.*

The *New Yorker* sometimes leads trends, but it has an exquisite sense of where its audience, which includes a major share of media leadership, is ready to go. It is not likely to be alone in questioning the near-hysterical view of "the environmental crisis" expressed by Vice-President Gore and leaders of large national environmental groups, who depend on mail-order public fund-raising. If the *New Yorker* questions the orthodoxy, it is safe for us to do so too.

I think Aaron would agree that now we can afford to reveal that we too do not believe that overpopulation and environmental pollution give grounds for thinking that the world is getting worse. Environmental disasters are not going to make the international economic and political patterns that we describe in this book irrelevant.

9. As Michael Novak has emphasized, all three characteristics are essential parts of our system. See Michael Novak, *The Spirit of Democratic Capitalism* (New York: Simon and Schuster, 1982).

CHAPTER 2

DEMOCRACY AND MODERN WEALTH
ARE NEW IN THE WORLD

Real peace—not only the absence of war but also freedom from fear of war—is what makes the international order in the zones occupied by modern mass-wealth democracies something new in the world. This chapter discusses the connections between modern wealth, democracy, and peace; the nature of the new kind of international order in the zones of peace and democracy; and the limits and uncertainties of our central hypothesis.

It is hard enough to understand the zones of peace and democracy when we look at them by themselves; if we tried to think about the zones of turmoil and development at the same time it would be impossible. The central point we make about the world order is that what we say in this chapter will not apply to most of the world—just the part we live in. And the dominating reality of the rest of the world no longer applies to the zones discussed here—although it did until recently.

While there have been many democracies through history, most of the countries of the zones of peace are a particular kind of democracy that never existed before a few decades ago—modern, mass-high-wealth democracies, where the ordinary people are materially extremely well off by historic standards. The only way a country can achieve such wealth is by having a highly productive citizenry operating a complex information-intensive economy—what can be called a "high-quality economy." Both the way these societies produce their wealth and what they buy with it pull them toward being democratic and peaceful (but do not guarantee those results).

We could use the label "technologically advanced" rather than the label "modern" to describe these countries, but "modern" describes social characteristics that make it possible for them to be "technologically advanced." Large amounts of oil make some small countries technologically advanced, but they do not produce modern economies. For our purposes, the most important thing about wealth is not what it buys but what produces it. What is important is the effects on the citizens of working and living in the kind of advanced economy that produces great wealth.

In a modern high-quality economy, almost all young people graduate from high school and many people have university educations. When they are young most people in these countries know their grandparents, and when they are old they know their grandchildren. They have relatively little experience with having close relatives die. Life is highly valued, families have few children, and the death of young people is shocking.

People in such wealthy countries are shielded from extensive experience with the violence of nature and from sustained physical adversity and hardship. Most of them work with their minds, and perhaps their fingers. Few people work with the strength of their backs or in occupations that involve violence. Success in such economies usually requires depending on other people, and on being dependable, on communicating effectively in a variety of relationships, on building a reputation and working for the future, on learning and teaching, and on motivating and coordinating the actions and interests of many individuals and organizations. And the people in modern economies learn to live with change.

Some of these effects of wealth and modernity came with the early stages of industrialization, which were characterized by the dominance of steel mills, railroads, and mass production of physical goods. But while such early industrial societies began the separation of people from the violence and primitiveness of nature, they were more violent and hierarchical than modern wealthy economies. Now the most advanced countries are characterized by the dominance of computers, electronic communication, and information industries, where subtlety, flexibility, and the motivation and organization of human creativity are more critical than mass and power. Selling, financing, and negotiating, as well as the productive power and efficiency of machines, determine who is successful. Persuasion rather than command is the predominant path to success.

While relationships in high-quality economies are by no means uniformly egalitarian, they are more egalitarian than in the heavy industry economies they are replacing. So it seems to us reasonable to believe that modern mass-wealth economies tend more strongly to lead people in the direction of democracy and peace than early industrial economies did.

High-quality economies also tend toward peace because they greatly reduce the importance of some of the things that people used to fight about. Modern mass wealth does not come from physical resources which can be taken from others and must be defended; it comes primarily from people's productive behavior, from a society and culture that encourages productive relationships. Countries become rich essentially by learning how to develop attitudes and relationships that enable people to work productively. The key to wealth is for people and society to learn how to make each hour of work produce more. (The technical definition of productivity is "the amount of the goods and services that people want which is produced by the average hour of work"—measured by the price at which the result of the hour's work is sold.)

In a modern high-quality society people have a large economic value. Their time is expensive. Training is expensive. People are the key to any organization's success. Large amounts of resources are used to protect people. Large costs result if someone is injured. Almost everything about the way the society operates makes it is clear that people are more important than things. One implication is pervasive: it does not make sense to sacrifice people to get territory or raw materials[1] because people are more valuable.

Moreover, the kind of work that makes a country wealthy cannot be done by conquered people who are reluctant or second-class citizens. Colonies cost far more than they produce. Certainly there are no natural resources—except conceivably the largest oil deposits—that are valuable enough to make it rational for a modern economy to go to war. It is very unlikely that there will be any case where aggression will make economic sense for one of the modern economies. Unfortunately, the fact that war would be bad economics for a modern country is no guarantee that a modern country will never go to war. But the reduction of economic reasons for war is useful, even if other reasons remain.

A striking fact about the world is that all twenty-four wealthy countries are democracies—excepting only Hong Kong, Kuwait, and Singapore.[2] We are using the category "wealthy country" to mean a country of at least 1 million people where people's life expectancy at birth is seventy-four or more years and where production per person is at least as high as in Portugal. Portugal is 40 percent as wealthy as the United States is now, or perhaps about as wealthy as the United States was somewhere around the time of World War I, although there is no way to make precise comparisons.[3]

The statistics also provide clear evidence that it is not wealth itself that is associated with democracy, but modern productive economies. There are four oil-rich countries with populations over 1 million (and four smaller ones).[4] None of these eight oil-rich countries is democratic. Conventionally they are called "wealthy," but because their wealth does not come from the productivity of their people, it is not associated with democracy. In contrast, most of the half dozen or so very small countries that are wealthy without having oil or other major natural resources are democratic. ("Very small" means fewer than one million people.)

Of course some democracies are not yet wealthy, which proves the obvious, that a country does not automatically and immediately become

TABLE 2.1

FOURTEEN SMALL WEALTHY COUNTRIES

	Democratic	*Undemocratic*
Oil wealth	0	8
Earned wealth	6	0

NOTE: This table is slightly more precise than is justified, because there is ambiguity about exactly which very small countries meet the standards of earned wealth and democracy. But the general message of the table is correct: democracy goes with earned wealth and it doesn't go with oil wealth.

wealthy by becoming a democracy. But the fact that essentially all wealthy countries are democracies is strong evidence that: (1) something about being wealthy makes a country likely to become democratic, (2) democracy may be necessary (or almost necessary) to become wealthy, or (3) both.

A good but unanswerable question is, Had Nazi Germany been democratic, would the German people have supported wars of conquest? At what material and human cost? Could Hitler have openly run death camps? Possibly, yet the far freer information available in a democracy might well have made a difference. While it is true that Hitler's Germany was a wealthy country by the standards of its time, it isn't clear whether or not such a dictatorship could have been an effective competitor in the current economic environment if it had not chosen war (although it is hard to imagine that it would have become poorer than Portugal).

Both South Korea and Taiwan, as their economies began to approach the most advanced stage, moved toward greater democracy from traditions that seem to offer little support for democracy. But we don't know the end of those stories yet. And the fact that we haven't yet seen a successful authoritarian modern economy doesn't prove that it cannot happen. We can't be sure that even the most ultramodern economy cannot become an aggressive tyranny.

A reasonable degree of humility requires us to recognize that there is a chance that any democracy, even the United States, might stop being democratic at some time in the future. No one knows enough to be sure how long democracy will last. However, as a practical matter, it is safe to make foreign policy on the assumption that the major democracies will continue to be democratic. But we have to remember that the history of modern democracy is short, that democracy may be fragile, at least in some countries, and that it may need to be protected against the storms of the future.

Germany and Japan are the major democracies that many people believe have the greatest chance of becoming nondemocratic again. (The United States is the only country that has been democratic since its beginning.) In both Germany and Japan democracy was installed by force after the defeat of the previous undemocratic regimes in World War II. Perhaps one of the reasons why democracy has survived in Germany and Japan, despite the fact that it was installed by force of arms over forty years ago, when many experts thought it was too alien to survive, is that both countries have modern mass-wealth information-driven economies. But there are some other important reasons.

Doubts about the German commitment to democracy are based on Germany's totalitarian and authoritarian recent past, on its nationalism, and the inclination toward hierarchy and authority in German culture. But for the following reasons, in addition to the nature of the German economy, it seems highly unlikely that democracy will be defeated in Germany in the foreseeable future.

First, the rest of Western Europe is strongly committed to democracy, and Germany, while nationalist, is also strongly Western European. It would be hard to convince most Germans that all the rest of Europe is wrong in thinking that only democracy is legitimate in Western Europe. Few Germans are willing to see Germany become a pariah in Europe, as it would if it gave up democracy. The American example also has great power in Germany. Unless the United States stumbles much more badly than it has since the depression, many Germans will feel that it is imprudent to go in a fundamentally different direction than the United States.

Second, while power, hierarchy, and nationalism are strong in German culture, so is respect for law, which can be a strong support for democracy (although it wasn't enough to protect against Hitler). Also a federal tradition is strong in Germany, and that too is likely to help provide protection for democracy.

Third, German democracy has been working well and strongly. Between the national government, the states (*Länder*), and local governments, there have been dozens of experiences with governments being defeated at the polls and peacefully turning power over to the opposition. Germans and the German government have been deeply and intimately engaged in a great variety of ways in working with the democratic governments of its European neighbors and of the United States. And there were substantial democratic roots in Germany before Hitler. Therefore, it seems very likely that democratic assumptions, values, and patterns of behavior have become widely and deeply assimilated in Germany. Altogether it is a very good bet that Germany will stay democratic.

Japan's future as a democracy is somewhat less certain. First, the Japanese are much less surrounded by democracy than the Germans are. They are Asian, and democracy is still felt to be an import from the West and not yet a widespread and strong part of Asian cultures. It would be much less hard for the Japanese to go a different way from Europe and America than it would be for the Germans (even though most Japanese have a good deal of fundamental respect for Europe and the United States—in addition to their negative feelings about these alien societies).

Second, democracy seems to have a kind of artificial feel to it in Japan, which may just be that it is Asian or Japanese democracy rather than American or European democracy, but which may also be a sign of its lack of long, historical roots. Until 1994, the national government had not experienced a ruling party being defeated and giving up power.[5] But even before that event, elections had produced substantial changes in Japanese governments, and powerful men had felt obliged to step down in response to voters' opinions.

Third, Japan does not have a strong tradition of respect for the superiority of law over individuals and governments. But, although devotion to law is usually one of the keys to preserving democracy, democracy does not depend only on law. It may turn out that other elements of Japanese culture, such as the great importance of shame and the desire for harmony, can provide strong protection for democracy.

But the basic reason for uncertainty about the future of democracy in Japan is that it has not yet been strongly tested there. Because of the Japanese role in the world and its position with respect to the United States, so far there has not been any strong temptation for the Japanese to give up democracy. Certainly their economic situation has given them little to complain about. Democracy will be tested only when a powerful and popular leader tries to move against democracy because there is some important reason to do so. If some day such an attempt fails because of resistance from the forces in Japan that value democracy highly, then Japanese democracy will have been tested. (But the fact that there has been no attempt so far may also be evidence that there is greater support for democracy in Japan than we understand.)

Our conclusion is that there is only a small chance that Japanese democracy will fail badly enough to contract the zones of peace. But, while the chance is small in Japan, it is even smaller in Germany.

Taken together this evidence strongly suggests that the effect on people of the experience of living and succeeding in modern information economies is an important reason why such economies are more compatible with freedom than with authoritarian rule. The evidence is strong enough so that we should have no doubt there is a substantial degree of contradiction between the nature and drives of authoritarian politics and the requirements of modern competitive economies, a contradiction which will be a strong force tending to keep a high proportion of the wealthy countries democratic. But neither the theory nor the evidence is strong enough to say that it is impossible for an authoritarian regime to operate an effective modern economy.

Even if the correlation between modern economies and democracy were stronger than it is, we would not begin to claim that economics determines everything. In the end democracy is a matter of politics, of ideas, of values, and of choices. We must expect that at least some democratic countries—including some of the most advanced ones—will face grave strains in the future. When they do, only the democratic values, wisdom, and character of their citizens will be able to assure that they stay democratic (and sometimes good luck may be needed too). But it is not unreasonable to think that the values and attitudes of those citizens may have been positively shaped by what they learned from working in their economies and from the qualities of life in their societies.

Democracy and Peace

We are interested in democracy here not because it is good or just but because of its tendency to prevent war and to reduce the importance of military power. There are at least three reasons why democracies don't go to war with one another.

1. In a democracy, major national decisions reflect the feelings of the people, and most people are reluctant to go to war because war is privation, war is death and disability, war is separation from loved ones, war is sacrifice. Democracies give those who serve and suffer a chance to elect the "don't send our boys to fight" party.

2. The patterns of behavior and the attitudes that political leaders need in order to become successful in democratic political systems tend to produce leaders whose strengths are in the use of political methods and whose experience leads them to think in terms of nonviolent ways of solving political conflicts. ("Leaders" include not only the head of government but also the principal people who influence the top person.)

When someone has succeeded all his life by responding to a crisis by calling his friends for help, organizing political coalitions, and by negotiating compromises, that person is likely to try the same kind of methods when his or her country is in a conflict with another. And the people the leader goes to for advice and support are likely to have the same experience and the same inclinations. Democratic politics tends to reject people who are perceived to be combative and unwilling to compromise.

3. Because widespread strong emotions are necessary to generate enough unanimity to authorize a war, democratic publics normally will only support wars against countries that they see as different and despicable. It is much easier for citizens of a democracy to hate a dictator than to hate a democratic government, and it is very hard to convince a democratic public that it should go to war against another democracy. There may be exceptions, perhaps Greeks and Turks or Koreans and Japanese, although even in their countries popular feelings may evolve significantly by the time these pairs of countries are stable democracies.

Whether a country is a democracy from the point of view of the international order does not depend on whether it has specific features of government that we think are good, like an appropriate party system, distribution of power, voting procedures, political rights, et cetera. And a country does not fail to be a democracy because it does things we think are wrong or undemocratic.

For example, most of us would say that it is undemocratic for a country to allow only men to vote. But in this discussion of the international order we have to say that a country whose politics are otherwise democratic is a "democracy" even if it does not allow women to vote. The reason is that a country where there is male suffrage is about as reliably peaceful as a country with both male and female suffrage. The democratic countries, such as the United States, that expanded their suffrage to include women experienced little change in the nature of their politics or the character of government as a result. Therefore female suffrage is a democratic value but not a practical necessity for a country to work like a democracy.

In sum, a country is a democracy for our purposes if its political system works in a way that reflects popular consent (thus giving those who would suffer from war the power to prevent it), trains political leaders to think in terms of political forms of conflict, and gives people a sense of kinship with other democracies.

While these are theoretical arguments, the basic fact of the greater peacefulness of democracies has stood the test of experience.[6] R.J. Rummel was one of the first to analyze the history of wars to compare the experience of democracies with that of other forms of government.[7] In this large body of historical experience democracies had a much lower chance of going to war than other forms of government—with equal opportunities. And the more democratic a country was, the less likely it was to get into substantial wars.

Moreover, throughout history democratic governments have also been less likely to use violence of all kinds than nondemocratic governments. That is, democracies use violence much less frequently against their own citizens as well as against foreigners.

Taken together all these statistics provide strong evidence that it is not just chance that two democracies have never fought a war against each other except in cases of civil war (see appendix 2.2 for a discussion of the significance of the U.S. Civil War as an exception). The whole statistical pattern of this large body of historical experience provides strong evidence that fundamental characteristics of democracy work against democracies going to war with each other.

Our conclusions are that wealth and democracy and peace go together. There are strong and deep reasons why the zones of peace and democracy are peaceful, and why they will stay democratic and not have any wars among themselves for a long time. The current domination of these zones by wealthy democracies is not just a coincidence, not just today's pattern to be replaced by tomorrow's as it replaced yesterday's. There have been fundamental changes that make the world different than it was in the past. We are on new ground.

This is not to say that we have reached the end of history. The future will hold new challenges, and perhaps new kinds of human disaster, that we cannot now foresee. But, while humility about the future is in order, we can recognize the ways in which part of the world has moved past some of the problems and dangers of the past. There is no point in worrying about the wrong things. The zones of peace and democracy should stop worrying about the kinds of military balance-of-power politics and wars that have dominated their history in the past. It is time to move into the future.

Nor does the achievement of wealth, democracy, and peace mean that life will be forever good in the zones of peace and democracy. We are not claiming that the world will necessarily be good and people will be happy because of the spread of democracy. Democracy solves some problems, but not all problems. It means no war; it does not mean no evil. Both theory and history give us plenty of grounds for worry about life in a wealthy, democratic, peaceful world. The dangers of that kind of world are probably the greatest dangers we face. We are going to need to find new ways to build good human character.

International Relations in the New "No-War" Parts of the World

Speculating about a kind of world that has never been seen before cannot be a high-confidence activity. Yet it does not seem right to focus on the importance of the zones of peace and then to say nothing about what will happen in these zones—other than that they will be peaceful (although that is saying a lot). The question is, How will the facts that war is out of the question and military power is essentially irrelevant affect relationships and conflicts within and among the great democracies?

To use a peculiar analogy, taking the potential for war out of international relations is in one way like taking the potential for sex out of human relations: It is hard to imagine the consequences of such a profound change. This is not to say that war is good, like sex; and certainly not to say that sex is bad, like war. But just as sex affects peoples' feelings even in apparently nonsexual situations, so the possibility of war has in the past always influenced international relations, even when war was very far away. It is hard to imagine what life will be like when such a pervasive influence is removed.

We believe that in the zones of peace the freedom from military dangers to national survival and the political impossibility of war with other democracies will gradually change familiar historic reality. The effect of war gradually becoming so much further in the background than ever before will eventually make a subtle but profound difference, a difference that is as difficult to imagine as the effect of completely taking sex out of human relationships.

Writing in 1923 about the British fleet for which he had been responsible as first lord of the admiralty, Winston Churchill commented:

> Consider these ships, so vast in themselves, yet so small.... On them ... floated the might, majesty, dominion and power of the British Empire. All our long history built up century after century, all our great affairs in every part of the globe, all the means of livelihood and safety of our faithful, industrious, active population depended upon them. Open the seacocks and let them sink beneath the surface, ... and in a few minutes ... the whole outlook of the world would be changed. The British Empire would dissolve like a dream.[10]

This is the heart of the former reality.

The difference found in the zones of peace today can be appreciated by thinking about the effect of opening the sea-cocks on the British ships seventy years after Churchill wrote this passage. Today nothing much would change. England would continue to be safe. Its influence might be reduced in some situations, but it would continue to have roughly the same place in the world. There would be neither panic nor any reason for panic.

Another way to appreciate the difference between the beginning and the end of the twentieth century is to consider the small recent movements toward regional separatism in Belgium and Italy. There has been long-standing hostility between Flemings and Walloons in Belgium, and in Italy the Northern provinces are impatient with the less-productive remainder of the country. These movements are not likely to come to much, but the dramatic "dog that did not bark in the night" is that no one in either country claimed that foreign governments had been stirring up separatist organizations in order to weaken the nation.

Early in this century charges of interference by foreign agents would have been an important part of the internal debate in Belgium and Italy, and they might well have been true. Separatism in Belgium and Italy would have been an important item on the agenda of every major government in Europe. Today it would not occur to the government of France or England or Germany or the Netherlands that it has any national interest in either promoting or resisting a separatist movement in Belgium or Italy. Certainly no European government would be concerned that its own power or safety would be seriously affected by the possibility of Belgium or Italy being weakened by internal separatism.

One of the main reasons most people don't appreciate how different the future will be in the zones of peace is that they fail to make one critical distinction. That distinction is between normal national security problems and threats to the survival of the country—that is, between ordinary problems and life-and-death threats. National security problems will continue and armies will still be needed; but in the great democracies the survival of the nation will not be in question.

People in the great democracies, even serious people who know history, will come to understand that their country's future will probably never again depend on its military strength or its military alliances. This understanding will have a profound effect, because there is such a fundamental difference between the possibility of losing money or even having some citizens killed, and the possibility that the country will be defeated in a war defending its territory and independence.

No discussion of the post–cold war world that we have seen has paid much attention to this distinction.[9] Therefore, if we are correct that the distinction is important, its political effect is largely in the future, because it depends on peoples' perceptions, and on confidence that can only be built over time. But even though the effect of this difference on international relations depends on changing perceptions and attitudes, they can begin to have an influence even before they are well articulated and explicitly recognized.

A word about our predictions. We do it the easy way; we say what will happen, not when. Some of the things we predict will happen soon; others will take longer. If we knew which was which we would say; but we don't. (And as our readers already guess, some things that we say about the future will turn out to be wrong.)

There is no reason why the end of war should mean the end of conflict, or even the end of hatred. In fact, the opposite can happen: freedom from the danger of war may reduce efforts to suppress conflict, freeing people to hate and to challenge.

In the new order, however, one of the most potent sources of conflict will be gone—nations will not have to maneuver to maintain a military balance of power. None of the countries of the zones of peace will be in military blocs worrying about becoming weaker than another military bloc. Nor will there be a need for concern for strategic pieces of geography, the sea-lanes, and choke-points of world commerce.

The New World of Geo-Economic Conflict

Part of the bad news about the zones of peace is that they may be zones of serious international conflict, primarily between the United States, Japan, and the European Union (EU). The real main subjects of the conflict will be economic—concerning trade restrictions, competitive subsidies, monetary policy, and the like—but some of the conflict will be transposed into other areas such as aircraft landing rights or even cultural exchanges.[10] One of the main characteristics of these conflicts is that they will be at most of flickering interest to the general publics in the countries concerned. There will be little conflict in fundamental national interests; the main conflict will be for marginal benefits.

The basic model is bargaining between someone who wants to sell his house for at least $100,000 and someone who wants to buy that house for less than $200,000. Negotiation can be fierce, both will benefit from a sale at a wide range of prices, but the zero-sum struggle over the division of the $100,000 of potential benefit may prevent any sale and thus hurt both parties.

The critical force that will shape many of these conflicts between democratic great powers is the degree to which special interests—within and outside of the governments concerned—will shape national policies. The typical dispute between countries will be based on a conflict between private groups—steelworkers or computer manufacturers, each protecting its own interest with little regard for the national interest. They will believe that whoever is hurting them is acting unfairly, whether or not it is true, and they will take whatever political measures they can to get their government to support them—starting with technical briefs to their foreign ministry and meetings with legislators and political leaders, going on to working with media and research institutes to sell the ideas that will gain political support for their interest. Governments must respond to political reality. While they can give some weight to the merits of the case and their view of the national interest, eventually they must send their diplomats to fight for those who have political muscle. And of course the government on the other side is in roughly the same position. The result is that the diplomats on neither side are representing the national interest of their country. They are representing the squeakiest and cleverest wheels in their political system.

Unless national governments are stronger than they have been, they are not likely to have the political strength or will to pursue their national interest. This factor will make most of the negotiations technically incompetent. That is, the negotiators—often on both sides—will be unable to represent the national interest of their own country and will not be able to make effective commitments concerning their country's future actions.

Conflict among the nations of the zones of peace will have two sources: money (jobs) and symbols. That is, it will be conflict based on either opposing financial interests or on issues that are of psychological or emotional importance. But the key fact is that none of this conflict will affect the fundamental interests and feelings of any of the parties to the conflict. No country's independence or form of government will turn on these conflicts. Nor will the outcome of the conflict make the difference between prosperity and poverty.

Some people will care a lot about the issues that divide the democracies, but they will not be issues that affect most of the country seriously. Most disputes are about economic matters. But although $100 billion is a lot of money, it is only a couple of percent of the U.S. annual production. It is not easy to find disputes between countries where as much as $100 billion is at stake. It takes a dispute that threatens something like a million jobs. All the oil in the ground of Alaska is not worth much more than $100 billion.

Of course people and countries often get very excited about disputes that don't really represent a lot of money. It is often impractical to find a way to use money to resolve a conflict, even where both sides would be willing to pay more than the real value in dispute to get a settlement. Nevertheless, in the long run, the economic value of disputes does somewhat affect their significance and political importance. People's crude perspective is influenced by perceptions of economic importance. While these perceptions are often wildly exaggerated, they cannot for long stay completely divorced from material interests and facts.

Increasingly people are coming to realize that each nation's well-being is much more affected by the quality of its domestic economic policy, and the quality of the work effort of its citizens, than by anything in dispute with any foreign country. There is virtually no conflict that a country can win that will do as much good for it as increasing its GNP by a percent or two for a few years. And there are no countries that do not have optional inefficiencies that cost a percent or two of GNP.

We have assumed economic conflict among the advanced democracies, and said nothing of how it may be alleviated. This is only because of our caution, not because we believe that such conflict is inevitable or that nothing can be done to make it less likely or less costly. We have assumed economic conflict because that tests the proposition that the great democracies will not go to war with each other—*even if* they are in extreme economic conflict. We have not discussed the practices and institutions that have been developed to limit such conflict, and how they may be improved, because we want to focus on the basic issues of war and peace. If we went on to say how advanced economic problems between great powers could be dealt with, it would reduce the attention paid to our main message—and perhaps our credibility as well. Besides, we don't know how to deal with the advanced economic problems. And if we devote more attention to how the great democracies could work to minimize economic conflict among themselves, we would be undercutting our argument about the unique importance of life-and-death issues.

Objections

Though our model of the next world order may appear deceptively simple, even commonplace, it is at odds with all current conceptions we know about, both in its causal structure and in its relative optimism. Perhaps the strongest argument against our view about the zones of peace was made by the distinguished scholar Elie Kedourie:[11]

> The idea that war between democratic countries is unlikely is an illusion. It is, broadly speaking, the same illusion that Immanuel Kant entertained when he committed himself to the thought in his *Perpetual Peace* (1795) that wars would be ruled out if every state were a republic and these republics united in a universal "league of nations." In a world of scarcity there must always arise a conflict of interests between two parties, or two

peoples, or two states which will covet the same possessions or advantages for (as they see it) the best possible reasons.[12]

While we agree that there will always be conflicts of interest—and ones that are worse than any conflicts about scarcity or possessions—we do not agree that democracies will settle those conflicts by war. Conflicts don't have to be resolved. Even though the conflict with the Soviet Union was not with another democracy, remember how reluctant we were to go to war. But maybe that only shows that democracies are reluctant to go to war with equal powers. Perhaps the danger is from conflicts between big democracies and small democracies. Maybe France will go to war with Belgium—or expect to settle a conflict on the basis of its ability to defeat Belgium in a war. Perhaps. We can't be sure. But it doesn't fit with our perceptions of how things work these days. And it might be hard to tell. France has other ways of exerting pressure in a conflict with Belgium, without suggesting that it might go to war. We can imagine a government of Belgium in such a conflict deciding to concede its position out of fear of French military action, or perhaps using that possibility as an excuse—even if France had not the slightest intention of making the matter a *casus belli*. But it is easier to imagine a government of Belgium getting stubborn with France, accusing France of trying to throw its weight around improperly, and getting enough international sympathy so that France would find it prudent to retreat. And most likely Belgium and France would eventually find some way of resolving their dispute in a way that would somehow reflect the fact that France's population and economy are more than twice as large as Belgium's. But it would also reflect the relative importance of the issue to the two countries. Belgium would be likely to get most of its way if the issue had much greater political significance in Belgium than it had in France. In brief, we don't believe that conflict between states must end in war or be settled on the basis of actual or potential military balance.

Some people, while conceding that the Western European democracies won't fight among themselves in Western Europe, express concerns about their getting involved in wars elsewhere. We discuss extensively the case for and against democratic intervention in wars in the zones of turmoil, but that would not be a war between two democracies.

It is not hard to imagine circumstances where one democracy could be inclined to intervene on one side of a war in the zones of turmoil and another democracy on the other. Our view is that this is unlikely to get to the point of battle between the forces of the two democracies, and that even if it did, they would be very likely not to let it turn into a war between their two countries. What could happen in the zones of turmoil that they would care enough about to go to war against another democracy? Recent experience has been that the democracies have shown great reluctance—many would say excessive reluctance—to get involved in anything dangerous in the zones of turmoil. The idea that two democracies would get so carried away by their involvement on opposite sides of a war in the zones of turmoil—even in Eastern Europe—that they would go to war with each other seems far away from recent experience.

Internal Divisions within States

There are divisive forces within most states, usually ethnic or historic distinctions. One of the things that has contained these forces has been the explicit and subconscious acceptance of national security needs for unity. In the zones of peace the unifying strength of national security concerns is likely to be reduced. At the same time, especially in Europe, international organizations are becoming more important. Because of the decline in the importance of national security concerns, the large states will gradually lose some importance compared to international institutions such as the EU and compared to subnational units of government. Because it will be less important for countries to hold together, it will be harder to prevent smaller ethnic or regional units from gaining increasing autonomy or some degree of independence. Small societies are more likely to be qualitatively strong than in the past, because quality does not require quantity. And in the current order there will be less doubt about the viability of small states. (See also the discussion in the third section of chapter 6, pp. 126–34.)

This process will be happening mostly outside the realm of national security (made possible by the reduced importance of fundamental security threats in the zones of peace and democracy). The fundamental security order will continue to be based on the major states. But there will be more smaller entities that do well.

Power in the New World

Theorists about international relations have always had trouble defining "power." While military power of various kinds was always understood to be an important component of "power," everyone agreed that there were other elements of power that could be important, and sometimes decisive. Economic power is also important, but what does it mean, how is it measured? Is the country with the larger GNP more powerful? The context for these questions is national sovereignty, which, because there is no international authority that can compel decisions, gives each nation the right to decide for itself.

In most discussions today about the future of Europe a great deal of emphasis is put on the problem of Germany's disproportionate power. This may well be an example of "old thinking," more in keeping with traditional realities than with the reality of the future. What kind of difference will it make that Germany's GNP will be one-third larger than France's (mostly because Germany's population will be slightly under 80 million and France's slightly under 60 million)? Germany will not be able to tell France what to do. When German companies and French companies are competing for business in a third country, Germany will not automatically be able to exert greater influence on the government of that country than France. For example, Switzerland or Turkey, in deciding some business question about which Germany and France disagree, will not necessarily decide in favor of Germany because it has a bigger GNP than France. Of course they know it is always good to improve relations with a country that has enough economic and political strength to help or hurt you in the future. But both Germany and France are big enough to help or hurt other countries. Whether a country has to be more afraid of (deferential to) Germany or France is determined more by other factors than by the fact that Germany is 30 percent larger. It depends on which cares more, on which is cleverer about getting its way, on the pattern of relationships, and many other factors.

Whether Germany or France will be able to help its companies more in their foreign activities depends on which country is better able to organize its diplomacy to the task of helping companies. The likely result is that France will be more effective in some countries, Germany in others. France will be more effective at some kind of help, Germany at others. There are thousands of these issues each year, and, as a practical matter, most of them are dealt with at a fairly low level in both governments; rarely do they become issues of weighing national power.

Wherever there are many issues they have to be dealt with on their merits. No country is going to decide that in all disputes between France and Germany it will prefer Germany. The result is that the outcome depends on the skill of the advocates and bureaucrats—in selecting issues, in focusing attention at the right places, in operating shrewdly. The "weaker" country may well do better overall than the stronger if it uses its diplomatic resources well.

But what about the councils of nations? Will Germany come to dominate because it has the larger economy? Undoubtedly there is some advantage to being the biggest, but that advantage is limited. To some extent things really are decided on a "each-nation-one-vote" basis. Other things are decided by an informal "weighing" of the two sides of a dispute. But such weighing is rarely precise. Germany's extra size is not nearly enough to give it a dominant voice in Europe. Any tendency for one country to try to dominate will usually produce enough negative reaction to balance the size advantage. Besides, as we have already argued with the voice of experience, when governments get their backs up, economic pressure does not work very well.

Will Europe have to accept Germany as its leader because it is the "most powerful" country? Not in any dangerous sense. Europe will not need to have a "leader" in the way that people are worried about. Germany will not be able to dominate Europe, nor to "lead" it, unless it pays due deference to the interests and sensibilities of the other European countries. If it fails to do so it will not be accepted as the "leader." Even if Germany continues to have a 30 percent or 50 percent larger economy than the other great European democracies, it would not be surprising if there were periods during which France or the United Kingdom—or some day even Italy—were the practical leader of Europe (although Germany may remain the monetary leader for a long time).

Another example of the kind of fear that comes from traditional thinking, and which seems inapplicable to the world as it is now, is the fear that anarchy in Russia is dangerous because Germany (and perhaps Japan) will take advantage of such Russian weakness to increase their own power. But how would this be done, and to what end? What would Germany hope to gain by being "twice as powerful" as France instead of "50 percent more powerful"? If Germany made an "alliance" with a Russian dictatorship, what would be the purpose or the benefit? Germany is not interested in being militarily capable of defeating France. Why should they, since they are not going to go to war? How much (if any) basic economic benefit could Germany get from some preferential relationship with Russia? Not much; probably less than they would lose from the adverse reactions of other countries. Recent political experience suggests that Germany would be eager to avoid entanglement in an anarchic Russia (even if there were no nuclear weapons involved). And if Germany does get involved, it will not win anything of value.

A Basis for Peace?

What counts about the zones of peace is that they are something new in the world. Without a government over them they are peaceful and democratic, and seem likely to continue to be so for some time. They will be a daily reminder to the world that the old message of history, that war is a natural and inevitable part of life, no longer has to be true. The zones of peace will be a demonstration that peace is possible among countries that used to fight one another—a model of how world peace may be obtained without world government.

Of course the theory that zones of democracy and peace can some day cover the whole world must be regarded with suspicion. If true, however, it describes a way that a state of affairs, long hoped for but seemingly beyond reach, may come about. Reasonable people have long asked how, without an ultimate world sovereign (*pace* Hobbes's *Leviathan*), could there be world peace? Given the unreasonableness of expecting world government, world peace has seemed an idle dream. But now we have a glimmer of how there can be peace without a peacekeeper. Just as that other self-organizing system, the international economy, creates economic growth without a world plan and without planners, so peace is possible through internal changes within powerful nations that, by their example, encourage others to change similarly.

No one can know whether democracy will survive in the United States or in any other country. We have given some reasons for thinking that the United States and the other great democracies will stay democratic for some time, but that question is not the subject of this book. Our argument is not that peace is safe in the zones of peace *because* all of the great democracies will stay democratic. Our argument is that *so long as* we and they stay democratic, there will be no threat of war among us.

The new fundamental in international relations is that the danger of a world war in the future depends less on international politics and military balances than on the continuation of democracy in the great powers, especially in the United States. In other words, our fundamental safety depends primarily on the domestic political character of our country and of the other great democracies.

Appendix 2.1
Expanding the Zones of Peace and Democracy

Some potential additions to the zones of peace are hard to define, but others are easy. When Mexico becomes democratic it will be part of the North American zone of peace and democracy. When all the countries of Central America—from Panama through Guatemala—are democratic, Central America will be added to that zone.

No countries can be added to the zone of the Antipodes. Eventually, however, the area that includes Indonesia and the Philippines will become a zone of peace, and there will be no point in thinking of the Antipodes as a separate zone.

Neither Korea nor Taiwan can become part of Japan's zone of peace until China does too. However, when China and Korea are democratic they probably will have a zone of peace even if Russia (or Siberia) is not yet democratic, because they will not have to get involved with Russia and Russia will not be a threat to their national survival.

The question of a zone of peace in Eastern Europe is more difficult. The countries on the border of Russia will not be in a zone of peace so long as Russia is not democratic. However, when Ukraine and Belarus are democratic, the Western European zone of peace can extend through the rest of Eastern Europe if the other Eastern European countries are democratic.

The zones of peace and democracy are not clubs that governments establish and into which they can invite any other country. Eastern European countries can be invited to membership in NATO or the EU or other European organizations, but no one can make a policy decision about whether Eastern Europe should be allowed to become part of the Western European zone of peace and democracy.

There is no formula for defining the borders of an "area." The practical definitions of areas depend not only on geography but also on perceptions and policy, and so they change from time to time. Roughly, we use "area" or "zone" to mean a contiguous territory within which the countries are necessarily concerned with each other, whether they like it or not. Unfortunately countries do not have much choice about which area they are in. No matter how democratic and peaceful they are, they cannot join the zones of peace and democracy if they are surrounded by nondemocratic countries.

An area becomes a zone of peace and democracy only when all the sizable countries in that area are democratic enough so that (1) they are confident they will not go to war with each other and (2) they believe that the strength of their military will not influence their negotiations with each other. For most of history that would be like believing a fairy tale, as it is even now for most nations.

Appendix 2.2
How Much of an Exception Is the U.S. Civil War?

In the U.S. Civil War, two democracies fought a long and bitter war against each other. How much should this example weaken our confidence that democratic countries will not fight each other in the future?

There are a number of reasons why the example of the U.S. Civil War does not contradict the arguments for the extremely low likelihood of wars between democracies in the future. But we have to recognize that it was a case in which governments that were reasonably representative of their citizens chose to go to war against another democracy and had substantial support from their citizens in doing so. (Of course the South was a democracy that insisted on preserving the institution of slavery, and the North was a democracy that had accepted slavery for more than seventy years.) And the decision to go to war was made by political leaders who had grown up in a democratic political system. So all the reasons why democracy usually prevents wars against other democracies applied—although in somewhat weaker form than they exist today, with the following special factors:

1. A civil war has unusual power to engage the emotions of a citizenry. And it has the unusual feature that both sides are defending themselves. One side is fighting for independence, the other side is fighting, not to expand its territory, but only to hold the nation together. Or each side is fighting to prevent something objectionable from being imposed on it.

2. While both sides in the U.S. Civil War were democracies, they both had much more limited voting franchises than do modern democracies. Women were excluded, as were slaves and many nonproperty owners. And Senators were elected indirectly. But we cannot claim that these facts were what made the Civil War possible.

3. The Civil War was the first in the most recent series of vastly horrible wars, involving mass armies and widespread civilian destruction. It came before the era of long-range weapons of mass destruction. At the time it began, there was probably less popular aversion for war than there is

now and than there is likely to be in the future.

4. The Civil War did not involve modern mass-wealth societies. Therefore the Civil War is not evidence against the hypothesis that fundamental characteristics of such modern societies reduce the likelihood of war.

Because of the example of the U.S. Civil War, and also for theoretical reasons, we have to assume that civil wars may occur within the zones of peace and democracy. This possibility does not change the relationships between countries in these zones. And the fact that there will not be military rivalries or competing military blocs within these zones means that any such civil war is unlikely to turn into an international war. Nor is the possibility of civil war likely to keep military forces at a high level or to increase widely the importance of military power in the zones of peace. And, unlike in the past, civil wars will not be encouraged by neighbors.

The factors that prevent democracies from fighting against each other are *tendencies,* not absolute imperatives; therefore they can be outweighed by other factors. Even international war is not absolutely excluded from the zones of peace, even if all the countries in these zones continue to be democracies. Nevertheless, the international order in these zones will be dominated by the extreme unlikelihood of war between countries within the zones, and it will not be much reduced by the possibility of civil war.

If we were gamblers or insurers, we would not give odds of 1000 to 1 against the possibility of a war between two democracies in the next century. As professional analysts we do not say that it is an established fact that such a war is impossible or that it will never happen. But we do say that something very new exists in the world. For most of the great powers, because they are democracies, it will become politically useless to try to influence policy by referring to the danger of a war with any of the other democracies. Citizens and political leaders will not take actions on the basis of concern about the possibility of war with another democracy. They may someday turn out to be wrong, but for many years that will be the political reality.

Notes

1. Julian Simon and others would argue that, strictly speaking, there are no natural resources; it is people alone who make lumps of inert material into something valuable. See, for example, Simon's *Ultimate Resource* (Princeton: Princeton University Press, 1987).

2. This count uses the Freedom House category of "Free Country" as the

equivalent of "democracy" and omits countries with populations less than 1 million.

3. If annual production is measured by GNP per capita adjusted to reflect purchasing power parity (PPP), this means all countries with a GNP per capita over $6,000. If unadjusted GNP per capita were used as the measure—with life expectancy—the list of countries would be the same but the lower limit would be $3,650 instead of $6,000. Various other measures would produce the same or insignificantly different results. The precise dividing line does not make much difference.

4. The statistical tip-off that these are not modern wealthy economies—in case you didn't know it already—is that all of these countries have life expectancies at birth of less than seventy-four years, despite their high GNP per capita.

5. Until 1977 Israel did not have any experience of the opposition party coming to power, and some doubted that it could happen. But then the Labor party did peacefully give up power to its hated rival Likud after forty-odd years in control of the Jewish government in Palestine and Israel (beginning before the State).

6. The theory was first put forward by Immanuel Kant two hundred years ago: "[When] the consent of the citizens is required to decide whether or not war should be declared, it is very natural that they will have a great hesitation in embarking on so dangerous an enterprise.... But under a constitution ... which is ... not Republican, it is the simplest thing in the world to go to war. For the head of state is ... but the owner of the state, and war will not force him to make the slightest sacrifice."

7. R.J. Rummel, *Understanding Conflict and War* (Beverly Hills, Calif.: Sage, 1975–81), vols. 1–5; and *The Conflict Helix: Principles and Practices of Interpersonal, Social, and International Conflict and Cooperation* (New Brunswick, N.J.: Transaction, 1991). See also the literature summarized in Kerry G. Herron, "Democracy and Proclivity to War," a paper delivered at the annual meeting of the Western Political Science Association, March 1993.

8. Winston S. Churchill, *The World Crisis* (New York: Scribner's, 1923), 1:123.

9. Robert Tucker's article, "Realism and the New Consensus," *National Interest,* Winter 1992/93, 33–36, is a partial exception.

10. Edward Luttwak coined the phrase "geoeconomics" in "From Geopolitics to Geo-Economics," *National Interest,* no. 20, Summer 1990.

11. In a private communication, after seeing a draft of this chapter, only a few weeks before his untimely death, Professor Kedourie significantly narrowed his disagreement with our position, but his words continue to reflect the views of a substantial school of thought.

12. Elie Kedourie and George Urban, "What's Wrong with 'Nationalism'? What's Right with the 'Balance of Power'? A Conversation," in U. Ra'anan, et al., *State and Nation in Multi-Ethnic Societies: The Break-up of Multinational States* (Manchester: Manchester University Press, 1991), 240.

CHAPTER 3

ZONES OF TURMOIL AND DEVELOPMENT

In the zones of turmoil, democracy is probably now at a temporary high water from which it is likely to recede before advancing again. All of the former Soviet empire except East Germany is now part of the zones of turmoil; much of it is likely to be in the hands of authoritarian governments in the next few years. And other countries in the zones of turmoil may also temporarily lose their democracy.

When democracy falls in Russia or other countries in the zones of turmoil, it should not cast doubt on the conclusion that democracy is going to spread through the whole world. The real trend in favor of democracy is not just the short-run change in the number of democracies. The real trend is the pattern of underlying forces that will determine the future. One result of that trend will be the spread of democracy through the zones of turmoil in fits and starts, with many countries spending a long time as marginal democracies, or temporarily falling back into authoritarianism before finally achieving stable democracy.

The failure of the Soviet Union and of communism permanently removes the last systematic challenge to democracy in existence. (This formulation deliberately leaves open the possibility that new challenges to democracy, not just resistances, will arise.) Even if authoritarian governments take control of all of the old Soviet empire, it will not be a reversal of the victory of democracy over communism because the authoritarian governments that may come to power in the former Soviet Union will not make a believable claim that they have a better or more idealistic system, and will not work together around the world to defeat democracy. They will represent temporary local failures, not a challenge to democracy. And eventually stable democracy will be achieved even in the social ruins created by communism.

The problem of understanding the significance of the likely resurgence of authoritarian government in the zones of turmoil illustrates why it is important to divide the world into the two kinds of zones. This division makes it is easier to see that the fall of new democracies in the former Soviet empire is only the kind of fluctuation that must be expected in the zones of turmoil, not a basic setback for democracy in the world.

The fall of democracy in the United States or several other great democracies in the zones of peace would be the end of the world order we are describing. The expected setbacks for democracy in the zones of turmoil are very different.

One reason to have confidence in the long-term prospects for democracy in the zones of turmoil—even in the face of the expected setbacks—is that no authoritarian claim to general legitimacy is being made, except by some Singaporeans and other Asians. This chapter discusses the other major reason for confidence about the longer run: the economic and political development process.

Although there will be many authoritarian governments in the zones of turmoil, democracies will be the only governments generally accepted as fully legitimate. We cannot be sure how long this statement will continue to be true, but it is true today and it is a fundamental feature of the current world order; if and when it ceases to be true, the world order that we are describing in this book will have passed, and we will have entered into another world order.

The exclusive legitimacy of democracy comes partly from the failure of communism and fascism, partly from the fact that there is no existing ideology that challenges democracy—with the partial exception of Islam—and partly from the example of the zones of peace. The fact that the rich and peaceful countries are all democracies is potent support for theoretical arguments in favor of democracy and for democracy's inherent appeal to human feelings. (Since no one would deny that democracy has significant defects, it is not discredited by its failings unless there is a better system available.)

Overall Perspective

Our overall picture of the zones of turmoil sees them as an immense, slowly boiling cauldron, agitated by powerful internal forces that are difficult to recognize and essentially impossible to control. One of the symptoms of the bubbling will be deadly violence within countries and between them.

But our picture is of zones of turmoil *and development*. The cauldron we see is not only bubbling, it is also slowly (but not steadily) changing in a predictable direction. Each fifty years, the fraction of the world still in the cauldron is likely to be smaller and the fraction in the zones of peace and democracy is likely to be larger.

We are confident about the power and direction of positive change because that change will be the result of a process rooted in fundamental factors described below that are influencing life in the countries of the zones of turmoil, factors that will do much of the shaping of the future of those zones. We are not talking about abstract historical forces. This is not a theory of history, like that of Francis Fukuyama (although it comes to similar estimates).

The nature and importance of the process that is taking place throughout most of the world is not fully appreciated by most analysts because it is relatively new. Also it is a process closely tied to economics and business, with which many historians and political analysts are not comfortable. But, despite the fact that the noise in the world will be made by short-run conflicts, we see them as mostly ebb and flow, and we expect that the lasting changes will be determined by the long-term processes described here.

As the current world order begins, life in the zones of turmoil, which fill most of the world, will continue to be ordered much in the way the world has always worked. Nations will be controlled by power and intrigue; the suffering of ordinary people will be the price of their rulers' folly and greed; and large-scale systematic violence will be a widespread threat. The fundamental conditions that now exist in the zones of turmoil, as well as the lessons of history, make it clear that these zones will be the scene of wars and revolutions, and of mass murders, famines, and epidemics caused by governments or by wars. Stability would be an impossibility. The modern media will give us a front-row seat at one scene after another of devastation and death.

The way to understand the future in these zones is to start by assuming that it will be like the past and then to adjust for new factors. We will not discuss here the traditional patterns that we can expect to see continued in the zones of turmoil. History provides many examples of the rise and fall of states and empires, of cities and peoples who prosper and rule themselves and then fail or are conquered. Good rulers are followed by bad, many noble experiments are tried but few succeed. Eventually the destructive specter of war marches across the land, destroying all in its path. Law yields to force, and the urge to plunder appears more reliably than the desire for public service. Ancient sources of hatred and rivalry abound, and modern technology provides new means for expressing them and additional sources of conflict, as well as making the brutal results visible throughout the world. These are familiar patterns; we need to focus on the new factors that will eventually be making the future of the zones of turmoil different from the past.

Military Facts

Since military force is still the ultimate determinant of what happens in the zones of turmoil, it is useful to say a little about basic military relationships before going on to the new factors. Unfortunately the Gulf War of 1991 produced some misleading impressions.

It helps to start by looking at ground combat and airpower separately. On the ground, the ultimate force is the mobile combined arms force based on tanks. If there are not too many obstacles in the terrain, nothing can protect against an armored force except another armored force. The ultimate military test, therefore, is the combat between mobile armored forces in open country.

An armored force capable of defeating another good armored force in sustained combat can be built only with years of high-quality effort by a large number of people. It must have expensive modern equipment and lots of money for fuel and ammunition for intense training. Tens of thousands of soldiers and officers must have spent many hours in rigorous, expensive training, with commanders who reject the pressures to reduce the pain and embarrassment needed to make training and maneuvers effective. The thousands of officers must have developed and must use a very complex set of organizational systems to handle supply, repair, transportation, medical treatment, and everything else quickly in the face of enemy fire and the need to move frequently. The soldiers must be disciplined and motivated so that they stick to the procedures necessary for coordination and effective fighting; they must have the initiative necessary to overcome the obstacles that arise in combat and be determined enough to move forward despite the excuses and temptations to passivity that combat provides. The officers, in addition to being well-organized and effective leaders, must have a sense of tactics, physical stamina, and the ability to operate under continuous emotional and other tensions and danger. The top leadership must be effective tacticians and strategists, as well as capable of meeting all the other requirements of managing a large organization in a complex political environment under immense pressure.

Only the most advanced societies can produce a high-quality combined arms force. Bravery and loyalty are not enough. Money is not enough. Widespread administrative skills are not enough. The ability to sustain organized effort, with attention to maintenance and planning, over many years, is not enough. All those things, and more, are required. A society that can produce a first-rate armored force can also operate an advanced modern economy. A society that cannot produce an effective modern economy cannot field a first-class fighting armored corps.[1]

Of course, the army of an advanced society is not automatically a first-class army. Producing a fighting army takes character as well as capacity. (Some would say it takes bad character, and if enough people say that, the army will not have it.) If the society does not believe in the importance of the fighting quality of the army, even an expensive army in the most advanced society can be too soft to fight well.

A first-rate armored force can defeat a second-rate enemy army several or many times its size. If it has enough time and space, it should be expected to defeat even an equally well-equipped army four or more times larger than itself. The reason is that a large army is an integrated organization, which a superior armored force can cut into pieces that do not function well separately and that can be defeated one at a time. Once a unit is hit so hard that it cannot maintain discipline and command, it loses all its fighting effectiveness, although, if given a chance, it can be put back together again.

While a good army has to be prepared to take casualties, normally in open combat between a good army and a second-class army, the good army suffers very few combat deaths. It would be reasonable to expect a first-rate force of 100,000 troops to defeat a third-rate force of 500,000 troops in a month of combat while suffering a few hundred combat deaths. (From February to May 1951, after General Matthew Ridgway took command of the UN force in Korea and forced the Chinese out of South Korea, the U.S. Army had a few thousand combat deaths, while the Chinese Communist armies lost half a million men dead, wounded, and captured. Israel has repeatedly had even better results against forces that had at least as expensive equipment as that of Israel.)

Modern airpower adds an additional dimension to combat. The first thing that airpower has to do in a war is to win the battle for air superiority and control of the air over the battlefield. The result of the battle for air superiority is usually that either only one force—or neither—is able to give air support to its ground forces on the battlefield. (Occasionally a stalemate in the battle for control of the air will leave both sides capable of limited air support, in which case airpower will not be a decisive factor.)

Once one air force has achieved enough air superiority so that it is free to operate without much opposition over the battlefield, it is able to provide great assistance to its army. In extreme cases, like the allied campaign against the Iraqi army in 1991, the air force by itself is able to destroy the enemy army's combat capability almost completely. This is possible when the air force is large and close enough to put many planes over the battlefield, the terrain is open, and the weather is not too bad. It is also possible when the opposing army's supply routes can be continuously attacked during the same period when it is forced to engage in mobile combat.[2]

While the exact value of airpower in a war depends on many specific factors and is changing with technology (and is controversial), as a rough rule of thumb one can think of air superiority as making an army capable of defeating an equal-quality army twice its size or of defeating a lesser-quality army four times its size. But an air force that cannot achieve control of the air over the battlefield does little more to help its army than protect it from the enemy air force.

The only air force in the zones of turmoil that might be able to prevent the United States from achieving control of the air is the Chinese air force trying to protect parts of mainland China. Everywhere else in the zones of turmoil U.S. airpower will provide democratic forces with the equivalent of at least an additional *two-to-one* advantage over any local army.

Few armies in the zones of turmoil are in the same class of fighting quality as the armies of the United States and some of the other great democracies. There are none in Latin America or Africa, except South Africa, which has a small first-class force. Much of Turkey's army would be first class if it had modern tanks. Israel has a first-class army of well over 100,000 after mobilization. There are no other first-class armies in the Middle East. But there are first-class units in the armies of China, India, and both Koreas, and probably several other countries in Asia. And of course it is possible that some of the countries of Africa or Latin America, such as Nigeria or Brazil, will in the future decide to create first-class armies.

This scarcity of first-class military units means that in general, on average, if the democracies fight local armies in the zones of turmoil, they will start with the equivalent of at least a four-to-one advantage in open battles—two-to-one from air superiority, and two-to-one from having first-class forces against second-class forces. Against many of the local armies, the advantage would be greater. Other factors, such as morale or strategy or situation, could either increase or decrease the advantage held by the forces of the democracies.

Before going any further, we should emphasize the uncertainties as well as the horrors of war. Realistic estimates of military strength must not lead to an arrogant quickness to use force. All military calculations are unreliable. No country should undertake a battle except for very good cause and with great reluctance.

In any war, chance and human error can be decisive. That one army is twice as good as another army does not mean that it is certain to defeat that army—only that it has perhaps an 80 percent chance of winning. Even an army that is three of four times as strong as its enemy is not certain to win a war. There is some probability, maybe one in fifty, that even a much weaker army will win any particular battle. Rarely are there enough battles for the law of averages reliably to prevail. And even victory can sometimes produce many more casualties than expected. Therefore it makes sense to be cautious and prepared for the worst. This is one reason why leaders prefer to have more force than necessary.

But one does not necessarily save lives by overstating the dangers of war. In the future, as in the past, many people are likely to die as a consequence of overrating enemy forces and excessive reluctance to attack.

Understanding what military forces should be capable of can also help in avoiding poor military leadership, which if not detected can be extraordinarily harmful. For example, the United Nations was being badly defeated by the Chinese in Korea at the end of 1950 when an accident led to General Ridgway's being put in command of the UN forces. Within six weeks after Ridgway took over, the UN army reversed the tide of battle, and in another five months it recovered all of South Korea and forced a greatly reinforced Chinese army to accept a cease-fire and begin negotiations. General Ridgway did not use any brilliant tactics, he just insisted that the American officers do what they had been taught to do in their manuals and schools. The difference between defeat prior to Ridgway and victory under Ridgway was not numbers, training, equipment, or strategy; it was competent military leadership.[3] Apparently U.S. military headquarters in Tokyo and in the Pentagon had not understood that the issue of military competence was decisively influencing the combat in Korea. And very little attention has been paid to the centrality of this issue in military histories of the Korean war (which is one reason why the question continues to be critical).

The false lesson that the Gulf War seemed to teach is that the democracies had to put an army of half a million men in the field to defeat Iraq. Since the prelude to the war seemed to teach the false lesson that the democracies had to be prepared to suffer thousands of casualties to defeat Iraq, the war itself only seemed to teach that sometimes good fortune keeps casualties low.

The course of the war showed that the military victory achieved by the allies in Iraq could have been achieved with confidence with fewer than one-third as many allied troops as were sent into Saudi Arabia, and probably with fewer casualties. Such a smaller force could also have taken most of Iraq (excluding the Baghdad area), also with very few casualties. Had that taken place, the deterrent lesson of the Gulf War—that only a high-quality society can compete militarily—would have been even more sharply etched than it was.

We emphasize this point because it shows why the democracies will continue to have the power to intervene decisively throughout most of the zones of turmoil—except parts of Asia—even if U.S. and other NATO armies are substantially reduced. Although it is possible, to be sure, that democratic forces will be reduced so much, or so weakened by the political and other temptations of peacetime, that they would lose the power to intervene against many of the armies of the zones of turmoil.

During the next few decades it is unlikely that there will be any military force stronger than the Iraqi army was at the beginning of 1991 anywhere in Latin America, Africa, or the Middle East (except Israel and Turkey). That is, there may be forces that are smaller and better than those of Iraq, or forces that are bigger and not so good, but in that large fraction of the world there will be no forces both bigger and better than the Iraqi military were.

There will almost certainly be wars in the Middle East and Africa during the next century. They may be as long-lasting and bloody as the stalemated war between Iraq and Iran, which took over a million lives. But it is important to understand that the forces fighting in those wars will not be forces capable of serious, sustained fighting against the forces of the great democracies.

Asia is so much more populous and economically advanced that it may have wars on a more serious scale. Korea today has well over a million men confronting each other in high-quality military forces, although the peaceful reunification of Korea is quite possible within the next five or ten years and will probably lead to demobilization of most of that force before the next decade is over.

Korea is an unusual case. North Korea, with a population of 22 million, is the most heavily armed totalitarian country in the world and is close to building its own nuclear weapons. But now that Kim Il Sung, who was its leader for half a century, has died, it is quite possible that North Korea will follow the path of East Germany, and for the same reason. Apart from nuclear weapons, North Korea no longer has any basis for a hope of victory. South Korea, which has twice as many people, is now militarily stronger (using only about 6 percent of its economy) than North Korea is (using a third of its economy for military purposes). South Korea is growing much more rapidly. And North Korea's international allies are failing, leaving it virtually isolated.

Conceivably there will be a period of danger when North Korea might try to use nuclear weapons to gain control of South Korea. But if that does not happen, or after the attempt is defeated, North Korea will have no reason to hold out against the inherent attractiveness of reuniting their country, which will have to be done essentially under the southern constitution. If North Korea stays communist and opens up at all, it will be ruined by the flood of North Koreans who will leave for the south. Therefore its only choices will be to continue its unnatural and useless isolation from its other half or to merge into South Korea. In the struggle for power that is possible now that Kim has died, those elements who promise unification will be able to attract more support than those who want to continue on a hopeless cause. In merger negotiations there would be no goals the North could usefully seek, except personal protection for the leadership.

The Taiwan-China confrontation, and that between India and Pakistan, are also large on a world scale and are not likely to end as soon as the Korean.

New Influences

The good news is that while conditions in most of the world can still be expected to produce turbulence and war, the same process that changed the zones of democracy has already begun to work in the zones of turmoil. The most reliable part of this process is economic development, which changes countries from poor agricultural and village-dominated societies to wealthy urban market economies, with much pain along the way.

Another part of the process is the change from traditional forms of government, mostly authoritarian, to modern complex political systems of popular representation, that is, to some form of democracy. (This century was dominated by a terrible detour to totalitarianism.)

The transition from traditional poverty to modern wealth is almost inevitable everywhere. Confidence in the transition to democracy must be more tentative. The elimination of historic poverty will be more universal and will come sooner than the general spread of democracy. And we are less sure that democracy is the final result of normal development than that wealth is. The basis for these judgments is presented next.

No doubt there are important connections between the two kinds of development. But the relationship is too subtle and complex for us to claim to understand. It is clear that either process *can* go forward without the other. And there are ways in which the two processes sometimes interfere with each other. That is, sometimes the process of moving toward democracy, or the results of democratic government in a country, can delay that country's economic development. Similarly, the changes produced by rapid economic growth can create social strains that may set back the movement to democracy in a country.

Nevertheless, we believe that generally the movement toward democracy and toward economic development are mutually reinforcing, and depend on some of the same basic social changes. Increasing education, the development of the rule of law and recognition of property rights, a reduced role for the state, and the gradual ascendancy of merit and reason over arbitrary power are examples of developments that usually help to bring both wealth and democracy.

Economic Development

Historic perspective enables us to see what is involved in economic development and gives a basis for believing that it will continue until most of the world is wealthy by historic standards. As recently as the beginning of the last century, most people in every country lived in villages and worked the land, ignorant and illiterate. Now this almost universal way of life is everywhere changing and on the way out. We cannot know yet whether it will be one hundred or two hundred years, or possibly even longer, before it will be gone. But there can be little doubt that by the end of the next century most people will be educated, living in cities, working in money economies, and much healthier and longer lived than their ancestors. Only small minorities will still be subsistence farmers living in primitive villages. The countries that are rich now do not have more natural resources than those that are still poor. Nor do their people have superior genes. All the rich countries were recently poorer than most of the poor countries are today. Now they are rich because they have learned to work differently.

Economic development is fundamentally a process in which a society learns how to allow its people to be more productive by learning new ways to work together. It gets easier to learn as there are more examples of more ways to be successful, and as the growing wealth of the rich world offers more and more opportunities to make money.[4] When others learn their own version of how to be productive, they too will be rich (i.e., rich in historical terms, as rich as Greece and Portugal are today).

To think about the question "How can we be sure that the poor countries will soon become as rich as Portugal and Greece have become?" one must first understand where wealth comes from. The traditional and obvious answers are wrong. Modern wealth does not come from physical resources—fertile land, or gold and mineral treasure. In the United States, for example, we spend only about 15 percent of our effort on getting all the raw materials we need out of the ground. And anybody else can have the same raw materials at a reasonably similar price. Our lives would not change dramatically if all the raw materials were free or if they doubled in price.

Modern wealth is made possible by the fact that modern workers of all kinds produce more than ten times as much with each hour of work as workers did a century ago. The reason we can be so productive is not that we are stronger or smarter or work harder than our ancestors. The reason is that our society now provides the support and opportunities that allow us to use our time and effort much more effectively than our grandparents could.

Other societies can learn some of the modern ways directly, without going through the process that we did when we were learning. Nobody has to start with giant, old-fashioned computers full of endless chains of vacuum tubes again or to invent electricity. But many of the social changes that permit people to work together effectively have to be learned a step at a time. People learn by making mistakes and finding out for themselves what is wrong with the way they have been doing things. When a society tries to copy a more advanced country, taking advantage of lessons it has not learned for itself, it will make new mistakes because it will not fully understand what it is copying.

When a child learns to act like an adult, it is not merely intellectual learning; the child has to go through a process of emotional and personal change to internalize each set of lessons before being ready to go on to the next level, and eventually to deal with the world on a mature basis. That learning and changing process of growth and maturation is called "development." Economic development, the learning and changing process that countries go through, is analogous, and involves similar difficulties, dangers, and traumas.

The obvious part of economic development is technological change—and advancing technology has indeed been necessary for the achievement of high productivity. But technological change, and the highways and power lines and factories associated with it, are as much a result as a cause of productivity. For both businesses and countries there is always more technology available than is being used. The level of technology that anyone actually uses depends not on what technology has been invented, but on how much each organization is motivated to make the changes necessary to use the best technology. Therefore, to a large extent the focus on technology misses the point. The driving forces toward more productivity are motivational and organizational.

To think about how productivity actually increases, a good example to keep in mind is the shipping clerk who figures out how to stack the boxes in the shipping room more efficiently so that he can ship more materials each week. When he does that, he is increasing his output without adding any new input. That is the definition of more productivity.

For the shipping clerk to make this change, he has to be smart enough to figure it out, which may or may not take much intelligence. More important, he has to conceive of himself as capable of inventing a useful change. He has to think that making such a change is part of his job rather than let the orders pile up until someone else solves the problem. The organization has to allow him the freedom to make the change. If he is not the oldest shipping clerk, he and the other clerks have to feel that it is all right for younger men to make suggestions. (If the clerk is a woman, she and the organization have to feel that it is all right for a woman to make suggestions.) And the organization must provide a basis for the motivation to make the change, either hope for a personal reward or a sense of participation in the success of the work.

Whether the shipping clerk and his organization are motivated and organized in a way that makes all this possible is likely to depend on the mores, values, traditions, and ideas of the society of which they are a part. Development comes in societies where more organizations have clerks who make changes that increase productivity. And the same motivation lets organizations adopt new technology.

Of course, most changes to increase productivity require something more than a better way of stacking boxes. Usually, many people are involved in the changes that increase productivity, and they all have to be convinced, or at least taught, to make the right response to the change. Often money is needed. Most organizations are resistant to change, partly because most individuals are inclined to be reluctant to change. Society is even more resistant to change, which almost always is bad for some people, even if it is very good for the society as a whole.

Because wealth comes from increased productivity, there is no limit on the supply of wealth. The only limit is on the rate at which it is increased. One country's growth does not get in the way of another's. (In fact, usually it helps.) Poor countries do not have any limit that affects how wealthy they can become. Like wealthy countries, they are limited in *how fast* they can increase their wealth. For each country, that is determined by how resistant it is to the continuous changes required for—and produced by —continuously increasing wealth.

Economists and others often believe that productivity gains are dependent on the availability of capital. They are partly right, but they miss an important part of the point. Many productivity gains do not require any capital at all—such as that produced by our shipping clerk. And many investments of large amounts of capital—by countries and by businesses—do not result in any increased productivity at all (because of mistakes or conflict or corruption or the dominance of other values).

Capital is neither necessary nor sufficient to produce increased productivity. If our shipping clerk's company believed that capital must be invested to increase productivity, it would have bought an expensive machine for the shipping room—or built more space—so that the clerk could handle the increase in orders, instead of allowing him to use his head. (Of course, none of this denies that capital is sometimes useful or essential.)

Some capital has to come from savings, that is, from sacrificing consumption, or from outside. But some capital comes from learning and changing ideas and values. Because of the resistance to change, it may be that such "soft" increases in capital—improvement in the quality and character of the labor force and of institutions—can grow only at about the same rate as "real" capital earns interest and profits.

But even "real" capital grows not just by diverting resources from consumption to investment. The value of capital is based on what it can produce. When a better way is found to use capital—like finding a new name for a factory's product that enables it to be sold at a higher price—that capital becomes more valuable. The result can be that the accounting books and national statistics show increases in physical capital that have not required any sacrifice of consumption.

The economists' formulas about how much capital a country needs in order to grow are partly a matter of the way that changes are reported. It is often more realistic to understand that the growth of capital associated with increased output is a *result* of the increased output, rather than the *cause*. It is true that if a country has more income, its total capital stock will be more valuable, but that does not mean that the country had first to find the capital in order to be able to increase its output. The two went together. Any society can increase its capital by becoming more productive without receiving any capital from outside.

We have said that a country does not need raw materials to get rich. Also that it does not need capital from outside. Also that there is plenty of technology available to it. So why aren't all countries rich? Don't the poor countries want to become rich?

The first answer is that most poor countries *are* becoming richer. During the past forty years most poor countries have been getting richer (i.e., increasing their real GNP per capita) at a rate of at least 2 percent per year. While that sounds slow, it is fast enough to double every thirty-six years, to get eight times richer in only a century. It is the rate at which England and the United States moved from poor to rich. After 40,000 years when no society learned to become rich, the gap between the first and last to start on the path is only a century or two.

Many poor countries are growing much faster than 2 percent per year per person because catch-up growth is easier than original growth (or perhaps because they are better societies for economic growth than we were).

But other poor countries are not growing, some are even getting poorer.[5] Why does this happen if economic growth is as "easy" as we say?

First, we do not say it is easy; we say only that it is natural, that every country can do it and that it does not require outside capital or natural resources. All children learn to walk and talk, but if you watch them, you can see that it is not easy.

When a country does not grow, it is not because it lacks anything; it is because something is standing in the way. Something in that country is preventing the natural increase in productivity from happening. What is standing in the way may be disorder or strong social resistance to necessary changes. But most often it is actions of the government that prevent growth. Just as there are many ways a company and its employees can behave that will prevent the shipping clerk from stacking the boxes in a new and better way, so there are many ways a government can behave that prevent its citizens from making changes that would make the country more productive.

Most individuals are motivated to try to earn more money, and even more are motivated to get as much benefit as they can with the money they have. Individuals' determination to do better for themselves, and the efforts and inventiveness that people exert for this purpose, have immense potential power. They are the ultimate source of all wealth. But whether the immense power of the efforts and thought of millions of citizens trying to do better for themselves will increase their country's efficiency depends on what is the easiest way for citizens to improve their position, and this depends on the incentives created by the government and society. It depends on whether these incentives channel the power of citizens' efforts toward increased productivity or in some other direction.

Of course, the first requirement for economic development is internal and external peace. War can destroy faster than people can produce, even if their productivity is very high. Even threats of war or anarchy can make it imprudent for people to invest time and money in the most efficient kind of work. The first need for government is to provide enough stability so that it is prudent for people to invest work and money in productive enterprise. Countries that have not learned how to achieve that degree of governmental stability will sometimes go backward. And a few years of negative growth makes it very hard to have high long-term average growth rates. (That is one of the reasons why it would be unwise to give great odds that China will grow faster than India in the next twenty-five years.)

If the government is arranged so that the easiest way people can help themselves is to get benefits from the government, or use the government to get benefits from others, or if people need to spend a lot of their effort protecting themselves against the government, then the country's productivity will grow slowly or not at all. If the government is arranged so that individuals will receive most of the benefits they produce if they are able to become more productive, then many people will become more productive, and so will the country.

What is needed to harness the natural forces of growth are peace, recognition of individuals' rights to own property, protection against violence, a sound currency (i.e., one that is generally accepted, can serve as a way of saving assets, and is a reliable measure of value), and a legal system that enables people to make binding contracts with one another. The latter makes the collection of debts possible. No collection, no loans. Any government that provides these things, does not interfere too much with prices or with normal drives toward greater productivity, and does not take too big a share of people's work, will find that its country is growing richer at a good rate. This is demonstrated by the fact that there is no example of a country that does these "simple" things and fails to grow.

Government is absolutely essential and deserves great respect. Governments are needed to be part of the solution, even though often they are the problem. In addition to the modest essential functions described earlier, there are other things that governments can usefully do to increase economic growth, such as providing the physical infrastructure for transportation and communication. And the government can or must do things for other purposes, such as redistributing resources to provide short-term help for the needy, protecting the environment, or reducing predatory behavior. And there is much optional activity that governments can do without damaging their countries' economies. But usually only governments, or the disorder from lack of government, and some religions are strong enough to defeat the natural drive toward increased wealth. And in every case where a country is failing to grow one can point to what its government is doing that stands in the way of increasing productivity.[6]

To summarize, wealth will spread through the zones of turmoil because of the force exerted by the following influences: widespread human talent and energy, competitive institutions, strong and diverse examples of how to become wealthy, and international markets. These forces are not magic. Some countries will likely stay poor for a very long time. Others will have long periods of stagnation or decline even after they start growing. But in each twenty-year period the whole group of still-poor countries will become wealthier, and some of them will cross the threshold to historic wealth, until virtually the whole world is at least as wealthy as Greece and Portugal are today—ten times wealthier than the richest society of the past. (We are not going to say anything about the different question whether the countries that are very wealthy today will continue to get wealthier.)

Confidence that economic development is coming does not mean forgetting the negatives of economic development, often a process even more
painful than adolescence. While modern ways are necessary, they are often
cold-blooded and nasty. Often they are adopted only by harshly rejecting
old virtues and values. And much pain results from the simple fact that
when change is rapid, parents and children have to grow up in different
worlds.

We speak of "modern ways," but these are often felt as "Western ways"
or "foreign ways." In addition to the inevitable disruption they cause, they
are often felt an attack on national culture or religion. Much of the history of the zones of turmoil can be written in terms of the different ways
that cultures respond to the "onslaught" of modernity—some of which will
be violent and irrational (see table 3.1).[7] Certainly this is one way to see the
current behavior of Iran.

The Development of Democracy

Are there forces that will make democracy spread, comparable to the forces
ensuring the spread of wealth? Here is our picture of what we can expect
and why.

Democracy will lose some ground in the next few years because the
shallow or questionable democracies that initially took the place of communist governments do not have strong roots and face tremendous problems. Also, most of the other democracies in the zones of turmoil have not
yet built the basis for stable democracy. (The only stable democracies in the
zones of turmoil are Israel and Costa Rica, and perhaps some of the tiny island republics.) By the law of averages, some of these shallow democracies
will fail at least once before finally achieving stable democracy. But very
gradually the number of people living in stable democracies will become a
larger and larger share of the world's population. (But even stable democracies can be lost.)

Democracy is hard to achieve because it is natural for anyone who has
power to become impatient with those who stand in the way of doing what
she thinks should be done and also to want to protect her position from
those who want to take power themselves. This is the traditional way for
those with power or authority to behave, and many people expect rulers to
behave that way. (Totalitarianism has partly a different basis.)

Democracy comes when most people believe that their government is
not legitimate unless it has the consent of the citizens—when enough
people feel strongly enough about democracy to risk their lives or their positions to reject the authority of a government that has not been democrati-

TABLE 3.1

REACTIONS TO CULTURAL CHANGE

I. *Nonviolent rejection of intruding culture*
  A. *Rational*
  Pharisees
  Slavophiles (Tolstoyan)
  Gandhi
  Latin Amerindians
  Négritude
  Dutch Guiana Bush Negroes
  B. *"Apocalyptic"*
  Essenes
  South African "Zionists"
II. *Violent rejection of intruding culture*
  A. *"Austere" and largely rational*
  Maccabeans
  Bar Kochba
  Wahabis
  Sepoy Rebellion
  B. *Manic*
  Zealots
  Some American Indian uprisings
  Boxers
  Mau-Mau

III. *Nonviolent synthesis with intruding culture*
  A. *"Talismanic" (or magical)*
  "Rice Christians"
  B. *Semitalismanic*
  Primitive Christians (Gnostics)
  "Afro-Asian socialism"
  (Pacific, as in Burma,
  Ceylon, India, etc.)
  C. *Rational*
  Sadduccees
  Brahmo-Samaj
  Meiji Japan (1880–1900)
IV. *Violent synthesis with intruding culture*
  A. *"Talismanic" (or magical)*
  Tai-Pin
  Lumpa
  B. *Semitalismanic*
  Bolsheviks
  Maoists
  India
  C. *Rational*
  Black Muslims

SOURCE: Herman Kahn, *World Economic Development* (New York: Morrow, 1979), 128. Reprinted by permission.

cally chosen and to insist on the freedom of opposition groups to organize and circulate information. Stable and effective democracy requires much more. Institutions have to develop, and people have to learn many difficult lessons about respect for differences, compromise, commitment to law, the limits to politics, and so on.

In this book we usually speak as if there are only two possibilities: a country either is a democracy or it is not. (We also distinguish between "shallow democracy" and "stable democracy.") But democracy can also be seen as a continuum. Countries that are already democracies can become more or less democratic. Countries that are not yet democracies can become closer or further from being democratic. Nevertheless, we believe that it is important to emphasize a sharp break in that continuum, a distinct threshold between democracies and nondemocracies, even if it is difficult to define the exact difference.

Aspects of democracy—such as increased respect for law, development of private property, and independent organizational life—are important to countries that are not yet democracies not only because they increase the chance that democracy will come to power and that, when it comes, it will be able to maintain itself in power, but also for their inherent value. In countries that have become democracies, becoming more democratic improves the quality of the democracy and may increase its stability.

The defining characteristics of democracy are that practical power does not come from force, that there are a number of different kinds and sources of power, and that ordinary citizens have at least a little power. The quality of democracy concerns the sources of power and the nature of the struggle to determine policy. In a higher-quality democracy, more power can be achieved from wisdom and integrity, from the ability to convince and represent people, and from other virtues. In a lower-quality democracy, these sources of power are relatively weaker; privilege, demagoguery, corruption, and conspiracy are more important. In a higher-quality democracy, decisions are taken in an orderly way, after widespread civil debate and negotiation. In a lower-quality democracy, the political process is more rough and tumble.

A democracy also achieves higher quality by becoming more inclusive. The quality of U.S. democracy improved as we gave more men the right to vote, as we eliminated slavery, and as we gave women the right to vote. (But we were a democracy from the beginning.)

The stability of democracy and the quality of democracy are different, although not unrelated. The stability of democracy depends mostly on two questions: First, how great are the sources of division and conflict (e.g., class, race, ethnicity, ideology, economic or military failure)? Second, how strong and widespread is the commitment to democracy and to the supremacy of the law? How many people feel how strongly that a government that has not been democratically chosen does not have the right to govern? How many people feel how strongly that no government has the right to break the law and to use force against lawful opposition?

A shallow democracy, where people do not feel strongly about democracy and individual rights, can survive for a long time if things go well. If a country is prosperous and not divided by strong conflicts, and if its government feels no urgent need to suppress the opposition, democracy may survive even without strong roots.

A major part of the battle for democracy has been won almost everywhere. The belief in basic democracy, that is, in the right of the people to choose the government, and the unique authority of free elections, is widespread. The practical procedural components of democracy, a belief in the superiority of law and the need for individual freedoms, is not so widely accepted. Nor is experience with compromise, respect for differences, loyal opposition, and mutual trust. And the belief in democracy is not so widespread and strongly held that rulers cannot easily be found who are ready to try to rule without free elections. And most people in the zones of turmoil are still able to accept nondemocratic government.

A critical recent advance for democracy was that one of the major traditional sources of authoritarian governments has been permanently weakened; most professional military officer corps no longer believe that they have a right to rule. Professional military officers in most parts of the world now believe in civilian supremacy.

This victory against military rule is not complete for several reasons. In some countries the military force does not have a professional officer corps (i.e., the officers are not "professional" in a sociological sense). In those countries civilian government is not protected by the new worldwide military professional consensus—and there are still a few military establishments outside that consensus. Also, many professional officers think that sometimes the military has an "obligation" to rescue the country from politicians' failures. But, unlike the past, such military governments will be generally seen by officers to be temporary and of doubtful legitimacy. And of course there will probably be occasions in the future when professional officers take over a government because they have the power to do so, even though most of their colleagues do not believe that it is legitimate to do so. Nevertheless, the problem of protecting civilian government from military takeover is significantly smaller than it was even twenty years ago.

Now that communism has destroyed itself—except in China, Cuba, Vietnam, and North Korea—the only major international source of legitimacy for authoritarian government is that part of Islam that believes in authoritarian, theocratic rule. Most of Islam is compatible with democracy but also provides alternative sources of legitimacy. And the claims of democracy are weakened in Islamic countries by democracy's association with Islam's perceived enemy, the West. And there are Islamic bases of support for the suppression of opposition and freedom of speech—just as there are Islamic bases of support for democratic principles.

One of the great mysteries of the future is the way that Islam will accommodate to the requirements of modernity. This accommodation will probably be driven by the desire to build modern productive economies, but it will also influence the speed with which democracy will come to the countries that are now Islamic.

And perhaps some other great religion, like Islam, or a new "anti-religion," like communism, might arise and keep a large part of the world from democracy for many years. It does not seem likely, but what we know about the future does not exclude such a possibility.

What will be the shape of the path toward democracy in the zones of turmoil? There is not space to describe all the patterns of struggle for stable democracy. In each country the situation is different. Where there are authoritarian governments, the most common pattern will be for the ruler to try to use some democratic forms—either for domestic reasons or to pay deference to international opinion. Rulers will find that they need to give these democratic forms increasing reality as their economies grow more complex, and they have to accommodate a complex variety of interests and keep in touch with a society that is becoming better organized. Each time a ruler dies or is unable to rule well enough to keep the society reasonably satisfied, there will be another chance for democracy. The potential successors may be so balanced that they keep each other from taking power and can agree only on elections. Or the new ruler may be so weak, because he cannot count on the loyalty of the sources of power, that he has to depend in part on the democratic elements within the country and give them more freedom and authority.

From time to time, increasingly powerful middle classes (produced by economic development) are likely to try to replace their authoritarian governments with democratic governments. Some of them will lose, some of them will win. Some movements for democracy will stay democratic, some will yield to the authoritarian temptation.

In shallow democracies or countries whose democracy has many defects, governments will from time to time feel pressure to squeeze democratic freedoms. If they go about it cleverly, and if the whole community is not strongly committed to democracy, they will succeed, and their democracy will become weaker, and their country may even become authoritarian. But if the attempt to deny democracy is too blatant, or if the community is determined to defend democracy, then the democracy will become stronger. After the failure of a number of such struggles to weaken the commitment to democracy, the democracy will become stable.

Most countries that do not have democracy will suffer a flow of talented people leaving to live under democracy. To protect themselves against pressures for democracy, authoritarian governments need to exclude information and influences from the democratic world. But they will know that their countries can develop only if they work with potential investors, customers, suppliers, and teachers from the democracies. The way to learn how to be developed is to learn what developed countries are like and how they work. Since the democratic world has most of the money, economic growth requires extensive contact with the democratic world. Therefore, the ideas of political legitimacy from that world will influence critical parts of the population in the zones of turmoil.

Economic development means that organizational competence and experience in using independent judgment is spreading through a society. Economic strength requires that tens or hundreds of thousands of individuals learn how to make decisions, take risks, and earn the trust and loyalty of others. Inevitably many of these people will be influenced by the attitudes of the people they deal with, people they are trying to learn from, in the democracies. This influence will be one of the ways that economic growth helps spread democracy.

It is not a naïve faith in the universal attractiveness or virtue of democracy that leads us to conclude that it will inherit the world. It is a practical judgment based on what has been happening through this century and on a consideration of the alternatives—a judgment that recognizes the cultural requirements of democracy and the cultural differences between many of the countries that are not yet democracies and those that are already successful democracies.

Nor is our conviction that democracy will gradually spread through the zones of turmoil based on a belief that democracy is an ideal form of government or that it does not permit a great deal of evil or that democratic governments necessarily or normally take care of their country better. We do not claim that democracy means good government. Democracies can be corrupt; and they are often so foolish that they prevent the economic growth that their citizens want, fail to protect citizens and the environment from dangers, waste vast resources, or produce a governmental stalemate that makes it impossible for people to plan or to make their own decisions. But democracies have the great advantage that they can be counted on not to kill large numbers of their citizens or let them starve to death. While this seems like too small a virtue to boast about, in this century well over 100 million people (more than the population of France) died from the absence of this modest virtue.[8]

Five New Forces

Five new forces will be working in the zones of turmoil to make their future different from their past. First is the all-encompassing process of economic development and the struggle for democracy we have just described at length.

The second major new factor that will influence the zones of turmoil is the growing practical political illegitimacy of nondemocratic regimes, of which we have spoken before. The two causes of this illegitimacy already mentioned are the lack of any systematic challenge to democracy after the failure of communism and the development of a professional military ethic of civilian supremacy. But something else may be even more important.

As long as the Soviet Union was generally regarded as one of the two superpowers, people did not feel comfortable speaking of the world as divided between democracies and nondemocracies because that would have been seen as taking sides in the cold war. Accommodation with the Soviet Union required downplaying the centrality of the distinction between democracy and other kinds of government. With the low level of ideological intensity in the developed democracies, this deference to communist sensibility became automatic and unconscious. Few people noticed that the reason why the distinction between democracies and nondemocracies was not more prominent was that making it prominent would have been an implicit criticism of the Soviet Union and its allies.[9]

Chapter 7 argues that one component of the policy of the democracies should be to promote and rely on the distinction between democracies and other governments. But in the zones of turmoil themselves it is already true that governments that have not been freely elected are not seen to have as much legitimacy as governments that have been. Of course, many people do not feel that way—or do not care. But in virtually every country an important fraction of the population believes that true legitimacy comes only from free elections.

The third new factor that will make the future of the zones of turmoil different than the past is that because modern wealth comes from human productivity, countries cannot get wealthier by taking things from other countries. War will virtually never be profitable for countries in the zones of turmoil.

Except for very small countries, natural resources are not valuable enough to be worth a war. Captured populations are not desirable, if for no other reason than that they cost more to support than the income they generate. The distribution of wealth in the world, the visible success of small countries without land or resources (e.g., Singapore or Switzerland), is a daily reminder that aggression is not the way to enter the path to economic success. Unfortunately, the unprofitability of war, by itself, does not mean that there will be peace. But it is a reason why the zones of turmoil can be expected to have less war than would be suggested by historical comparisons.

The fourth new factor in the zones of turmoil is the example provided by the zones of peace and democracy. Never before have countries had such a demonstration that sustained peace is possible. The zones of peace will also show how countries that have a long history of fighting with one another can deal with disputes and conflict without war, and without heavy armament programs. The example provided by the zones of peace will also demonstrate that wealth is possible and show what successful countries are like. And it will show that democracy can survive for generations in a variety of cultures, with a variety of forms. The people in the zones of turmoil will be armored against arguments that democracy is impossible and will be provided with examples of many tools that have been successfully used to overcome its difficulties.

Finally, the future of the zones of turmoil can be made different from the past because the great democracies have the power to intervene, free from competing security concerns and conflicts. Chapter 8 considers the democracies' dilemma in deciding when and how to intervene in the conflict and violence in the zones of turmoil.

Wealth, democracy, and peace are different from happiness or human progress. There is a solid basis for expecting that wealth, democracy, and peace will be spread through much of the zones of turmoil by the end of the twenty-first century. But we cannot say whether more people will be good or happy at the end of the century or at the beginning.

We can point to the practical forces moving toward wealth, democracy, and peace. But we do not know of historic forces assuring progress toward a better world, toward increased human happiness, virtue, or well-being. In fact, it is apparent that wealth, power, freedom, and knowledge are not only eagerly pursued goals that will increasingly be attained but are also sources of profound new dangers and challenges. Someone else will have to write the book that predicts whether or not decadence and evil will do more to determine the quality of life than wealth, peace, and democracy.

Notes

1. This leads to the question of how the Soviet Union could have had a first-class army when it turns out that their economy was at about the level of Thailand's. There are several answers. First, their army had not fought a first-class enemy since World War II. We do not know how many of their divisions were really capable. Second, the Soviet Union was the supreme example of a large society that focused such an inordinate share of its resources and leadership on its military that the rest of the economy was starved.

2. An air force can prevent the massive supplies of fuel and ammunition required by an army engaged in mobile combat from reaching the front. But it is rarely, if ever, possible for an air force to cut off supplies enough to severely damage

an army at rest, because an army at rest requires ten or a hundred times less supplies than one engaged in mobile combat.

3. It was not, as some think, a difference between defeat and a draw. In June 1951, when the ceasefire was reached and negotiations begun, the Chinese army had been so badly defeated that it could not have prevented the UN from moving north and occupying Korea up to the narrow neck of the peninsula, north of the northern capital Pyongyang. The taking of most of North Korea at that time would probably have resulted in fewer UN casualties than the Chinese and North Koreans inflicted in two years of static fighting accompanying negotiations, after the ceasefire had given them a chance to recuperate and reinforce.

4. A short explanation of economic growth, in terms like those used in this discussion, is contained in chapter 2 of Max Singer, *Passage to a Human World* (New Brunswick, N.J.: Transaction, 1989). Long and complex discussions and explanations of economic growth are found in the following works: Theodore W. Schultz, *Investing in People* (Berkeley: University of California Press, 1981); Theodore W. Schultz, *Transforming Traditional Agriculture* (New Haven: Yale University Press, 1964); N. Rosenberg and L.E. Birdzell, Jr., *How the West Grew Rich* (New York: Basic Books, 1986); George Gilder, *Wealth and Poverty* (New York: Basic Books, 1981); Herman Kahn, *World Economic Development* (New York: Morrow, 1979).

5. About three times as many people live in those less developed countries that grew at least 1.8 percent per year per capita from 1965 to 1989 as live in countries that did worse.

6. While it is very difficult objectively to weigh the burdens and benefits of a government, one crude measure can be used, at least at the extremes. If two-thirds of a country's workers are working directly or indirectly for the government, it is likely that the government will prevent economic growth. If 15 percent or less of the workforce is working directly or indirectly for the government, then the government is probably not preventing economic growth. In between, the question is more difficult.

7. See also Edmund Stillman and William Pfaff, *The Politics of Hysteria* (New York: Harpers, 1960) and Vittorio Lanternari, *The Religion of the Oppressed* (New York: Knopf, 1963).

8. Since World War II, none of the famines has been in a democracy—although democracies have had many crop failures. See Amartya Sen, *Poverty and Famines* (New York: Oxford University Press, 1981). See also R.J. Rummel, *Death by Government: Genocide and Mass Murder since 1900* (New Brunswick, N.J.: Transaction, 1994).

9. Some would argue that the United States also downplayed democracy because some of the regimes the United States supported against communism were not democracies.

CHAPTER 4

WHAT DIFFERENCE DO NUCLEAR WEAPONS MAKE?

Nuclear weapons will not affect the fundamental character of the next world order, but they will cause trouble and possibly great tragedy. (They are fundamentally evil because they have the potential power to kill so many people. They have been a necessary evil, but it may be possible to make them an unnecessary evil.)

At the end of the cold war there were perhaps fifty thousand nuclear weapons divided between the United States and the former Soviet Union and perhaps another five thousand in the rest of the world, of which about half are in China, with the rest divided among England, France, Israel, India, and Pakistan. The two most important questions they raise are these: Do the former Soviet weapons make Russia significantly more powerful than it would otherwise be? Will nuclear weapons increase violence in the zones of turmoil or make events there dangerous to the zones of peace? (The weapons in the zones of peace do not represent more than a theoretical threat to these zones because the countries there all know that democracies will not use nuclear weapons against one another.)

Can nuclear weapons make Russia a major threat to Western or Central Europe? No. Russia's nuclear weapons give it no offensive power. (But as long as a Russian nuclear force is large and competent enough to be theoretically capable of outmatching the European nuclear forces, the Russian nuclear weapons do urge upon Europe a security link to the United States, because hypothetically Europe needs the U.S. nuclear forces for deterrence, at least until Russia has become a stable democracy.)

The Russian weapons pose no offensive threat to Europe because there is so much deterrence and fear of nuclear weapons in the world. Since 1945, no one has been able to use nuclear weapons for offensive purposes. The closest thing to a use of nuclear weapons for a military purpose other than deterring other nuclear weapons has been NATO's use (the U.S.'s use) of nuclear threats to deter a Soviet attack on Western Europe. But there was probably ample deterrence of that threat without the nuclear weapons.

The only possibility of using nuclear weapons effectively is if they are supported by political sympathizers, or political groups that can be manipulated, in the country being threatened. The efforts the Soviet Union made along these lines had only limited objectives, and they achieved only limited success, but an extension of that approach was the best chance they had of achieving a decisive victory over the West. A Russian dictatorship would not be able to organize such support and therefore could not use its nuclear weapons in that way.

There are, finally, no prizes available that Russia might hope to obtain by threatening the European democracies. There is no territory in Central Europe that Russia would be helped by taking. Even a nasty military government of Russia will know that what Russia needs is trade, investment, and aid from Western Europe and that it cannot use military threats to get such things.

Since there is great reluctance to attack a nuclear power, the Russians could get defensive benefits from their nuclear force—if they needed them. But why would the Western Europeans want to attack Russia? And Russia can be strong enough, even without nuclear weapons, so that it has no reason to fear attack from its neighbors. This is meant in both senses: It is not likely that the neighbors will attack; and if they did, Russia should be able to defeat the attack without even thinking about needing nuclear weapons.

Although Russian nuclear weapons might improve Russia's position in relationship to Ukraine, which could develop a serious military force in a few years, Russia will be better off if neither country has nuclear weapons than if both countries do, even if Russia has many more. Without nuclear weapons, Russia is likely to be able to win any war with moderate cost and damage; with nuclear weapons on both sides, any war risks major destruction in Russia. Generally, nuclear weapons favor the weak and irresponsible, not the powerful and responsible. And although Russia may turn out to have some irresponsible (reckless) governments, it will not want to plan on it. (Ukraine may have a stronger case for needing nuclear weapons, but it too would be better off in most cases if neither it nor Russia had any at all.) It would be too expensive for Russia to keep its nuclear force at a level where it can be a match for U.S. forces if the United States wants to protect itself. So Russia's nuclear force does not provide much of a basis of achieving superpower status—whatever that is.

It is likely that Russia will reduce the size of its nuclear arsenal by perhaps 90 percent—to some three thousand weapons. This does not depend on a relatively democratic or friendly government staying in power. It is the result of the fact that maintaining nuclear forces is expensive, and because Russia would get no substantial benefit from continuing to keep thirty thousand nuclear weapons instead of three thousand. Presumably the United States will continue its effort to encourage Russia to make such a reduction, although Russia is likely to do it in any case. (Maybe Russia will keep six thousand; the exact numbers do not make much difference.) Since they will not be trying to keep up with the United States, they will not care much whether the United States agrees to comparable reductions, although they may make a show of seeking equivalent reductions from the United States.

In brief, with or without nuclear weapons, Russia will be much stronger than its neighbors, not strong enough to take offensive action against the Western European democracies, and significantly inferior to the United States. That is, Russian nuclear weapons will not significantly influence the strategic balance in the world.

Nuclear Weapons and the Relationship between Zones of Turmoil and Zones of Peace

Nuclear weapons are unlikely to give any country or group in the zones of turmoil the ability to take offensive action against any of the countries of the zones of peace. But the democracies will be reluctant to intervene in conflicts in the zones of turmoil against a country armed with nuclear weapons. The ability to deliver a few nuclear weapons against cities in the zones of peace could be an umbrella to protect aggressors in the zones of turmoil from interference by the democracies. But the weapons could not enable such aggressors to threaten the survival of the democracies.

While it is likely to be not too expensive for the democracies to build defensive systems that provide a substantial degree of protection against ballistic missiles and other military delivery vehicles from the zones of turmoil, such systems cannot be perfect. (The possibilities are described later.) And even if the cities of the zones of peace have sufficient protection against missile attack, they will remain vulnerable to covertly delivered weapons because clandestine weapon delivery is much more difficult to prevent by purely physical defense measures. And it is much easier for a country or a group to produce a mass-destruction weapon that can be carried on a ship or as air freight than to produce such a weapon mated to a missile delivery system, particularly if that missile delivery system has to penetrate missile defenses.

Many countries and groups will have, or will seem to have, the ability to make nuclear, chemical, or biological weapons that can be hidden on a ship and that, if released in the middle of American or European cities, would cause hundreds of thousands of deaths. It seems highly unlikely that it will ever be possible to design a reasonable physical defense against such a threat. Weapons weighing over a ton or even several tons each can easily be concealed on small boats brought into ports over several weeks' time. And many places have or will have the ability to make a nuclear, chemical, or biological weapon of that size that might well kill hundreds of thousands of people if released or detonated in the middle of a big city. And the technology of long-range detonation arrangements is trivial. What can be done to protect against someone announcing that weapons of mass destruction are hidden in ten cities and can be exploded on command? While this scenario is not realistically likely, it is such an obvious idea that governments are likely to have to deal with the question.

Protection against clandestine weapons can be provided only by police and intelligence work and by deterrence, measures which are generally effective but are certainly not perfect. A general world regime of law and arms control could reduce but not eliminate the possibility of such a threat, but it is not clear that this is a promising approach. No faintly practical arms-control arrangements could prevent everyone from acquiring the technical capability to build such weapons. In other words, this is one of a number of potential weird threats and dangers that we have to learn how to live with, even as we work hard to reduce it as much as possible.

Deterrence against clandestine weapons presents quite different problems from the traditional deterrence relationship with the Soviet Union, even if the analytic structure of deterrence is essentially the same. The deterrent threat is likely to have to be against the individual or small group that is being deterred, not against a country. The deterrent probably does not need to be massive, but it does need to be as rapid and precise as possible. If weapons are the deterrent, the key physical problem will probably be timely target identification and location.

It is really "compellance," rather than deterrence, that is needed to deal with this threat. The United States would not be satisfied by the ability to retaliate or preemptively destroy the threatener without destroying the weapons. It would need to be able to compel the threatener to reveal the location of the weapons so that they could be disarmed. The basic sequence would be: (1) A democratic police action against X; (2) X says "desist or I will release my weapons in your cities"; (3) democracies say, "Tell us where the weapons are or we will destroy you"; (4) X says "If you destroy me, the weapons will be released." Now the democracies need a threat against X that will prevent X from retaliating for his own destruction. For some Xs, it is hard to imagine such a threat.

It is not clear whether this kind of scenario is realistic enough to justify serious concern or substantial military programs. But those who oppose a missile-defense system are likely to use the possibility of clandestine weapons as a reason to avoid building a defense against missiles. So this scenario will be considered even if it is pretty far-fetched. (Former Secretary of the Air Force Harold Brown invoked such a possibility in a newspaper article opposing strategic defense.) Most ordinary people would not consider the fact that there is a danger from clandestine weapons to be a sufficient reason not to buy protection against those threats for which substantial protection is possible.

While no one can rule out the possibility that clandestine weapons of mass destruction will be used against, or to threaten, London or Rome or New York, it should be clear that uncomfortable—or tragic—as such threats or attacks may be, they would not alter the nature of the international system or make great gains for whoever tries to employ such "suitcase bombs."

Since an increasing number of countries or groups are likely to have the physical ability to cause hundreds of thousands of American deaths by attacking U.S. cities with nuclear, chemical, or biological weapons, one of the few fundamental objectives of U.S. national security policy must be to provide as much protection as possible against this possibility. The basic threat is from missiles, but weapons might also be delivered clandestinely. Bombs dropped from airplanes are probably not a major possibility except as a kind of clandestine attack (i.e., civilian planes penetrating by disguise).

Nobody is going to try to go to war with the United States. A threat is most likely to arise in connection with U.S. efforts to stop aggression, preserve peace, or protect democracy in some part of the developing world. But conceivably a threat could come from a nonrational "Idi Amin" engaged in a local or internal conflict.

The basic concept is that the United States does not want anyone to have the power to kill hundreds of thousands of Americans—whether or not there is any reason to think that someone would be motivated to try. Also, the United States does not want its choices in responding to developing-country conflict to be constrained by fear of having U.S. cities attacked.

Physical defense against developing-country missiles is becoming a realistic option at budget levels in the range of $5 to $8 billion a year, starting in 1996. By the next decade such programs could make any dictator with a small number of missiles very doubtful that he could land a missile on a U.S. city. Our defense system would have a good chance of stopping an attack of at least a few tens of weapons aimed at American cities by any country that had not had a very expensive and advanced program of missile improvement designed to defeat our defenses. (And an even better chance of stopping most weapons from such an attack.)

Two broad kinds of missile defense have been developed in recent years. Ground-based defenses are probably more effective against substantial attacks, but they have to be located in the general area of the target. Defenses that would protect our mainland would not protect Europe (or Hawaii).

Space-based defense—the so-called "brilliant pebbles" type—uses hundreds of satellites kept in orbit and programmed to maneuver to collide with any ballistic missile that goes more than twenty miles up in the air and then heads back to attack the ground. One set of satellites can provide protection to all cities in the world against all countries now likely to acquire missiles.

The space-based system works by spreading satellites evenly through a band of space around the earth. But only the satellites that are fairly near to a missile's path while it is in the air can be used to block it. If the defense system is relatively inexpensive and has only 500 or 1000 satellites, they have to be spread fairly thinly. Only a brief part of the trajectory of short-range missiles is high enough to be intercepted by the satellites. So only a small percentage of the satellites would find themselves close enough to intercept a volley of short-range missiles launched simultaneously, and those few satellites could stop only an equal number of missiles. Of course, if there are more satellites, or the missiles are flying over a longer range, a larger attack could be stopped by this system.

Since a space-based system does not defend a particular area on the ground, and since it does not use weapons based in a particular location, it has special advantages for use by an international agency or a partnership of countries.

Ground-based systems can also use a much smaller set of satellites to provide target information to ground-based interceptors (the "brilliant eyes" system). If the United States is using a set of satellites to support our ground-based defenses, we could let other countries use the information from the "brilliant eyes" too, so they could build their own defenses more cheaply. And the satellites could also be used to make it much easier for us to provide temporary local defenses in other parts of the world. Later, even better systems of worldwide protection, using lasers without large numbers of satellites, are likely to make it possible to stay ahead of minor-power offensive-force technology. Also systems which use high altitude, long-endurance drones are likely to be able to provide protection against short-range missiles in some circumstances.

Most of the arguments used against missile defense during the cold war no longer apply. It is clear that a reasonable degree of effectiveness is practical. There is no enemy that can respond to defenses by building a massive offensive force. The various arms control arguments, including concerns about stability, do not relate to the defense of cities against miscellaneous dictators in the zones of turmoil. The only question left is whether the degree of protection that can be bought is worth the cost.

The nation will have to decide whether to spend one-tenth of 1 percent of our GNP to prevent countries from being able to attack our cities with missiles. This choice would be easier if we could expect that beginning in a few years, and for a long time, there will be a number of nondemocracies with missiles and chemical or nuclear warheads that could reach the United States. But it is more likely that it will be a decade before such a threat to the United States definitely exists, and thereafter there are likely to be at most one or a few nondemocracies at any one time capable of threatening the United States with missiles.

There are likely to be more countries that could attack some city not in the United States, such as Rome or Calcutta. If, for example, Iraq, in order to deter the alliance attack against it, had been able to threaten to send a nuclear-armed missile against Rome, we would have been almost as deterred as if they had threatened Baltimore. And if Europe had bought a ground-based system so that Rome could not be threatened, an Iraqi threat against Calcutta would still have been a serious deterrent. So some of the strategic reason for being able to defend U.S. cities requires being able to defend all cities.

The main argument against the value of missile defenses is that they do not provide protection against covert attack, the "suitcase bomb." But there are many situations in which someone would have a missile threat against the United States but not have the threat of covert attack. For one thing, missiles can be aimed at the United States in minutes, while it is likely to take months to arrange a covert attack.

We are cautious enough to think the United States ought to buy protection against military threats, even though that protection leaves the danger of covert attack unsolved. We believe that the United States should begin to build a missile defense system. We think we should have such a system even if all nuclear weapons are outlawed, because someone may cheat, and in any event a defense is needed against missiles with chemical or biological weapons. Also, when missiles can attack a particular window from thousands of miles away, even ordinary high explosives can create an unacceptable vulnerability.

Currently there is more political objection to a space-based system than to a ground-based system, partly on technical grounds, but mostly because of the residue of traditional cold-war attitudes and congressional pork-barrel considerations. Therefore it probably is prudent to start with the ground-based system and add the satellites that can protect other parts of the world later. The U.S. military budget is now nearly $250 billion a year. Our recommendation for a defense against missiles would take 2 or 3 percent of that amount.

Nuclear Weapons in the Zones of Turmoil

The importance of nuclear weapons will probably not come from the wars they win or the numbers of people they kill, which are likely to be small. If the weapons turn out to be important, it will probably be because they influence the nature of international political conflict in the zones of turmoil.

There are two possibilities about the future of nuclear weapons in the zones of turmoil. The possibility that seems most likely now is an increasingly "nuclear world." In a nuclear world the general expectation is that more and more countries are going to acquire nuclear weapons and that sooner or later they will be used. North Korea may soon join Russia, China, India, Pakistan, Israel, Ukraine, and Kazakhstan, as nuclear powers in the zones of turmoil. And there is a good chance that one or more of the oil-rich Moslem countries will succeed in buying some of the Soviet-built weapons by then or in making their own, in part with material or technology coming from the former Soviet Union.

In a nuclear world the democracies are likely to reject a policy of preventing aggression or protecting democracy in the zones of turmoil because of the danger of having to act against a country with nuclear weapons.

If eight or ten countries in the zones of turmoil have nuclear weapons in the year 2000, which other countries might get nuclear weapons in the following few decades? There is a good chance that Latin America is close enough to being a zone of peace and democracy that nuclear weapons will not come to that continent. Both Argentina and Brazil have moved away from their programs. It is quite possible that they will never again be able to imagine using nuclear weapons against each other.

Sub-Saharan Africa is not likely to have nuclear weapons for a few decades. Whether they get nuclear weapons later, as they have more economic development but still plenty of conflict and nondemocratic government, depends on what happens in the rest of the world before then. A democratic, black and white, South Africa will not need nuclear weapons. An authoritarian South Africa might well get nuclear weapons.

Most of the big powers of the Asian zones of turmoil already have nuclear weapons or are on their way to getting them: China, India, Pakistan, and Korea. In a nuclear world in which China and Russia have nuclear weapons, a unified Korea might continue the nuclear weapons program begun by the North, even though there is a good chance that it would be a democratic country.

If the world continues to be nuclear, the chances are probably about equal that Southeast Asia—Thailand, Malaysia, Burma, Vietnam, and Indonesia—will or will not get nuclear weapons in the first decades of the twenty-first century.

The Islamic zone, across North Africa and much of Asia, is the likeliest candidate for the further substantial spread of nuclear weapons. These countries can easily imagine fighting one another—there have been dozens of wars and near wars among them in the post-World War II period. There are also a variety of conflicts along the line where Islam meets its non-Islamic neighbors, and of course the Islamic (especially Arab) conflict with Israel, which is assumed to have nuclear weapons. While none of the Islamic countries have developed economies, a number of them have enough oil money to be able to buy nuclear weapons in a nuclear world. (In effect, the West has fueled a large share of its automobiles with Muslim oil paid for with Western weapons, including the material and technology for building weapons of mass destruction.) So if we continue to have a nuclear world, it would not be amazing if there were five or ten Islamic nuclear powers from Morocco to Pakistan by 2020. Fundamentalist Islamic governments may approach issues in ways that surprise us because they have not yet developed the kind of ideas for justifying compromise with which we are familiar.

Nuclear weapons tend to balance each other or perhaps to provide political advantages, but rarely are there situations where it is useful actually to explode nuclear weapons. Israel is the exception. Because Israel is small and its primary enemies' goal is to destroy it, Israel's enemies are probably the only groups that could achieve their goals by exploding nuclear weapons—using them to destroy the majority of Israel's population. And those enemies have often had governments that did not put great value on the lives of their own citizens.

Because Israel also faces some real danger of being destroyed by military attack without nuclear weapons, Israel has a substantial reason for having its own nuclear weapons. As long as Israel is thought to have nuclear weapons, it may get some deterrence from them, which may prevent some fighting and casualties or even prevent an unlikely Israeli defeat. And in the event that it could be defeated, Israel might protect itself, at least once, with nuclear weapons, if the Arabs did not have them too.

But no matter how good its nuclear weapons are, Israel's danger would be increased much more if its enemies acquired nuclear weapons than it would be if it lost its own nuclear weapons and its enemies were prevented from gaining possession of such weapons. But that alternative—no nuclear weapons in the hands of either Israel or its enemies—may not exist. The experience with Iraq demonstrates that it is very difficult to prevent rich dictatorships from getting nuclear weapons. And if the dangers of nuclear weapons or materials escaping from the former Soviet Union are not sharply reduced soon, it will become much more difficult in the near future.

Apart from the Arab (Moslem) conflict with Israel, it is quite possible that a nuclear world would provide very few military explosions. There were nearly forty years of cold war between two sides with nuclear weapons and no military explosions. It is fair to say that the "natural" condition of nuclear weapons is to be unused. In most cases they are most useful to those who have them if they are not exploded. But that does not provide any guarantees. If there is a nuclear world for the generations before the zones of turmoil become democratic and peaceful, it seems likely that nuclear weapons will be exploded at least a few times (apart from use in an effort to destroy Israel). If they are used against cities, millions of people could be killed—although probably only a fraction as many as were killed by communists outside of wars.

Radioactive fallout from nuclear weapons and indirect or ecological damage resulting from nuclear explosions will produce only a fraction of the damage and deaths that would be produced by exploding nuclear weapons in cities. While fallout would cause many deaths outside the zone of combat if large numbers of weapons were exploded near the ground, the numbers would not be large compared to the number of people otherwise dying of diseases and accidents and would not substantially change people's life expectancy in any country not in the war itself.[1]

What is the harm if ten or twenty countries in the zones of turmoil have nuclear weapons? We have already said that it is unlikely that many of these weapons will be used by the nuclear countries or that they will kill very many people—compared either with the numbers killed by nonnuclear wars, by governments, or by such causes as smoking.

Of course, the first harm is the possibility that we are wrong and that many weapons will be used and tens of millions or hundreds of millions of people will be killed. Nuclear weapons have the possibility of getting out of control. Countries can produce thousands of them. They can be made very large. Through unimaginable circumstances, there can be wars in which many thousands of them are used and hundreds of millions of people are killed. Even though this is extremely unlikely, the possibility is inherent in the nature of nuclear weapons. Therefore we should be more distressed about nuclear weapons than is implied by thinking only about the reasonable possibilities.

The next harm is the possibility that the presence of nuclear weapons might slow the movement to democracy and peace. But it is difficult to know whether, if India and Pakistan, for example, continue to have nuclear weapons, the chance that they will go to war with each other will be increased or decreased. Nor is it clear whether the nuclear weapons will make it easier or harder for them to achieve stable democracy. Plausible theories can be spun in either direction. Both may be right; that is, the nuclear weapons can produce forces for peace and forces for war—and forces for and against democracy—at the same time. The theory does not give any solid basis for judging which effects will be stronger.

There are few data. The French and British nuclear weapons seem not to have a noticeable influence on either their democracy or their peace. The United States and the Soviet Union had nuclear weapons aimed against each other for more than forty years. Many think the nuclear weapons prevented conventional war between the two countries. We would argue that because of Soviet caution, war would have been unlikely even without nuclear weapons, but that is only speculation.

It is clear that having ten or twenty nuclear countries increases the chance that another twenty or forty countries will eventually acquire nuclear weapons. This multiplies the risk that the weapons will be exploded and kill a lot of people. Also, if nuclear weapons become much more commonplace, they may lose some of their mystery and magic and begin to be used like other weapons. On the other hand, if two countries having nuclear weapons are less likely to fight each other, then the spread of nuclear weapons might prevent more wars.

While countries with nuclear weapons may be strongly inhibited from using them, individuals and nongovernmental organizations are quite different. The world might be a substantially worse place if terrorist groups like the Sendero Luminoso of Peru or the drug lords of Colombia had a few nuclear weapons. The more countries that have nuclear weapons, the more likely it is that some weapons will escape from governmental control and be acquired by groups that might use them or that might have an accident with them.

Our conclusion is conservative but not hysterical. While it is not clear that a nuclear world would necessarily be much worse than a nonnuclear one, the chance that it would be horrible is great enough so that *there are few things more worth doing than preventing the spread of nuclear weapons*. And the case is much stronger for anyone who cares about the future of Israel.

Two Possibilities for the Future

The good news is that, while a nuclear world is the more likely possibility, some form of nonnuclear world is also possible. If a "nonnuclear world" were defined as a world in which nuclear weapons are impossible to build or in which no nuclear weapons exist, then it would no longer be possible. But we use the phrase "nonnuclear world" as the label for any world that avoids most of the dangers of a nuclear world. It is fair to say that a world in which the general expectation is that the number of nuclear powers is not likely to increase and in which no one thinks that nuclear weapons are ever likely to decide an international crisis, would be a nonnuclear world.

It is almost a cliché to point out that the fall of the Soviet Union dramatically increases the likelihood of an early spread of nuclear weapons, but the simultaneous good news has been less recognized. The fall of the Soviet Union may also create opportunities to change the world into a nonnuclear world.

Currently the first of these effects is stronger. With worsening chaos likely in the former Soviet Union it seems improbable that the thirty thousand Soviet-built weapons will all stay well guarded and in the control of national governments. There is a good chance that, for some of the next five years, major parts of Russia, Ukraine, or Kazakhstan will not be controlled by any national government. And even today many units of the Russian government are effectively out of the control of the government. Since countries and groups will pay millions of dollars for each of these weapons, there are strong incentives to find ways to get hold of a few of them to deliver to eager customers. We can see no basis for thinking that it is as much as an even-money bet that none of the Soviet-built nuclear weapons will get to countries outside of the former Soviet Union in the next few years. This is a danger for the world and a major threat to Israel.

But the fall of the Soviet Union also has created the first real opportunities in forty years to move toward a nonnuclear world. Some of these opportunities have already become visible. The likelihood that most of the Soviets' thirty thousand nuclear weapons will be dismantled and destroyed has already become a political reality, and with it the assumption that this dismantlement will permit the United States to eliminate a good fraction of its own nuclear weapons. It has become very likely that there will be only one-half or one-quarter as many nuclear weapons in the world at the end of this decade as there were at its beginning.

Since there was little chance that all the nuclear weapons would have been used even if there had been a war between the Soviet Union and the United States, the main importance of the reduction in the numbers of nuclear weapons that it is the first step in the right direction in over forty-five years. This reduction in numbers of weapons can be used by statesmen to make it begin to seem possible to move toward a nonnuclear world. Also, it reduces the chance that weapons will escape from governmental control.

For Ukraine, Belarus, and Kazakhstan, the main reason to keep some nuclear weapons is to avoid being dominated by Russia's nuclear weapons. For Russia, the main reason to keep some nuclear weapons is to protect against Chinese nuclear weapons. (And of course it is natural for any government to keep the weapons it has, at least if their maintenance cost is not too high.) In all cases the decision will reflect not only national interest but also internal political considerations.

For China, the main reasons to keep nuclear weapons are to protect against Russian nuclear weapons and not to accept a status inferior to the Western nuclear powers'.[2] China's leaders, more than any others, believe deep in their bones that their country is a permanent great power with or without nuclear weapons. They believe that because of its huge population China would be invulnerable if nuclear weapons did not exist; nuclear weapons are the only real danger to China. If they believed it to be possible, they would prefer a world in which there were no nuclear weapons.

Most of the leadership of the U.S. government has lived so long with nuclear weapons that they have forgotten the fundamental strategic understanding that existed when the nuclear force was started. For the United States, nuclear weapons were a necessary evil. If others had them, we had to have them. If the Soviet Union had the military power to overwhelm Western Europe, the United States had to have nuclear weapons. (This was never as true as generally believed, but that is a more complicated story, which is now only of historic and theoretic interest.) U.S. leaders do not generally recognize that since the United States is a rich country with the size and population and wealth to be unarguably a great power, it would now be better off if nuclear weapons had never been invented.

Since nuclear weapons are used primarily to deter or threaten, they give advantage to governments that are, or can effectively pretend to be, desperate, irresponsible, or crazy—governments that do not care if their people are killed or their cities destroyed. In a confrontation between a country that has a small number of nuclear weapons and a "reckless" government, and another country that has many, higher-quality nuclear weapons and a normal democratic government, the country that has the smaller force is likely to be helped more by the nuclear weapons. So nuclear weapons can be useful for reckless dictators. Nuclear weapons can also be useful to weak countries that have strong aggressive neighbors. But the United States does not come within that category either.

Of course, the other big value of nuclear weapons is for "prestige," to improve a nation's status, to demonstrate that it is one of the greatest powers. If nuclear weapons are the sign of being a great power, they are levelers. Great Britain and France and China were "leveled up" by their nuclear weapons to join the Soviet Union and the United States at the top level, marked by veto power at the United Nations. But this is a trap. If any country that has nuclear weapons is automatically accorded high status, then Britain and France are leveled down to India, Ukraine, and Belarus, with more to come. Fewer countries will be able to match England and France when measured by history and civilization and wealth and democratic tradition than will be able to match them in having nuclear weapons.

So the national interest of the United States, Russia, and China would all be served if nuclear weapons could be eliminated and so cease to be the measure of great-power status. The situation of Russia and China would be especially improved if their small, unpredictable neighbors did not have nuclear weapons. If these three countries were willing to give up their nuclear weapons, then much of the reason for the British and French weapons would be gone, and they could be convinced to join the larger nuclear countries in giving them up.

The great powers could not give up their national nuclear forces without first creating a nonnational nuclear force to protect them against cheaters or against someone who later builds a few nuclear weapons. While history provides little basis for confidence in the effectiveness of nonnational forces, the requirements on this particular nonnational force would not be very demanding. Its only mission would be to retaliate against anyone who uses a nuclear weapon, and it would be very unlikely ever to be called on to act. It is important that it be expected to act if nuclear weapons were used, but, in fact, in the unlikely event that nuclear weapons were used, it probably would not be critical whether or not the international force retaliated promptly or reliably. And especially after a few years, most people would not expect the international force ever to be needed. Nevertheless, no country can responsibly give up all its nuclear weapons unless some nuclear force exists to protect it against the possibility that a number of concealed nuclear weapons remain or may be built in the future.

A negotiation concerning the actual composition and arrangements for the nonnational nuclear force would be difficult but would not require resolving critical mutually contradictory national requirements. The issues will be as much symbolic as real. The key points are that the nonnational force—essentially a technical agency—has to have such a large, high-quality force that no one could hope to match it with a clandestine force, and it must not be at the service of any individual nation.

We disagree with the view that any international organization that has a monopoly of nuclear weapons is automatically a world government—because no one could defy it. The reason this view is wrong is that it is quite unlikely that an international agency assigned the task of retaliating against any use of nuclear weapons would try to or could succeed in using its weapons to try to command obedience from nations.

Of course the question of preventing misuse of the force has to be dealt with. The nature of the problem depends on how the agency is constituted. For example, whether the agency recruits its personnel as individuals or is staffed by units provided by national military forces; whether it is specially created by a few countries—such as the current nuclear powers—to do only one task or is a unit of the UN. But it is by no means impossible to create an international force with a monopoly of nuclear weapons without that force becoming the master of the world.

If the great powers agree to create a nonnational nuclear force and give up their national nuclear forces because they agree that they all have a strong interest in making a nonnuclear world, they will have the power and the determination to induce the lesser nuclear powers to give up their national nuclear forces too. India, Pakistan, Israel, and North Korea (much less Ukraine, Belarus, and Kazakhstan) cannot stand against the five major nuclear powers on this issue.

So the end of the Soviet challenge provides—for the first time in forty years—an opportunity to rid the world of national nuclear forces and to create a reliable basis for a nonnuclear world. It is impossible to say, however, whether the leaders of the United States and China will recognize and seize this opportunity.

The best chance was in the first days of the new governments that followed the Soviet Union. The next chance may come with the beginning of a new presidential term in the United States. The chance may get better when the old men of the current Chinese leadership are replaced by a new generation. (It is only secondary characteristics of the current leadership—inertia and suspicion of the United States—that stand in the way, not their fundamental view of China's interests.)

Since the opportunity to eliminate all national nuclear forces may not be taken (or may not really exist), we should also ask whether it may be possible to create a nonnuclear world without going as far as eliminating all national nuclear forces. Can the world be made nonnuclear through some kind of minimal nuclear pluralism, even if the United States and China keep moderate-size nuclear forces? The answer may be "yes."

It is not inconceivable that Russia and the other three former Soviet Republics could be convinced to give up all their nuclear weapons to get rid of the danger from themselves and one another, and in return for anti-missile defenses and for deterrence commitments from the United States against China, plus economic assistance and trade. Such an idea would be much more attractive to Russia if England and France agreed to convert their national nuclear forces into a "European Nuclear Force" in which Germany and Russia have an equal say and whose only mission is to deter attack on all European countries, including Russia. This would improve Russia's protection against China, link Russia with Europe, and take away the superior position of England and France. The benefit to England and France from this proposal would be the nuclear disarmament of the former Soviet Union and possibly a permanent basis for Germany to stay nonnuclear.

If the United Kingdom and France and all the former Soviet Republics were to give up their national nuclear forces in favor of a European Nuclear Force, it would not be unreasonable to think that India and Pakistan could be induced at least to stop their weapons programs where they are, if not to give them up altogether. Korea might also be stopped. Or they might participate in an "Asian Nuclear Force" largely in the hands of China, which would not be more objectionable than the Chinese force. The result would be such a strong trend toward fewer nuclear powers that the general expectation about the future would change, and a nonnuclear world might be created.

In a nonnuclear world, in which normal countries do not get nuclear weapons and in which realistic people can expect that nuclear weapons will not increasingly dominate events, programs to prevent countries from getting nuclear weapons will not be seen as fruitless efforts to hold back the tide, and such programs may be pursued more seriously by governments than they have been up to now. In such a world, political leaders will find it less likely to think about starting a program to get their own nuclear weapons and it will be more difficult for them to do so. The chance of nuclear weapons spreading would be sharply reduced.

There has been virtually no discussion of the idea of a European Nuclear Force (ENF) to take the place of the national nuclear forces of Britain, France, and Russia. The idea has not been considered, even though the creation of such a force to provide deterrence against nuclear attack on any country in Europe, in place of the six existing European national nuclear forces, would serve the national interest of all countries involved.[3] Furthermore, giving Germany a role in the control of the ENF equal to that of Britain, France, and Russia could solve the problem of the increasingly anomalous difference between Germany's nuclear status and that of Russia and Britain and France—an anomaly that could someday become a source of trouble. If the diplomatic obstacles to creating such an ENF can be overcome, doing so may be the only practical way to make a major step toward a nonnuclear world.

Unfortunately the United States cannot create an ENF; only the Europeans can do it. However, if the United States were going to build a missile defense system that could also be used to protect Russia and the rest of Europe, then the United States could propose to provide that protection in connection with an ENF, which would put the idea of an ENF on the table and also make it more attractive to all parties.

Minimal nuclear pluralism might work with three or five (or even seven) national nuclear forces, but the larger the number, the more likely it is that other countries will decide to acquire their own nuclear weapons and that government decisions will be based on the assumption that sooner or later many countries will have nuclear weapons. A nonnuclear world probably requires eliminating all major nuclear forces except those of the United States, the Asian Nuclear Force, i.e., China, and the European Nuclear Force.

As we begin the current world order, there is a fork in the road, created, like the world order itself, by the fall of the Soviet Union. One road is a more nuclear world, spurred by materials and people and technology from the former Soviet Union. The other road takes advantage of the end of the U.S.-Soviet conflict to turn around and to go back toward a nonnuclear world. Within the next few years, we will find out which fork has been chosen; they are both within the same world order. We believe the nonnuclear road is a healthier, safer one for the world and that there is a better chance to get on that road than most experts realize.

Notes

1. These statements are not absolute certainties. One can imagine extreme circumstances where the outside or indirect effects of nuclear wars in the zones of turmoil would be much worse. But there is no reason for believing that the probability of such extreme circumstances is as high as one chance in ten, and it is probably a hundred or a thousand times lower for circumstances that would destroy a substantial fraction of the environment or kill a substantial fraction of the world's population.

2. Chinese leaders probably believe that the United States would not hesitate to use nuclear weapons against China if there were no Chinese nuclear weapons to deter the United States.

3. This counts Kazakhstan as European.

CHAPTER 5

WHAT THE LAST WORLD ORDER
LEFT BEHIND

The dominant feature of the world order that began with the defeat of Nazi Germany and ended in 1991 was the cold war. The end of that conflict and the radically changed position of Russia are what has allowed the current world order to begin. Before looking at the future of the former Soviet Union, we should notice why the cold war so suddenly and irrevocably ended and what we can learn from it.

A decisive clue is the fact that no communist coup was attempted against Mikhail Gorbachev until August 1991. That no communist sought to depose Gorbachev before then is the most powerful evidence of how sick the Soviet Union was. Well before the summer of 1991 it was apparent that Gorbachev's actions were destroying the communist system. But nobody from within the system tried to take power to stop Gorbachev because nobody could put together a group that believed they could make the system work. Nobody had a better idea. Nobody believed strongly enough in his own ability to fix things to have the strength to take power. And when the coup attempt came, it lacked enough conviction to succeed. They were all correct; if they had taken power, there was nothing they could have done that would have worked.

The cold war ended because the Soviet Union lost; its system worked so poorly it could not continue. There was no compromise. Nor did the Soviet leaders become convinced of American goodwill. They kept trying as long as they could, but there was no way they could sustain their system.

We in the Western democracies did not win it, they lost it. The war did not end because we got smarter and adopted better policies, and it certainly was not because we became more "peaceful." Of course, if we had not had the determination to keep holding out, we could have lost—so there is a sense in which we won, and we can take some pride in our accomplishment. But we should be humbled by the realization of how wrong we were about so many things, and how many people died because of the mistakes we made. Churchill said that World War II should be called "the unneces-sary war"; democratic performance against the communists was only mod-estly better than it was during the rise of Hitler.

The lesson of the cold war is that some conflicts are not symmetrical. There is not always moral or other equivalence between the two sides in a war. Sometimes one side is right and the other side is wrong. The cold war shows that when faced with an enemy who wants to destroy you, and who is too powerful or dangerous to conquer, the successful strategy is to keep holding on until the enemy collapses or changes. Neither sympathy nor em-pathy with the enemy, neither compromise nor accommodation, can solve the problem in such cases. Struggle, strength, patience, and confidence in your cause are what is needed, although practical accommodations that make the conflict less destructive or dangerous to both sides sometimes make it easier to last to the end.

The Fallacy of Normalcy

Several fallacies are common in discussions of the future of the former So-viet Union. One is the historian's error of thinking that some form of the old patterns of relationship between the Russian empire and Europe will be re-created. This view is probably wrong for at least three reasons: First, as a result of the economic development of Western Europe, the Russian em-pire has fallen so far behind that the traditional balance is changed for at least several generations. In the year 2000, Russia will be lucky to have as large a GNP as Italy. Second, the Western European countries have all be-come stable democracies, but no nation of the former Soviet Union has become more than the flimsiest democracy. This new distinction will be critical to the future relationship between the two areas. Because of the rise of mass wealth and democracy, Western Europe is fundamentally different from the way it was when its traditional relationship with Russia existed. Third, the traditional view does not take into account the immense effect of the moral and psychological harm done to the Russian empire by commu-nism.

The second common fallacy, more subtle and widespread, is the as-sumption that current governments are in control, that some kind of rea-sonable and familiar politics is working, and so it is likely that if there are important governmental changes in the future, they will be reasonably peaceful and orderly. A better picture to keep in mind for a perspective on future developments in the former Soviet Union is one of revolution gone awry. Not that the specific dynamic of former revolutions is relevant. But the experience of events getting out of the control of the participants, of actions leading to dramatically different results than intended, and of none of the major figures at the beginning continuing as important influences at the end is likely to hold for the former Soviet Union.

The assumption of relative normality and continuity is not so much an intellectual as a psychological error. It is very hard for almost anyone—and especially for the people responsible for operating a government—to accept fully the possibility of chaos, of rapid and unpredictable change, of events being out of their control. Such a possibility is frightening, for it seems to make impossible any rational policy. Moreover, it would not be diplomatic for a foreign ministry to say that its policy is based on the assumption that another country is going to fall into disorder, which might seem to be an unfriendly encouragement or hope for such negative events.

It is not that commentators argue that the existing governments are stable or dispute an assertion that disruption and radical change is a good possibility. Instead, governments and commentators verbally agree about, and then ignore, the possibility of disorder, acting as if they were dealing with relatively normal governments and political processes. And the few individuals who would want to act differently, or at least to try, find it too hard to explain the mistake and cannot get enough support to break through the wall of complacency and denial. As a result, the public and official discussion is largely divorced from reality.

Partly because of this fallacy of known-preferred-to-unknown evils, foreign governments keep trying to sustain whatever government exists, first in the Soviet Union and then in the Commonwealth of Independent States and the constituent Republics. The unspoken assumptions are that any government is better than none, that it is easier to deal with fewer governments than many, that current governments are to be preferred to the unknown results of their downfall, and that outside support for the existing government may enable it to survive. The known is not so much actually preferred as clung to out of fear of the unknown. (But there are still reasons to prefer the Yeltsin government to what will follow if it is overthrown.)

At any particular time, the standard assumptions may be correct; frequently, however, they are not. Hindsight will almost certainly demonstrate how often they were wrong. But it is very difficult for governments—or those engaged in the normal formal discussion of policy—to give up these assumptions, and often hard to know what to do if these assumptions are rejected.

Another form of the fallacy of assuming relative normality is made by many of those who are calling for U.S. support of "democratic forces" and seeking guarantees of human rights and democratic processes. Regardless of how high a priority one gives to the objective of achieving democracy, it is an ineffective strategy to pursue that objective by always supporting the more democratic group against the less democratic group, regardless of which, if either, is in power. It is also poor strategy always to condemn a government for failing to protect civil and political liberties.

The U.S. experience in Iran is an example of how harmful a simpleminded commitment to democracy can be. We undercut the shah because he was insufficiently democratic, and his fall produced massive death and suffering, less immediate democracy, great international problems, and quite possibly a setback in Iran's long-term path to stable democracy.

Effective support of the long-term interests of democracy will be very difficult. It requires a strategy that takes into account the likelihood of violent change and extensive disorder. It may be that the most we can do for democracy in the former Soviet Union in the next few years is some kind of principled testimony to our beliefs, without much effort to influence events. Though we might succeed in asserting our faith in democracy, we are likely to fail at installing, and especially maintaining, democracy. (We will return to the question of what we can and should do at the end of this chapter.)

Another error in much discussion of the former Soviet Union is forgetting how hard and important it is to have a government—any government—and assuming that all of the former Soviet territories will have real governments. But stable peaceful government is difficult to achieve, and it is unclear whether the current governments can survive or how soon how much of the former Soviet Union will achieve stable government. In some ways it is now more realistic to think of Russia as not having a real national government. It has a ceremonial government and is actually ruled by many diverse powers, some of which are in parts of governments, some not.

The Future of the Former Soviet Union

It is impossible to predict the future of the former Soviet Union. But some things about its unpredictability can be foreseen with reasonable confidence. We cannot make policy without using some assumption about what is coming. If we do not make explicit predictions, it means that we are assuming that things will continue as they are, and it is easy to make better predictions than that. So we have to try to say as much as we can about the unpredictable future of the former Soviet Union.

First and foremost, it is unlikely that any substantial overall organization will survive. Nor does this make much difference—neither to the constituent Republics nor to the outside world. If there are ties among the

Republics, they will not be important enough to make the Commonwealth of Independent States or any successor a real international actor. The Republics will dominate the Commonwealth of Independent States or any successor, rather than vice versa.

This prediction is not at all bold. The heritage of central rule by Russia has been horrendous. And, contrary to general impression, only weak incentives exist for the Republics to tie themselves together, and they are poorly equipped for the especially delicate task of establishing and sustaining effective links between independent countries.

Theoretically, there are many possible ways in which the former Soviet Union could be organized, from a single federal state to dozens of independent states. The possibilities that would be of some significance to the rest of the world are a single entity that includes Russia, Ukraine, Belarus, and the Moslem Republics; the possibility of a combination of Russia with Ukraine; the possibility of a single Moslem unit incorporating most or all of the Moslem Republics; and the possibility that Russia would be significantly reduced in size by the separation of Siberia and perhaps other territories. Other variations would not make much difference except to map makers.

People think that possible combinations of Republics are significant because they might create a larger economic market and currency zone, because they might create larger powers for international politics, and because they might prevent conflict (i.e., there is an assumption that there is more danger of conflict across international borders than within them).

There are rich and successful countries of all sizes, from little Switzerland to mid-size Taiwan to giants like the United States. A large internal market is not necessary for growth or prosperity as long as international trade is as open as it has been. Many of the benefits of integration can be obtained by specific agreement among fully independent countries—covering tariffs and trade or infrastructure projects such as railroads and communication systems. While there may be limited economic incentives for the Republics to get together, these benefits are certainly not large enough to dominate the political forces of division.

For a group of Republics to gain power internationally from being united they need to be tightly integrated. If there is only a "community" or "commonwealth" or "association," then the real power will be in the capitals of the constituent Republics, not in the "confederal" capital. Which means foreign diplomats will be concerned about the politics of the Republics, not about the words of a central foreign office that will have to look to its real Republican masters for key decisions.

Ukraine or the Moslems could be part of a fairly major international power by linking themselves to Russia, but they would be dominated by Russia; and even combined with Russia they would be no more than a third-rate power unless and until they become qualitatively stronger.

The Moslem states joined together would be a fairly substantial addition to the Moslem world—population about 50 million (compared to Indonesia 190 million, Pakistan 110 million, India 90 million [11 percent], Iran and Turkey about 55 million each, and the Arab countries 80 million, of whom about 55 million are in Egypt). They would almost double the size of the Turkic component of the Moslem world. Of course, they would have the same effect if they came in separately. (About 10 percent of the Moslems of the former Soviet Union are related by language to Iran rather than Turkey.)

But even if the Moslem Republics united into a single country, they would not be a major factor in world affairs and would be only a third the size of Russia and less than one-twentieth the size of their neighbor China. Their situation is a little like that of the countries of Central America. They would get some advantages from being a single country (and some disadvantages), but people are reluctant to move away from the experience of separate governments, and even together they would not be large compared to their neighbors. The Central Asian Moslem countries may have less separate national consciousnesses than the Central Americans, but they are also larger, much more spread out, and have less history in common.

In the unlikely event that Ukraine united with Russia the most important effect would not be the increase in Russian power, which will be much more determined by internal events than by a one-third increase in population and the addition of the considerable Ukrainian assets. The major effect would be the removal of Ukraine from Eastern European politics, where it would otherwise be, with Poland, the dominant power, and the bringing of Russia/Ukraine into the heart of Eastern Europe. The effect of Belarus joining Russia would be similar, but much smaller, since its population is only 10 million. Poland especially would worry more if Belarus or Ukraine was reattached to Russia.

Russian Prospects

There are three major questions for us about the future of the former Soviet Union. The big question is whether the Russian government can succeed at the most basic level. Can it come through the rest of its transition without a period of violent disorder that ends with an army takeover (though probably not the current army)? If Boris Yeltsin or a lawful successor can get through the next three years without a break in the rule of reasonably constitutional government, that will be success. But if the government is removed by force—whether of mobs or military units—or if the politics of terror and assassination returns, that will be failure. If basic legality is preserved, and violence is only local or intermittent, or can be suppressed by the government before it becomes endemic over large areas for long periods of time, then Yeltsin or his successor will have beaten the odds and succeeded.[1]

The second big question is whether there will be fighting between Russia and any of the Republics. In particular, will serious conflict or war develop between Russia and Ukraine? Will the current border between Russia and Ukraine survive, leaving at least 10 million Russian speakers and much traditionally Russian land in Ukraine? How will northern Kazakhstan, which is populated almost entirely by Russians and other non-Kazakhs, be transferred to Russia? It is unlikely to stay part of Kazakhstan.

Third, what will happen with the millions of Russians living in the other Republics (in addition to the 20 million who are in the areas of Ukraine and Kazakhstan just outside the Russian border) and the millions of peoples from the other Republics living in Russia? Will there need to be an exchange of populations, as there was between India and Pakistan and Greece and Turkey?

There are a number of reasons why it is unlikely that the Russian government will survive, and why it will be difficult for Russia to establish a stable government. We would argue that as a real government it has already fallen and is now a zombie government. And a stable *democratic* government is even less likely in the short term.

First, the former ruling class—about a million people in the families of the Communist party upper ranks—must be replaced. They have been accustomed to more power, privilege, and higher living standards than they will have in the future. They will either have to be forced to give up these benefits or to find a new basis to justify them. So far, perhaps a majority of them have found ways to preserve power and/or position. Their resistance will exact a high political price.

Second, it may be necessary to deal with a demand for punishment or justice by Russian victims of communism. The children and parents of the tens of millions of Russians murdered by the communists have had to keep silent because it was dangerous to complain. If there seems to be an opportunity to call for justice, to demand that the guilty be punished, millions of Russians can be expected to come forward with demands or to act privately. It is hard to imagine the power of the feelings and fears involved or the impact they can have on efforts to preserve peace and order in Russia. The millions of victims and the hundreds of thousands or millions of the guilty will have to find a way to live together—perhaps by continuing to ignore the past, but who knows?

Third, since communism was a totalitarian system, it prevented the development of independent organizations such as political parties, trade unions, interest groups, religious organizations, and the like that could be a foundation on which to build political structures and relationships. Democracies grow in societies that have all sorts of groups, and the growth of democracy makes the proliferation of groups even richer.

Fourth, communism almost systematically worked against the human qualities of character and attitude necessary for government: respect for others and for differences, experience and willingness to negotiate disagreements and to make compromises, respect for law, confidence in the community and in the government, a basic respect for truth, willingness to trust others, understanding of the idea of a loyal opposition, among others. Some people say that Russian culture and tradition were always an obstacle to anything but autocratic government; however true that may be, it has been made much worse by three generations of communism.

Finally, the economic system must be built from the beginning, and almost all existing institutions and practices must be replaced. There is no base of guilds or private farms or businesses or other institutions or systems to build on. Until a new economic system can be created, it is likely that living standards will continue to decline, and dramatic shortages of basic goods may recur from time to time. These worsening economic conditions will obviously increase the difficulty of establishing stable government.

There are two other reasons to think that it will be some time before Russia is able to achieve a government that can follow any reasonably coherent foreign policy that requires substantial national resources: the power of organized crime in Russia, and the continuing rise in Russian mortality rates.

Organized crime reaches farther and has greater power in Russia now than it ever did in Italy.[2] It is possible to see the power of organized crime as a "stabilizing" force and observe that it provides services and a kind of order that has some value to the society. Also it involves more continuity with past arrangements than is often realized. But any values organized crime provides come at a high price and bode ill for the future.

We mention the role of organized crime not as a moral judgment, but because politics has laws almost as inexorable as the law of gravity. While these laws are difficult to formulate precisely, or to prove rigorously, we think that they ordain that in a changing society stable political order cannot be built by criminal groups.

Organized crime may find ways of avoiding internal conflict for a while—there are certainly ample spoils for everyone to divide without fighting. But sooner or later temptation will overcome prudence, and power clashes will shake the order.

The foundation of government is comprised of institutions, habit of mind, and laws that are strong enough to overcome the stresses that disorder society from time to time. Unless criminal organizations create such foundations, the order they provide is temporary at best.

The demographic evidence that Russia lacks a viable government shows that, since 1989, every country where the communist regime collapsed has had a striking increase in death rates. Conversely, every country where the communist regime is still in power (China, Cuba, Vietnam, and North Korea) continues to have high but slowly falling death rates.[3]

The worsening mortality rates from Leipzig to Vladivostok cannot be fully explained by poverty, poor medical care, alcohol, and pollution. Nicholas Eberstadt, of the Harvard Center for Population and Development Studies and the American Enterprise Institute, asserts that "in the modern world ... significant and general increases in mortality *always* betoken either social instability or regime fragility, or both."[4]

It occurs to us that profound disorientation, caused by the realization that there is no government to hold society together, may help to explain the extraordinarily high death rates of Russians, and perhaps East Europeans. (Between 1989 and 1991, however, East Germany too saw a 25 percent increase in death rates for people in their late thirties, although the East Germans have no reason to doubt the strength or survival of their new government.)

We argue that both the scope and power of organized crime and the falling birth and rising death rates in Russia are additional evidence that the Russian government is illusory. Since the illusion does not fool the Russians, they are frightened and experiencing distress so extreme as to sharply increase their death rates.

The idea that Russia's great natural resources will prevent it from being a poor country is a misconception. No large country can be wealthy on the basis of natural resources. When Russia gets its oil resources working properly it will get from $200 to $800 per capita from all its natural resources, almost entirely from oil. That is, the difference between the cost of removing natural resources from the ground and the selling price of these resources will be on the order of $60 billion a year. While this is substantial, it is not enough to make Russia a rich country. Russia's benefit from raw materials will be less than the benefit it would get by increasing its growth rate by a couple of percentage points for a few years. Apart from oil, its natural resources will provide less than $5 billion a year of profit. For example, their annual diamond production is only $1.5 billion, from which production costs must be deducted.

Russia now produces some 3 billion barrels of oil a year, but much of this is fairly high-cost oil. A very rough guess is that after decent production technology is fully installed, ten or more years from now, they will continue to be able to produce 3 billion barrels a year at a cost equal to half its international price, which would mean that they would make about $40 billion per year profit (plus or minus 60 percent). They will need to consume most of that oil themselves, even if they use oil much more efficiently than they have in the past.

Probably Russia's new economy cannot really begin to be developed until the organizations that have been responsible for the economy are completely disbanded—perhaps with their office buildings turned over to citizens to make over into apartments.

While the economic agencies continue, they make it more difficult, if not impossible, for the new economy to get started. Until the familiar sources of direction and support no longer exist, many citizens will not understand that they have to figure out for themselves some way that they can do something useful. And while the bureaucrats continue to sit at their desks, making calls and moving paper, even people who are ready to act on their own will find it hard to understand that they can do business without waiting for approval from anyone and that they do not have to be afraid that whatever they do will be spoiled as the result of the system or of some bureaucrat's personal interest.

Since the average factory in Russia had more than twenty times as many employees as in the United States, few factories will be efficient enough to continue, and almost all manufacturing will have to be done in new organizations. Also, the existing distribution system is almost completely irrelevant and inadequate to the task of bringing large numbers of new small producers together with over 100 million consumers. New enterprises will have to be built for every one of the dozens of steps between raw material and final purchase. But since almost everything had been organized in huge enterprises and government agencies, few people have experience working in or managing small companies.

Eventually they will be able to organize everything they need. It does not all have to be done at once. But they probably will have to begin nearly at the beginning. Since they start with adequate clothing and shelter from before, and no longer have to devote one-fourth or more of their effort to making guns, almost the only thing they have to produce for themselves at the beginning is food—and if necessary the world will donate most of that.

So they have time to build the system of production and distribution. If there were peace, sound currency, and minimal sensible government policy, they could create the beginnings of a new economy in a few years that would double their production every ten or fifteen years, perhaps even faster at first. But it probably cannot start until they disband the economic ministries, which so far have had enough power to protect their jobs and to prevent the passage of laws and regulations that would free Russians from the thousand threads by which their state entangles them. They may continue to be able to do so until there is a complete breakdown of the government (i.e., until there is no government that can print money to pay them their salaries and give them the fig leaf of an excuse for coming to the office). The political strains to be expected from such a process are obvious.

What will happen if the government does not survive? If Yeltsin falls (other than by free election or natural death), the chain of legitimate authority will be broken. There may well be no accepted way for a new government to gain authority. People will come to power by coup, by use of military force, by the power of mobs in the streets, or by conspiracy, possibly with help from parliamentary factions. But whoever comes to power by these methods is vulnerable to being replaced by such methods. A new government's first priority will have to be to control the potential sources of power. Until the preservation of power is assured, little priority can be given to trying to govern the country. There could be three or six or a dozen changes in control before a regime comes to power that is stable enough to use most of its effort to improve the country.

The question of who controls the central government of Russia is not of concern only to politicians; the problem of disorder goes much deeper than the struggle for control of offices in Moscow. If the central government is too weak to provide authority throughout the country, the questions of power and control will have to be answered in every locality. The police will not stand against groups who do not accept their authority unless they are confident there is a government to support them and, if necessary, troops to back them up. Or, if there is no higher authority or power, in some places the police may decide that they are the rulers.

The fundamental question in every place is, Who must the individual with a gun, or the crowd that demands its way, obey? Then, when that question is answered locally, by someone establishing power or authority in a village or a neighborhood, what higher authority must the local power obey, and why? When the central government is too weak and divided to establish its power and authority through the country, these questions all become open, unless they are settled by general consent or by force. And the experience of communism has gravely weakened the sources of community agreement and the prospects of a general consent. Although the Russian masses have a deep desire for order and fear of anarchy, little inclination to ideological division, and great reluctance to destroy the small basis of legitimacy that exists, these feelings are not enough to provide reliable protection against a breakdown of government.

The more the patterns of past authority are broken and lose their acceptability, the more questions of authority and order become open. The unprecedented fact about Russia is that almost all the arrangements and institutions that have ordered life for the last three generations are badly tarnished or fundamentally defective or both; the Communist party, the courts, the trade unions, and the bureaucracy can all be expected to be replaced fairly soon. In the meantime, although one might like some patterns of order to hold together for a few more years so that they can be replaced in a peaceful and orderly—and even democratic—way, they are likely to come under immense pressure from the need to handle the great changes and bitter struggles of the transition from communism. Few of the institutions, practices, and relationships are likely to be strong enough to handle the strain. New links from people to local power to regional power to central power—and among various local and regional powers—will probably need to be forged, and the only fire that can forge such links is the fire of struggle for power.

In any place where the local order keeps the danger of random brigandage low enough so that people can work and buy, ordinary life can go on. Most people will not be directly involved in the struggle to control the local source of power. ("It is his problem who he has to take orders from or to whom he has to pay taxes.") But if the struggle for power leads to fighting, or if the local power becomes too busy protecting itself to maintain local order, then ordinary people's lives are disrupted. And if the local power protects itself by paying off, the people for whom it provides order will have to provide the resources for the payoff. So the cost to them of having order can become high.

These issues affect everyone's life. In order to eat, people have either to grow food or earn money and spend it to buy food. They cannot do either unless they are protected from individuals with guns who are ready to eat what others produce. Police cannot be counted on unless there is an accepted system of power from the local policeman up to the national border.

It is fairly easy for families and communities to develop systems for protecting themselves against individuals with guns (by giving their support to the local police or in other ways). But then such local self-protection organizations or police have to protect themselves from the wandering company of soldiers, perhaps with a few armored cars or tanks. Local police or even militia cannot engage in combat with real military forces. Usually the answer is for the local authority to pay off the military force in some way. (After all, how much can it eat or carry?) But when military force can bring a large payoff, someone usually tries to organize larger military forces to get the benefits of systematic control over larger territories —or simply to get a share of the payoffs going to the small military forces.

Organizing larger areas and larger forces can be done by negotiation or by force. People normally prefer negotiation, but there is usually some of each. And since the process is essentially outside the law, whatever arrangements are made must be sustainable by force, or they will not survive. There may be many layers between the lowest level of government and the central government of Russia, and on all levels the borders between territories are subject to dispute. So there is much room for conflict, even before any questions of policy or ethnic rivalry come into play, and there is also animosity among some ethnic groups.

This basic traditional picture is only the beginning of Russia's problem. Ordinary life is not merely local. It involves trade between communities and through large regions. Trucks and trains carrying goods can move only if there is enough protection. The chain of power and authority has to be established over wide regions before regional economies can operate well. And if people are to be able to work to provide what they need, they usually have to have a little more than protection from bandits.

Barter is inefficient; for people to be able to trade effectively there needs to be an accepted currency. But if the Russian government keeps the power to print money, it is almost certain to succumb to the temptation to print enough money to buy what it wants. (That is, to keep on paying salaries to people it is afraid to put on the street.) This will have the result of reducing the value of the ruble (extreme inflation), and eventually making it unable to fulfill the functions of money. No foreign stabilization fund or other mechanism that leaves the government of Russia with the power to print money will solve this problem.

If the ruble loses value people will do business with foreign currencies, but business organizations will need to be developed to import and distribute the foreign currencies efficiently, and they will be somewhat awkward to use.

A banking system can increase the efficiency of the money system—if it is allowed to operate with foreign currencies. But once people are using banks they are vulnerable not only to bandits but also to "governments" and to many kinds of swindles and more subtle forms of robbery. If these become too prevalent people have to stop using the banks, and there will be some return to local subsistence economics.

At any time a government of Russia can provide a stable new ruble by creating a "currency board" that has the power to issue only as many rubles as it has hard currency reserves to back the ruble. A recent advocate of such currency boards, which have been used in many places (including for a while in Russia many years ago), is Professor Steve H. Hanke of Johns Hopkins University. The advantage of a currency board is that it can provide an inflation-proof ruble, that is, one that will hold its value as well as the hard currency it is tied to. The disadvantages are that the ruble would have to be tied to some other specific currency, and money would be needed to buy the board's initial reserves. The basic costs of a currency board ruble are comparable to the costs of buying foreign currencies to use as money in Russia.

To get beyond the most primitive forms of trade and production, people need to be able to make agreements that they can rely on. They need to have some confidence that conditions will not change so fast that it becomes foolish to act for the future. They need to have reasonable protection for their right to receive their share of the benefit of their work, even if it will not come for some time. Although we usually assume that all these things come "naturally," they do not; Russia will have to build systems and arrangements that provide these basic foundations of economic life.

The reason why Russians can prefer their current bleak situation to what they had before can be seen from its analogy to a young man who becomes a drug addict at age twelve, finally gets off drugs after many years as an addict, and then goes through a very difficult delayed adolescence. Even bad adolescence, although it involves much suffering, is better than drug addiction because the addict, although he has many pleasant moments and achieves a kind of stability, is on a road to nowhere. Eventually he has to get off drugs and grow up and go to work. Success on the drug road does not put anyone farther ahead on the road of real life; it just delays the start. Adolescence, in contrast, however tough, is a road that is going somewhere. It leads to maturity and the ability to live. It turns out that Marxism-Leninism was a very long-term opiate, but now Russia has kicked its habit and is in painful recovery.

So the Russian people, however much they suffer as they struggle to replace communism, are better off than they were before. Although the road they are on now may be long and painful, it is a road that leads somewhere. Furthermore, although their current road may be bloody, it will be safer than the communist road, which killed some 50 million people, excluding wars.[5] Even if the disorder following the replacement of communism becomes very bloody, it is very unlikely that more than a fraction as many people will be killed.

The brief summary is that it is more likely than not that Russia will suffer both instability of its national government and intermittent loss of government control over much of its territory. Also, there may be violent conflict between Russia and the other Republics.

Revulsion against Communism

Today, everybody knows that as an intellectual matter communism is discredited, although there are those who argue that it is only the Soviet Union that has failed, not the idea of communism. Even before the Soviet Union began to come apart, there was a theoretical consensus in the West —including intellectuals and the left—that the Soviet government was not to be admired and that the West had to protect itself against the Soviet Union.

Before long, something much different will begin to happen. The discrediting of communism will become emotional rather than intellectual. A widespread revulsion against communism will develop, like the revulsion against fascism that developed after Hitler's defeat and the exposure of his regime's crimes and atrocities.

There was a large strand of intellectual opinion that saw the U.S.-Soviet conflict as a symmetrical struggle between two morally equivalent powers. And the post–cold war discussion to date gives little basis for appreciating the psychological power of the revulsion against communism that is likely to begin in the next five to ten years. In parts of our population that traditionally thought of communism as "a good idea carried too far," this revulsion will be one of the most important features of the first decades of the current world order.

The trigger that will gradually turn intellectual rejection into emotional revulsion will be all the human stories that will come out of Russia. Millions of witnesses against communism will be eager to come forth and testify against its crimes. (Many will testify falsely for selfish reasons.) Official files will become increasingly available. The stories will be too dramatic and have too much human interest to ignore. They will be everywhere and never-ending. Our TV sets and papers will be full of stories of communist venality and corruption. First the stories will be on the news and in documentaries, then as staple plots of fiction they will become part of the next generation's basic understanding of the world.

Those who do not care about politics will read only the stories that have sexual or other spicy features, but no kind of story will be lacking. No one will be able to escape the sense of Russia as a country that had been pervaded with decadence, immorality, and evil.

Underlying that revulsion will be the fact that in addition to preventing Russia from even having an economy that could feed and take care of its people, while European countries were becoming wealthy, communism inflicted vast harm on the country's physical environment and the health of its population; spread arms, terrorism, and conflict throughout the world; killed more of its own citizens than all the people killed by war during this whole century,[6] and denied freedom to those it did not kill.

The murder and repression are well known. But why the immense pollution in a system not driven by the profit motive? In addition to the lack of democracy that permitted fanatical overemphasis on production (especially military) compared to consumption, the communist central-command economy was so inefficient in its use of materials that it consumed much more energy and material than the capitalist economies for equivalent output. And most important, the government did not care at all about the health of the people, who had no say in what the government did.

But much of the emotion will come from the backlash of the fact that communism did all these things in the name of an ideology that challenged God and religion and enlisted the moral support and sympathy of idealistic people all over the world. Soon disillusion will gradually turn to anger and revulsion, and feelings of sympathy and respect will begin to backfire.

This wave of feelings will be helped to grow by the fact that there will be virtually no groups with an interest in defending communism. In fact, the opposite; under the tide of opinion—as under the tide against fascism following the revelations of Germany's crimes—it will be tactically or psychologically almost impossible to sustain reasonable nuances or distinctions if they seem to defend any aspect of communism or communist regimes. (Just as it was for a long time imprudent to say that Hitler killed 5 million Jews, not 6 million.) Even those people or groups that might have some sympathy with communism will need to avoid seeming to justify anything done by the communists in order to preserve their audience and their effectiveness.

The consequences of this *volte-face* in the intellectual world will be immense but are still unfathomable. The effect on the Russians themselves will be different. But it is difficult to believe that the effect on them will not be profound, in ways that are beyond imagining, although a widespread return to religion is almost certain to be one of the major responses.

Russia's Foreign Policy

It is unlikely that the Russian government in power at the end of this century will have short-term expansionist ambitions or will make efforts to be a world power. Whatever the character of the Russian government, and whatever the ideas and personal inclinations of its rulers or its masses, it is likely that Russia's fundamental weakness will force its government to avoid ambitions beyond the territory of the former Soviet Union. Russia will be poor, inward looking, nonideological, engaged in annoying conflicts on its borders, lacking self-confidence, aware of the low regard in which it will be held abroad, and desiring help from the democracies. It may also still be either internally unstable or so authoritarian as to be disreputable, or both. It will also be engaged in a very arduous and demanding process of building internal economic and political structures and institutions. And it will be aware that most of the power and wealth in the world are held by democracies who regard aggression as illegitimate.

For a political party to maintain relatively unified continuous power over a domain and population as vast as the Soviet Union for a seventy-four-year period as changing and challenging as the reign of the Communist Party of the Soviet Union was an extraordinary "technical" achievement. It cannot be explained just by ruthlessness and ambition—which have never been in short supply. On the stage of world history, it is an outstanding evil accomplishment achieved by technical human and organizational inventions and disciplines as demanding as those required to achieve the marvels of modern engineering.

The Communist Party of the Soviet Union succeeded in maintaining coherent power for nearly three generations by a subtle combination of ideology and organization. The weaknesses of the ideology and the widespread loss of belief even among party members did not prevent that ideology from performing functions essential to keeping the party together and in power. But now the party is gone, and there is no alternative source of moral and psychological authority or of a salient basis for unified control or a sense of invincibility.

If Russia comes under the control of old Communist hardliners who try to restore central control by reversing many of the changes of recent years, it will be almost impossible for them to succeed for more than a few years at most. Vital supports of the amazingly successful system of power that had been constructed in the Soviet Union have been irreversibly destroyed. However ruthless the hardliners are, however many millions of people they are willing to kill, they have very little chance of being able to maintain a government with enough internal strength to carry out external initiatives (especially since their only experience is operating within the Communist party system and they are not long on creativity or charisma).

While no proof is possible, the authors believe that their effort would be doomed, not necessarily because of the appeal of freedom, reason, and conscience, but by the traditional human facts that have always made unified continuous power difficult—ambition, selfishness, individual rebelliousness, illusion, and the vastness and complexity of Russia—combined with the tremendous difficulty, especially for an oppressive system, of coping with the damage done to the Soviet Union by communism.

In conflicts with its neighbors, the other pieces of the former Soviet Union, Russia is unlikely to have substantial territorial ambitions. (The issues of eastern Ukraine and northern Kazakhstan, regions that are occupied mostly by Russian speakers, are special cases and are likely to be settled in the next few years.) Experience with the Soviet Union will have taught Russian rulers not to desire to govern other peoples. They will understand that imperialism is dead and that adding to Russia territory occupied by Moslems or other nationalities will not add to the strength or wealth of their country. On the contrary, in an international order dominated by nations at once democratic and technologically advanced, only increases in quality will enable nations to compete, whether in war or in peace. Any Great Russian feelings will be expressed by efforts to dominate neighbors, not to incorporate them (at the most, Finlandization). Conceivably Belarus, Ukraine, and one or more of the Baltic states might be exceptions to this policy of nonacquisition.

What Happened to Soviet Power?

Our argument that the world order does not need to take into account the possibility of a strong Soviet Union or Russia for at least a generation seems to defy a law of the conservation of political matter. A moment ago there were two superpowers, each capable of threatening the independence and survival of the other. Now there is only one. What happened to all the Soviet power? All the land and people and resources and weapons are still there. Why do we not need to take account of the possibility that Russia or somebody else will be able to put it together again? Why is the possibility that old-line Communists will be restored to power in Russia not a major national security threat to the United States or Western Europe?

Part of the power was lost by the division of the Soviet Union, but only a small part. A large piece of the power is temporarily lost by the internal disorder in Russia, and it is correct to recognize that this loss of power can be reversed if a strong government is able to gain full control of Russia. But, although this can happen, it cannot happen soon, and not before a large price is paid through internal conflicts.

A major share of the power loss is economic. First, while the rest of the world continued to grow, the Soviet Union began first to stagnate and then to decline because its system was inadequate for a modern economy.

A new economy will probably be built, but the losses during the transition to a new working economy will rob Russia of at least the equivalent of twenty years of growth. Second, much of the apparent economic power did not really exist—it came from the Soviets being overrated, by the Central Intelligence Agency and almost everyone else. Third, they were in the past able to mobilize nearly a third of their economy to support their international power, leaving not much more than two-thirds for consumers and for investment. It is unlikely that any future government of Russia will do that.

The most important reason that the power that made the Soviet Union so dangerous has disappeared and cannot be restored by Russia or any other successor is that so much of that power came from the Soviet Union's ability to use communist ideology and a massive system of political agents, allies, supporters, and sympathizers in programs of deceit and political warfare. Because of this, the Soviet Union, with the unintentional cooperation of people all over the world, was able to establish a largely false understanding of history and reality that was a major share of its political power. Most Soviet victories from 1945 on depended primarily on its ability to use these assets and skills to deceive its victims and the democracies.[7] But even if old-line Communists came back to power, their ability to sell lies would have been destroyed by what has happened in the last few years.

Ideas have consequences. The idea that the Soviet Union was a progressive force and that, therefore, a moral act was one that helped its Communist party was a long time dying. And without it, Russia will be an ordinary nation but not a world force. A major source of Soviet power has disappeared from the earth; it no longer exists to be picked up by someone else.

Political matter is not necessarily conserved. The current world order does not include great power in the territory of the former Soviet Union. The pieces of the Soviet Union will be ordinary parts of the zones of turmoil, not requiring any more special attention than Brazil or India or Indonesia.

Russia's Place in the World

The first fundamental fact shaping the current world order is that Russia has inherited only a minor fraction of what made the Soviet Union a superpower whose challenge shaped events for nearly half a century. Not only is the new Russia not the Soviet Union, it is not even traditional Russia. Not for many years, if ever again, will Russia stand in its traditional relation to

Western Europe. As discussed above, Russian weakness results from its poverty relative to Western Europe; its internal disorder (which has barely begun); its need to make peace with its destructive and disillusioning past; and its need to construct a whole social, economic, and political system almost from the beginning.

One result of this immense change is that a Russian military threat will not be a rational basis for a military alliance among the Europeans, much less for a military alliance between Europe and the United States. The alliances that were originally organized to protect against the Soviet Union may continue, and may still be valuable, but any attempt to justify them by a military danger from the East will be fatally flawed. Unless a better reason can be expressed, they will become like stale fish.

Chapter 4 explained why Russia's nearly thirty thousand nuclear weapons cannot make her strong. But what happens with these weapons will determine which of two nuclear paths the world will follow. The likely path is that some of the Soviet-built weapons (or components or technology) will get loose during the turmoil and will find the tens of millions of dollars that will be searching for them and hasten the spread of nuclear weapons to Moslem countries and some of the rest of the world. This is the greatest danger to the rest of the world from the turmoil to be expected in the former Soviet Union. It implies that we should be working very hard, not for promises, and not to concentrate the nuclear weapons in Russia, but to get as many nuclear weapons as possible out of the former Soviet Union, or under effective international control, to be dismantled beyond the reach of defecting colonels, entrepreneurs, and mobs.

Fortunately, a new Russia, which does not see the United States as its enemy, whose government is not comfortable with responsibility for nuclear weapons, and which has no confidence in its ability to stay in power and maintain control, may provide an opportunity to turn the world onto a different nuclear road, toward a nearly nonnuclear world.

Dealing with Russia on nuclear weapons, or on other matters is not at all the same as dealing with the Soviet Union. We do not have to be afraid of Russia because it does not have the other sources of power that would have made it possible for the Soviet Union to use nuclear weapons as part of a combined military and political campaign that could have been a genuine threat to the United States. Also, we do not have to concede Russia's right to the nuclear weapons it possesses, as we did the Soviets'. Russia cannot claim to have the Soviet Union's rights unless it accepts responsibility for the Soviet Union's crimes. Since Russia does not claim that the United States is its enemy, as the Soviet Union did, why should it keep a nuclear force aimed at the United States?

We need not let the fallacy of normalcy lead us to apply to Russia either the assumptions and attitudes that governed diplomatic relations with the Soviet Union or the assumptions and attitudes that apply to normal countries. Russia is not entitled to be treated as we treated the Soviet Union. (The Soviet Union was not entitled to be treated the way we treated it, but that is a different story.) Nor need we treat Russia as a great power. Nor should we automatically give Russia and the Republics the respect and freedom from consideration of their internal affairs that we give normal sovereign states. Russia is the heir to the defeated aggressor in a vicious war against the democracies.

This is not to say that Russia should be treated as Germany and Japan were after World War II. We are not entitled to decide whatever we want about how Russia shall be run, nor should we want to. But Russia does not have any basis in right or in realpolitik for getting the benefits of Soviet power without responsibility for Soviet crimes. We do not think that Iraq is entitled to nuclear weapons; why is Russia or Kazakhstan entitled to have nuclear weapons? Of course, it is not clear what we should do about the Soviet nuclear weapons in the possession of Russia and the other Republics, but in deciding what to do we should not assume that they are entitled to have them, just because no one challenged the Soviet Union's right to have such weapons.

Russia is the heir to a government that inflicted immense damage not only on its own people and territory but also on the rest of the world. It is the heir of a government that systematically flouted the normal practices of international diplomacy and worked to destroy democratic governments and international peace. Therefore, other nations have much more right to a say about what happens in Russia than they do about what happens in, for example, Chile or Kenya. Russia should not be treated like a pariah or international criminal. Our basic relationship to it should be benevolent, as it should be to all countries that are not active enemies. But it will be many years before it will have the right to be treated like every other sovereign state. Most important, we should insist that Russia is not entitled to equal treatment with France and Germany because it is not yet a democracy.

The United States and the other democracies should be willing to contribute to the recovery of Russia and the other Republics. We should not try to impose hardship or weakness on them. But it is wrong to help them without requiring that they stop selling advanced weapons to nondemocracies in the zones of turmoil and take their military forces out of countries that have requested that they be removed, such as the Baltic states. Certainly if the other European nuclear powers are willing to give up their national nuclear forces, it is appropriate that we *insist* that Russia and the other Republics do so also. By "insist" we mean making compliance a requirement of any U.S. trade, aid, or investment.

President Yeltsin has genuine (although imperfect) democratic credentials because he was elected by popular vote. We should give him special personal credit because of the democratic source of his authority and try to strengthen his position and help him gain and keep power. But this effort has such a low chance of success that it should be carefully limited. It is not useful to turn a blind eye to the realities in Russia. It is not a democracy. Yeltsin controls very little. He will be helped, not hurt, if the United States holds Russia's lack of genuine democracy against it in negotiations.

Since Russia claims the Soviet Union's permanent seat on the UN Security Council with a veto power, we should not hesitate to assign it a measure of responsibility for Soviet crimes. This is one of the reasons why we should not support any Russian efforts to have primacy over the other former Republics. There is no reason why the nuclear weapons from Belarus, Ukraine, and Kazakhstan should go to Russia instead of being dismantled and destroyed outside of the former Soviet Union. The United States and the rest of the world has no stake in the unity of the former Soviet Union and should not do anything to encourage the other Republics to be represented by the Commonwealth of Independent States or any other central authority. Nor do other nations have reason to oppose centralizing efforts either.

Neither its support for Yeltsin nor anything else should lead the U.S. government to count on the current Russian regime's surviving. In fact, our private assumption in designing our policy should be that the current government is so temporary that it cannot make effective commitments. The United States should be much more focused on actual physical deliveries because Russia's promises are not valuable.

There is some small chance that Russia will descend into such complete chaos that the United States and other democracies will need to provide food to prevent starvation and to deliver that food with our own people because there will be no organized government capable of distributing it or protecting those who provide help. That is, circumstances may tempt us, or even put pressure on us, in effect to take control of Russia or part of it. There may be no government, or the government that is trying to end the chaos may be so unsure of itself that it would welcome U.S. dominance.

There are strong arguments against taking an opportunity, if it comes, to impose democracy on Russia, more or less as we imposed it on Japan and Germany, either alone or in combination with Europe or a few of the great democracies. Russia will be very hard to govern democratically, even if it is allowed to break into smaller pieces. Germany and Japan had strong human and historical assets for building democracy that Russia lacks; and we Americans have less confidence in ourselves than we did in 1945.

Nevertheless, America did succeed in Germany and Japan. Russia and the world would be much safer if democracy were successfully imposed on Russia. And if America did not impose it, democracy would be unlikely to come for many years after a breakdown in government in Russia.

We cannot judge whether the United States should take an opportunity to impose democracy on Russia if one comes. Our first inclination was to reject the idea out of hand, but now we are afraid that perhaps the possibility should be given serious consideration and that the answer may depend on the specific circumstances.

Almost everybody recommends that the United States use its various sources of influence to achieve one objective or another in Russia. Some want us to try to protect democratic government; others focus on trying to preserve stability; others want to avoid violence or preserve unity. We think that all these policies are mistaken because there is too small a chance that America can succeed with any of them by manipulating the levers that we have in our hands. (Part of the problem is that it is almost impossible to understand the rapidly changing situation there well enough to manipulate the levers very wisely, but even with perfect wisdom we think the levers are not strong enough.) And two things are wrong with pursuing unrealistic objectives. First, our efforts may do more harm than good, and by trying to influence the outcome we assume more responsibility for it. Second, the pursuit of unrealistic goals can produce real costs. Hopeless efforts to preserve unity among the Republics may prevent us from pursuing the most effective approach to preventing harm from Soviet-built military technology. Useless efforts to preserve stability can cost many tens of billions of dollars of taxpayers' money (with no appreciable benefit to any needy people). And fruitless efforts to protect democratic government may lead us to compromise principles in ways that make it harder to support those principles elsewhere.

Foreign policy toward the nations that have emerged out of the former Soviet Union, including Russia, should mostly be subject to the same principle that the United States adopts toward other struggling nations: modest benevolence. Emergency humanitarian aid is likely to be necessary from time to time. Caution should be exercised, however, in not providing aid in such a manner as to weaken the recipients' agriculture or other industries on which it must depend in the future.

It is difficult to resist the argument that the United States must support

Russia or Poland or Hungary on grounds that averting trouble now would be less difficult or expensive than dealing with it later. Perhaps, but we doubt it (even though it was strongly urged by as experienced a statesman as Richard Nixon). For one thing, though these nations may do great damage to their own people and nearby countries, they are (with the usual partial nuclear exception) not a threat to us or to other democratic nations. For another, our aid cannot be enough to make these countries successful if they do not take the actions necessary for economic growth to become possible. There is no more reason to give aid uselessly to the former Soviet Union than elsewhere. And there is no reason for the United States to give more than its reasonable share in such aid. Joshua Muravchik and others have argued for an active U.S. program to protect democracy in Russia because of the danger if Russia again comes under authoritarian rule.[8] We disagree. A bad Russia is less dangerous than he thinks, and a decent Russia is much less possible than he thinks. That is, we see less chance that we can save democracy in Russia and much less danger to the world from a new Russian dictatorship. (Of course, we would be willing to do something to protect democracy in Russia, but we would not invest very much faith or treasure in the enterprise.)

Notes

1. By an equally significant measure, the Russian government has already failed as a government: It cannot make enforceable decisions. Yeltsin does not govern his own administration. Ministries do not necessarily obey the president; offices do not necessarily obey their ministers; local branches do not necessarily obey their national headquarters; local governments do not necessarily obey the national government; and no one feels obligated to obey the law. On this dimension the question is not, Will the government fail? but instead, How soon can Russia achieve a real government? The answer probably is, Not until Russians build the necessary foundation, and that will take decades.

2. Claire Sterling, *Thieves' World* (New York: Simon and Schuster, 1994).

3. Murray Feshbach, ed. *Environmental and Health Atlas of Russia* (Moscow: PAIMS, 1995).

4. Nicholas Eberstadt, "Demographic Disaster: The Soviet Legacy," *National Interest*, 36 (Summer 1994): 53–57.

5. See Robert Conquest, *The Harvest of Sorrow: Soviet Collectivisation and the Terror-Famine* (London: Hutchinson, 1986) and *Stalin: Breaker of Nations* (New York: Viking, 1991). See also R.J. Rummel, *Death by Government: Genocide and Mass Murder since 1900* (New Brunswick, N.J.: Transaction, 1994).

6. Conquest, *The Harvest of Sorrow* and *Stalin*.

7. This point is presented, with examples, in Max Singer, "U.S. Vulnerability

to Soviet Political Warfare," in *Arms Control: The American Dilemma,* ed. William R. Kintner (Washington, D.C.: Washington Institute Press, 1987).

8. *Commentary,* July 1992.

PART TWO

New Policy Thinking for the
Real World Order

CHAPTER 6

SUPRANATIONS AND SUBNATIONS— REBIRTH OF FEDERALISMS

This chapter recommends three separate policy ideas. While these propos-als are not essential either to the basic description of the world order that is the primary purpose of the book, nor to the overall policy approaches we suggest in the next chapters, they are included because we think they are good ideas. (Much of section B and the first part of section C also describe some specific features of the world order.)

A. Reforming the United Nations

A dramatic improvement could be made in the United Nations in a short time if the democratic member countries organized themselves into a bind-ing caucus to coordinate their participation in UN decisions. Exactly how dramatic the effects of this action would be depends on the voting formula to be used within the caucus, but in any case the United Nations could be transformed into a more responsible force for improving international or-der.

Today, some 99 of the 183 members of the United Nations are democ-racies, if a generous definition of democracy is used (see table 6.1).[1] We be-lieve that the great democracies should work with the governments of these 99 countries, which together have half of the world's population, to im-prove the quality of the United Nations and to decide how the United Na-tions should respond to disorder in the zones of turmoil. To do this the democracies will need to create a small organization to be a binding caucus to coordinate their participation in the United Nations.

The UN Democratic Caucus (UNDC) would have a formal member-ship, open to all democratic UN members, and a small nonpolitical staff paid by its member governments. Its basic activity would be coordinating the votes and other participation of its members within UN agencies. The power of the caucus would come from the prestige of democracy and the fact that, by voting as a single bloc, the members of the caucus would al-

TABLE 6.1

SUMMARY OF DEMOCRACIES IN THE UNITED NATIONS

	Countries	Population (in millions)
Leading democracies (narrow list)	22	800
Other democracies	77	2,000
Total democracies	99	2,800
Total UN member countries	183	5,600

NOTE: This table uses the mid-1995 list of UN members. See appendix 6.1 of this chapter for the names of the 99 countries on the lists of democracies. These designations are for illustrative purposes only—largely based on the 1995 edition of Freedom House's survey "Freedom Around the World"; they do not claim to be careful or final judgments.

most always be able to determine UN decisions. (This would be true even if the caucus were smaller, because a narrower definition of democracy was used, and perhaps almost as true with a caucus of only the 40 or so "stable democracies"). As a practical matter, the UNDC would almost certainly have effective control of the United Nations (except where Security Council action is required).

No country would be obligated in advance to comply with the decisions of the caucus unless it had agreed to be bound by them. The only thing the caucus would have the power to decide is how the members vote in the United Nations (or exercise other UN rights).

One of the major concerns of the UNDC should be to increase the UN's integrity by supporting standards of civility of debate, financial responsibility, UN adherence to its own rules and procedures, truthfulness in UN statements, objectivity and fairness in UN reports and studies, and consistent application of principles in UN actions.

It will be objected that many democracies do not maintain such standards at home, which is true. But the United Nations is not a government; if it does not earn the respect of nations, it has little power. Besides, at the international as well as the local levels, the community should have higher standards than the lowest common denominator (i.e., more in keeping with the aspirations of its members than with their worst performance).

Although many times the United Nations acts in an exemplary manner, and it has a number of valuable accomplishments to its credit, its poor habits have earned it a bad reputation. UN agencies and bodies often flagrantly violate UN rules and principles. The United Nations often does not observe its own rules concerning the selection and behavior of staff. Most of UN staff and agencies are extremely wasteful and inefficient. UN groups like UNRRA and UN peacekeeping forces make arbitrary and one-sided decisions, ignoring relevant law and facts to favor countries that have strong majority support in the General Assembly. In official UN debates the delegates frequently say things that are not true, ignore the law, break UN rules, and are otherwise irresponsible and foolish, without suffering any consequences.

There is no point in debating whether the United Nations has done more good or more harm in the past. Its past contributions demonstrate that it has valuable potential for the future. If through a UNDC or in some other way the United Nations develops higher standards and greater integrity, it will become more respected and thus more useful and effective in the future. But it has done more harm than it should have, enough harm that it ought not be given a greater role in the world before the causes of its faults are dealt with.

If a UNDC is organized, there are strong arguments for limiting its membership to stable democracies that have high levels of protection of civil and political rights so that the member governments would have a good deal in common, would seldom be embarrassed by other members, and would almost never need to consider removing a member. But we believe that if any country has a genuine—even if incomplete—commitment to democracy, a reasonably freely elected government, and some kind of democratic political process that influences basic decisions, that country should be in the UNDC, even if it has not yet achieved stable democracy or a full acceptance of human rights.

Democracy would be encouraged by using a less demanding standard for UNDC membership, and no great harm to the effectiveness of the caucus would result from having some members whose democracy, in practice, is temporarily dubious. What is important is that the character and decisions of the caucus are determined by undoubtedly genuine democracies.

The result of having a low threshold for admission for membership is that occasionally it will become necessary to remove a country from the caucus because it has fallen below the minimum standard for democracy and has become authoritarian. Removal from the democratic caucus would be a useful sanction to apply against a country that retreated from democracy, and it would be much easier to apply than most sanctions. It would not cause innocent citizens to suffer; it would not require sacrifice from the countries imposing the sanction; and there would be no enforcement problems.

Membership in the UNDC may help to bind some marginally democratic countries to the democracies and strengthen the internal democratic forces in those countries. Often when an authoritarian regime takes over a democracy, it tries to disguise what it is doing, pretending to be democratic. A respected international democratic forum, which can authoritatively determine when a country has gone so far in violating democratic standards that it is no longer a democracy, will help those within the country who are trying to keep the country democratic. Of course this will not work in all countries; some authoritarian regimes will not be influenced at all by the threat of being thrown out of the UNDC.

Another question is whether a democratic caucus should include even the very small democratic members of the United Nations, such as Barbados, with a population of 250,000—only one tenth of 1 percent as big as that of the United States. We believe that all the democratic members of the United Nations should be included, and that the UNDC should be as universal an organization of democracies as the United Nations is of countries.

But to make the UNDC more effective, we believe that Barbados's vote in the caucus should not be equal to that of, say, the United States or France. We suggest that the UNDC use a voting formula that gives countries with many people and a high level of economic development more votes than countries with few people and lower levels of development.[2]

In the possible allocation of votes discussed in appendix 6.1 the United States would have forty votes, Barbados and other very small countries one vote, and the big four European democracies would have twenty votes each. Such a system of weighted voting is more democratic than the current UN voting system because it gives more weight to people and less to sovereignties.

The illustrative system also gives some weight to economic development, which is not an undemocratic thing to do. It parallels the practical reality in any democracy. Real power necessarily depends on resources, the ability to organize (which is a kind of resource), and many other factors. In a democracy, each citizen does not have equal practical power but only an equal opportunity to acquire power. (Each citizen has equal dignity, which is comparable to the counting of sovereignties in the UN voting system.) In the United States, an individual's vote is more a symbol of his or her equal dignity than a way of providing equal power. Very rich people would not be noticeably more powerful if they each had one hundred votes in national elections.

In addition, there is some justice in giving those who contribute more a greater say in how their contributions are spent. (The rich countries contribute a much bigger share of UN funds than their share of votes with the sample allocation shown.) Without such weighting, decisions are made by those who are spending other countries' money.

It is especially appropriate to have weighted voting in a voluntary organization like the UNDC (as there is in business corporations) because such an organization does not have quasi-governmental powers or sovereign dignity. Using a weighted-voting system in a democratic caucus at the United Nations would preserve the UN principle of equality of sovereign nations while providing a basis for decisions that reflects the principles of fair representation and the realities of democratic power.

It is not possible to know for sure how a UNDC would actually work, but weighted voting is international dynamite. It would give the major democracies a better chance of being able to assure that the democratic caucus will be an organization that uses sound and responsible standards and procedures in making its decisions—quite different from much previous experience with the United Nations. This development would make it necessary for the U.S. government to support sound procedures and principles more than it has in the past.

Because the UNDC would be an organization composed entirely of democracies, where the distribution of voting power reasonably reflected the distribution of power and responsibility among all democracies, it would be likely to become an international forum more deserving of our respect than any that has been available before. The UNDC (or the United Nations as controlled by the UNDC) could be the organization that the United States needs in order to decide when to intervene in conflict in the zones of turmoil. In the UNDC, the elements of the world whose voices we should care about can be expected to use fair and responsible procedures to answer the hard questions involved in democratic intervention to reduce conflict and violence, and we would have a fair degree of representation in making those decisions. We would have good reason to follow a policy of accepting the decisions of the UNDC.

Of course, the United Nations is involved with more than limiting violence in the zones of turmoil. If a democratic caucus restored the UN's integrity and made it more representative, there would be pressure on the United States to pay more attention to all United Nations programs and decisions than we have in the past.

A stronger United Nations would not be a threat to America's independence or its national security. The limitations in the UN Charter and U.S. veto power in the Security Council protect U.S. national independence. If the UN's power grows because of the success of the UNDC, it will do so step by step on the basis of experience and accomplishment, and the United States will have substantial voice in the decisions about whether to give it more responsibility. While there are ways in which this process could go dangerously wrong, the improvement in the United Nations could turn out to be valuable, and the process is not so rapid and powerful that the United States cannot afford to let it start if it wants to make sure events do not get out of control.[3]

Whether to have weighted voting is not an all-or-nothing question. It involves two primary choices. First, how much difference should there be between the biggest and most-developed country and the smallest and least-developed country? That is, should the United States have twice as many votes as Barbados, 20 times as many, or 200 times or more? (The U.S. level of population and economic development is more than 2000 times as high as that of Barbados.) Second, how much weight should be given to population and how much to other factors, such as wealth or level of economic development?

The illustrative voting system shown at the end of this chapter gives each of the 26 most powerful countries either 10 or 20 votes (except the United States and Japan, which are given 40 and 30 votes respectively). There are also 16 countries with 5 votes and 26 with 2 votes, which leaves 31 countries with 1 vote each. With this illustrative allocation, the United States and other major, stable democracies would have nearly a majority with 255 out of 553 votes in the caucus. In the United Nations itself, these countries have 22 of 183 votes. The sample allocation of votes is roughly based on a formula that gives equal, but much less than proportional, weight to both population and level of economic development.[4] The system avoids having an abstract mathematical quality by using only 5 levels of voting power (except for the United States and Japan), instead of assigning exact vote weights to each country (e.g., 9 or 17 votes).

Although all this sounds too complicated and arbitrary to negotiate, appendix 6.1 shows why, once the principle of weighted voting is accepted, the choices needed to assign the number of votes to each country are reasonably clear-cut and possibly a plausible outcome of negotiations. (Partly this is because just about the same political consequences would be produced by any one of a number of different distributions of votes.)

The appendix also shows a much weaker alternative system of weighted voting, where each country has either one, two, or three votes. In such a system, the United States would have 2 percent of the votes, instead of 7 percent, and the leading democracies together would have 30 percent of the votes, instead of the 47 percent they would have in the illustrative "full" weighting system.

The small democracies that would superficially seem to be the losers from a system of weighted voting would have to decide whether they wanted to participate in an organization such as the UNDC in which they did not have as many votes as other members. In effect, they would have the choice between having their votes outweighed by the big democracies in the UNDC, or continuing to have their votes outweighed by the large number of nondemocracies in the UN membership.

The smaller democracies would be better off if the United Nations were dominated by the larger democracies. Because of ideological attachment to democracy and the greater power and prestige of the democracies, almost all the small democracies would probably join the UNDC. They would want to align themselves with the strongest and most admirable group, and to have an opportunity to express themselves in UNDC meetings, which would be the decisive forum, even though their vote would have little effect.

The basic operating principle of the caucus, as stated, would be that all participants agree to vote in the United Nations according to whatever decision is taken by majority vote in the caucus. But it would not be necessary to make an absolute rule that a member of the caucus had to use its UN vote in accordance with the decision of the caucus in every single case. So the United States, Britain, and France could retain their Security Council veto power,[5] although in most instances it would be politically difficult for one of the democratic powers to veto a Security Council resolution that the UNDC had decided to support. And small democracies would not have to be compelled to use their UN vote against their own strong national interest or against strong political opposition at home.

The caucus would not have to make decisions on issues about which the democracies were badly divided. And if the caucus did not act, each of its members would be free to vote as it pleased. So there would be two safety valves preventing countries from being too unhappy about having to vote with the caucus. First, on some issues, the caucus would decide not to act, or not to require its members to vote according to the caucus decision. Second, there would be provisions for individual members to be freed of the obligation to accept caucus decision on matters of strong direct interest or other strong conflict.

As a practical matter, on most votes, most of the members will not care much about which way they vote. The real question for many of the small democracies will be whether to agree to use their vote to support the democratic caucus or to stay out of the caucus so that they are free to trade their vote for some other advantage.

The UNDC would probably control the United Nations, and rarely lose important UN votes because there are few bases for the nondemocracies to be united enough to overcome the UNDC votes. Few nondemocracies would be ready to join an overtly "antidemocracy bloc." Many of them would pretend or aspire to be democratic, so they would be reluctant to vote against the UNDC on matters of importance unless they had a strong national interest in doing so—and on any particular vote few would have such a strong national interest. The fact that the democracies have most of the money would also make many countries reluctant to vote against them without good reason.

If a democratic caucus with weighted voting were created, it would, without any amendment of the UN Charter, have the result of changing the United Nations into an organization where most decisions outside the Security Council were actually made on the basis of weighted voting power instead of one-state, one-vote. It would in effect change the United Nations from an organization in which most of the voting power is held by small and/or poor nondemocratic countries to one in which the effective voting power more or less reflects the realities of the world, where advanced modern democracies have the bulk of the practical power. This effect would be the result of the small democracies' agreement generally to vote in accordance with the weighted vote of the UNDC, and the fact that the UNDC would have enough votes and other advantages to win most UN votes. This would be a revolutionary change in the nature of the United Nations, though it would not change its legal structure or authority.

The caucus could probably also be effective in raising the standards of behavior in the United Nations. It is rarely practical for an individual country to try to take action as a matter of principle against violations of UN rules by UN staff and individual member governments or to try to get other countries to uphold standards of decent parliamentary behavior. But once the caucus decided to speak out against violation of such standards, all members of the caucus would be obliged to join the protest. And the caucus would create regular procedures and channels for raising questions about improper actions by the United Nations or its agencies or members, without an individual member having to take on the burden of being the crusader for virtue.

A caucus of democracies at the United Nations would also raise democratic consciousness in the world by providing an institutional expression of the connection uniting all democracies. There is now no worldwide organization of democracies. The only major international institution whose charter provides that only democracies can be members is the European Union.

Creating a caucus of democracies would involve fewer difficulties and dilemmas than almost any other kind of new international organization. No member would be giving up its power or authority to the caucus, except the power to trade its UN vote. The financial cost would be trivial because the caucus would not have projects of its own and would have a small staff. The cost of the caucus could be paid for with the further reduction in UN waste that the caucus could achieve, even though substantial administrative and financial improvements were made with democratic leadership in the late 1980s.

A caucus of democratic members of the United Nations, unlike a new organization of democracies, would not require challenging or rejecting the United Nations. In fact the caucus would serve both to improve and to strengthen the United Nations. (For this reason, people who are against any international authority at all would have reason to oppose the UNDC.) Because of the caucus's lack of formal power and legal authority, many decisions about exactly what it should do and how it should operate would not need to be made in advance and could grow gradually out of its experience.

The UNDC would be a good opportunity to try out the idea of weighted voting for a broad international organization.[6] Creating a new formal organization would require a large commitment involving many risks and difficult issues. But by trying weighted voting in an informal organization attached to a continuing institution, we can find out how it would work in practice, while only making a commitment that we could back away from relatively gracefully if it did not work out. After seeing how the process works, we could decide how much to use it. If it did not work, the United Nations would continue as it had been. (Of course, substantial benefits cannot come without effort and risk, so it would be silly to pretend that creating a UNDC, even though informal, would not be a serious step with significant difficulties and dangers.)

WOULD A UNDC IMPROVE THE WORLD?

A very strong case can be made for a modest use of the democratic caucus idea to restore the integrity of the United Nations, but without expanding the UN's role in the world. It is undesirable to have the United Nations hanging around in its current disreputable condition (even though its behavior has improved recently) if there is a way to make it more decent.

The experience with the United Nations has given many people a strong feeling that supranational government is dangerous and likely to do more harm than good. While we share the negative judgment about the UN's past performance, we believe that much of the bad experience with the United Nations is the direct and indirect result of the cold war, which is gone and will not come back, and that a UNDC could improve the United Nations so much that the experience we have had with it in the past would not necessarily tell us much about how it would work in the future.

But if the integrity of the United Nations is restored, if the United Nations becomes a serious, responsible, reasonably representative international organization, there is a possibility/danger that the United Nations will become more powerful, which raises broader questions.

It is easy to believe that the zones of turmoil would be improved if the United Nations became more like a supranational government that could preserve peace, give a little protection to the struggle for democracy within countries, and prevent governmental mass murder. The zones of turmoil may well need more supranational government than they now have. As Stanley Hoffmann sees it, nervously moving between fear of American aggression and his desire for the United States to intervene in domestic affairs where he thinks it desirable:

> A central question is how to get international consent on lifting the immunity conferred by "domestic jurisdiction," an immunity that can have deadly consequences. A new standard worth working for would justify collective intervention by international or regional organizations, or by states with these agencies' consent, whenever domestic disorders or policies threaten a region's peace or security, and when fundamental human rights are violated on a large scale. We must remember that when states are in conflict, preventing war through diplomacy is possible, whereas when the troubles are domestic, under present international law, nothing can be done, as with Yugoslavia's slide into civil war.[7]

We are not sanguine about agreement on such circumstances, nor about the wisdom of what may be agreed on to deal with the full range of domestic and international conflicts that Hoffmann seems to have in mind. More modest objectives, such as encouraging peaceful resolution, even though that may not always be possible, or discouraging some forms of violence, should perhaps suffice for now. Hoffmann's despair, in short, comes from setting objectives beyond what human institutions are capable of accomplishing.

The beginning of wisdom, we think, is not the lesson that Hoffmann would have us learn from the slaughter in the former Yugoslavia (discussed in the next chapter), namely, that more authority to intervene early was needed to prevent what occurred. The lesson we take is that even when some people see what is coming, there is often insufficient political or bureaucratic support for courses of action that could be useful. Without moving troops the United States had much more power to change Serbia's cruel policy than it was willing to use. So did the European countries. But in addition to bureaucratic and political resistance to a precise diagnosis, action is inhibited by common consciousness that the deep and intractable character of the conflict casts doubt on any clear prescription.

Many people believe that the world also needs more supranational government to decide how the environment should be protected, to make protection against health risks and international commercial chicanery more consistent and effective, and to provide for fairer distribution of income. We think that the world is more likely to suffer from too much effort by supranational government to produce these benefits than by too little effort. (Unfortunately, the world can suffer from both too much and too little at the same time.) Our view is that supranational government would create new dangers, while most of the benefits it might provide could be gained by use of agreements among national governments, without more supranational government.

Since the world obviously needs supranational government that "does enough but not too much," should we not try to move toward some kind of supranational government that will do essential tasks, while being organized in a way that provides protection against going too far? That is not an unreasonable goal. And the UNDC approach is a reasonable way to pursue that goal. Nevertheless, someone who is much more afraid of too much supranational government than of too little should resist the UNDC idea, because it is impossible to make supranational government more feasible, effective, and attractive without increasing the risk that there will be too much of it.

A compelling argument for going ahead with the UNDC idea is that anarchy is inherently undesirable and dangerous and that in the long run, international anarchy, a world of hundreds of national governments not subject to any judge or legislature or international authority, is not fully civilized. Since ultimately we must come to some form of international legal order, some form of world government, this argument runs, it is a good idea to take cautious steps in this direction. Since we have to get there eventually, steps that have good procedural protections against going too far, such as the UNDC idea, are the right way to go.

But we are not completely sold by this argument. The analogy between the lack of government in a territory—anarchy—and the lack of a supranational government over the hundreds of nations of the world is not decisive. The problem of finding ways for a few hundred governments to work together is not the same as finding ways for millions of people to share the same space. It may well be that hundreds of nations can find ways of preserving the peace and cooperating and coordinating with one another as much as is necessary or useful, without creating a government that has authority over them.

Peace is the biggest issue. We have already argued that democracy provides strong protection against war between democratic countries. As Immanuel Kant, who is usually dismissed as utopian, asked, If all the countries of the world are democracies, why would a supranational government be needed to preserve peace? Until that happens, maybe the United States can do about as well as possible if it has to intervene in the zones of turmoil by improvising, as it did in the Persian Gulf conflict.

Airline safety is an example of what may seem like a natural subject for supranational government. But there is no reason why an international agency to protect the safety of air travel cannot be given as much authority as it needs without creating an overall supranational government. Federalism includes the intertwining of governments, not necessarily the creation of a hierarchy of one government over another.[8] So national governments can give an international airline safety organization all the authority it needs. Any other particular kind of international cooperation or coordination can also be done by agreement among national governments, without creating an overall international or world government. There already is a rich network of international authorities that are dealing reasonably successfully with a variety of problems that require international cooperation, without overall supranational government.

Of course, it is probably true that it is harder to give an international air safety organization the authority it needs by getting agreement from hundreds of national governments than by having an international legislative body enact a law. But experience shows that it is by no means impossible to get the necessary international cooperation by negotiation, and the extra difficulty may be a price worth paying for insurance against the potential dangers of an international legislature. Even if there were a "world government," the political problem of getting agreement would continue.

Our conclusion is that whether it would be good for the United States, or for the world, to have an improved United Nations with more power depends on whether the greater problem for the world is too much or too little supranational government. Some questions are so tough that they have to be left to the reader.

One reaction to the idea of a UNDC is that it is impractical, that it would be impossible to get agreement from so many countries to such a complicated proposal. (Some will say "fortunately," others "unfortunately.") Those who think that countries are too selfish to agree to such an idea should ask who would benefit from it. Superficially, at least, it is the large democracies, principally the United States, Japan, and the European "big four," especially the last of these. If the United States proposed such an idea to these five countries why would a selfish point of view make them reluctant?[9] (Of course, resistance to following the United States or any one of many other national inclinations might prevent agreement, even if selfish national interest would favor it.) If the six countries then announced that they contemplated forming a democratic caucus at the United Nations in whose decisions they would have forty, thirty, and twenty votes each, and issued an invitation to all the other democracies to join and participate in the consideration of a proposal along the lines presented, would the invitees not attend? Would not many democracies want to join the great democracies in such a caucus, even if they might prefer to organize it differently? They would have something to gain by participating, especially those being offered ten or five votes. If many of those invited decided to accept an invitation to such a caucus, why would many democracies stay out?

Perhaps some countries that were not invited would complain, arguing that they are really democratic and so are entitled to membership in a UNDC. But this would not prevent the UNDC from being created. It is good for a prospective organization to have countries fighting to become members, particularly if they do so by insisting that they are democratic. The UNDC would not be seriously damaged if a few too many countries were included.

Apart from the normal complications that always make action difficult, the main obstacle to the idea is probably U.S. inertia. Of course the proposal does not have to come from the United States. But recently no other country has tried to act as a world leader.

B. A Single "Europe" or Two "Europes"?

The EU, which is a European approach toward limited supranational government, is now committed to a common passport for all the citizens of all its members. This means that any citizen of any member state can live in any other member state and find a job there, about like a local citizen. This is wonderful, but unfortunately it makes it impossible for countries such as Poland and Turkey to become full members of the EC for at least a generation. It is neither reasonable nor politically possible today to say that as many Turks and Poles and Bulgarians as want to move to Paris will have the right to do so.

There are two groups of ideas about what Europe is geographically, and two debates about what institutional form Europe should have. The narrow view of the geographic and cultural Europe is limited to the Roman Catholic and Protestant countries of Western and Central Europe, perhaps extending east to Greece along the Mediterranean and to Estonia along the Baltic. The sense of communality within this group includes religion, history, art and literature, economic development, and democracy. Of course, there are significant differences within narrow Europe. The Protestant

North and Catholic Mediterranean are quite distinct. The richer countries are twice as rich as the poorer ones (more than three times as rich as Poland). Democracy is much less deep in Greece than it is in England and France. And so on.

There is also an alternative strong view of what Europe is, one that extends much farther to the east, including the Balkans, Eastern Europe, Russia, the Caucasus, and Turkey (see table 6.2). This broader view of Europe includes Slavs and the eastern branches of Christianity and some Moslems. The broadest Europe is defined by a sense of differentness from Asia and Africa, a differentness that is partly racial and partly historical and cultural. This broadest sense of Europe could even include most of the Mediterranean countries that have long had connections with Europe, especially Tunisia and Lebanon, as well as Turkey. Europeans do not feel much more different from the Maghreb than they do from Russia, and probably less than from Turkey. All these people are felt to be from related families and to share the same history in a way that other Africans and Asians do not. (They also share what is generally thought of as one color.)[10]

When it comes to the question of the political meaning of "Europe" —how "deep" the institution of Europe should go—there are two debates with at least as many strands. The fundamental drive, about which there is the most agreement, is that Europe should be as big a trade bloc and common market as possible, to compete most effectively with the United States and Japan. The biggest fly in this ointment is the desire of Western European farmers to be protected against competition from Eastern Europe.

The two debates about what institutional form Europe should take are these: How much should the government of Europe do? And how much should it be answerable to the European states rather than to European citizens?

Some Europeanists see Europe as eventually replacing the nations as the main government. They want the government of Europe to do more —in social policy, foreign policy, and the like—and they want it to base its authority on its own institutions and the citizens directly. France, in contrast, wants the government of Europe to be more important and do more, but to continue to be a government of states. Many of the English, and others, want Europe to be primarily an economic and trade reality, with other matters left to the individual states. Finally, there are those who do not want Europe to take over more governmental functions, but who on trade matters want it to act more nearly as a direct government, not as an agent of national governments. They would like the EU to become an effective negotiator on trade policy, with the power to act, and therefore the power to make concessions in order to win concessions from the United

TABLE 6.2

POSSIBLE PARTS OF AN EXPANDED EUROPE:

A SUMMARY

	Population (millions)	GDP ($ billions)
Narrow Europe (all Protestant and Roman Catholic) (4 large countries; 5 small and middle-sized countries; 2 tiny countries)	280	3,500
Very rich countries GNP per capita = $13,000; population = 224 million		
Moderately rich countries GNP per capita = $7,000; population = 56 million		
Other elements that could be included in fullest Europe		
1. Other rich Protestant and Roman Catholic countries (U.K. and 5 small countries)	90	1,200
2. Other "non-Slavic" countries (Rumania and 6 small countries)	60	300
3. "Slavic" countries (Poland, Ukraine, and 8 small countries)	160	600
4. Moslem countries (Turkey, Azerbaijan, and Albania—plus Moslems in the Balkans, Bulgaria, and Russia)	70	200
5. Russia	150	600
Totals (38 countries)	800	6,400

NOTE: There are five former Soviet Republics of Central Asia with fifty million people, 25 percent of whom are Russian, having a total gross domestic product of roughly $100 billion.

States and Japan. Now, primary negotiation on major issues must be done with national governments because the EU can accept only what its member governments have already agreed on.

In other words, there are two sides of two issues: narrow or broad coverage, and independence or responsiveness to national governments, and there are advocates for each of the four possible combinations of the two sides (narrow and independent, narrow and responsive, broad and independent, and broad and responsive). And of course there are many varieties of compromises that try to or seem to avoid the two harsh dichotomies.

All four of these positions have to address the separate question of which Europe, small Europe or big Europe, should be the goal. Here realities intrude on the argument. Some issues, such as social policy and labor policy, are not suitable for a group of states as diverse as a broad Europe.

Only some forms of integration are suitable for a broad and diverse group of countries: removal of internal trade barriers, external trade policy, peaceful settlement of national disputes, insistence on at least minimal standards of political and civil liberties, coordinated environmental protection policies. A broad Europe devoted to these tasks would be a powerful protection to the well-being of the Eastern European countries and would speed their economic development.

If such a broad Europe existed, the psychological and political cost of being outside "Europe" would be so great that each of the Eastern European countries would have to join and to accept the compulsion to allow their citizens to have civil rights.

The two fundamental obstacles to getting agreement on a broad Europe to do these jobs are the problem of disentangling broad Europe from narrow Europe (deep Europe from shallow Europe) and the reluctance of Western European farmers, who are now protected by special exceptions from the rights that East European countries have as associate members to sell in the common market. Technically it would be possible to continue such exceptions if those countries became full members. But West European farm interests are likely to fear that their political position would be weaker if Eastern European countries became full members of the European organization.

The forms of integration that are suitable only for a narrow, more homogeneous Europe include free migration of persons; common social, labor, and welfare policies; and close enough psychological identity to create moral responsibility for one another's citizens. We all have obligations, of course, to all other human beings. But the degree and immediacy of the obligation depends on the closeness of the connection. The obligation is clearly stronger for members of the same family and for members of the same nation. Adding new commitments has to be done realistically. If people believe that they cannot fulfill the newly implied obligation, they will not accept it; the result will be that the intended common identity will not be achieved. People do not feel embarrassed that citizens of another United Nations member state live in conditions that are "unacceptable" for citizens of their own country. With a strong "European" identity, a citizen of Europe would have to feel embarrassed if other Europeans lived in unacceptable conditions.

The forms of integration that are possible for either a broad Europe or a narrow Europe, but are more appropriate and easier to achieve in a narrow Europe, include some common regulatory and environmental regimes, various forms of economic planning and industrial policies, and elements of an integrated foreign policy. The desirability of movement in these directions is more controversial.

Fortunately, the future evolution of European institutions will not be as much influenced by security considerations as it has been in the past. Military concerns will soon be of little importance to the countries that would be in a narrow Europe. The Eastern European countries that may have nondemocratic neighbors would have a slight security gain by being included in a broad Europe. But the ability and willingness of Western Europe to protect an Eastern European democracy from a nondemocracy would be nearly the same without the institutions of a broad Europe as with such institutions. Security issues will be an inadequate or distorting basis for constructing the institutions or the political base of either a broad or a narrow Europe, but especially for a narrow Europe.

In principle, two partially overlapping "Europes," a broad one and a narrow one, could exist at the same time. The broad Europe could have the powers and do tasks suitable for a heterogeneous group of countries; the narrow Europe would have fewer and more homogeneous members and would be more fully integrated. The countries of narrow Europe would also be members of the broad Europe, and in fact would be the dominant part of broad Europe.[11]

Broad Europe would be the trade bloc that would compete with the United States and Japan. Trade negotiations would be carried out by the institutions of broad Europe, institutions that would presumably be responsive to national governments.

Narrow Europe would make it possible for those countries that want to pursue political integration and maintain or increase the momentum toward centralization (welfarism, industrial policy, *dirigisme,* or whatever) to do so. Those countries that do not like those directions could stay out, or get out, of the narrow Europe. This would probably include Britain. (Some countries would not be allowed to join the narrow Europe; but their exclusion from an optional "second Europe" would be much less harmful than excluding them from the only "Europe.")

Our view is that it would be desirable to develop an articulated vision of broad Europe as a practical goal of policy, and to begin to move toward implementing it, because broad Europe could improve the chances of democracy in Eastern Europe, make economic development arrive faster, and perhaps help to preserve peace there. Finding a way to make broad Europe real would also make it possible to keep Turkey in Europe. Enabling Turkey to be part of Europe would be a great virtue—for Turkey, for Central Asia, and for the Middle East. One of the few current issues that is likely to shape history is the need to find a way that Turkey can continue to be oriented toward Europe.

The key requirement for making broad Europe possible is finding a way to make it compatible with the current narrow Europe. Such a narrow and deeper Europe is probably necessary, in addition to a broad Europe, if for no other reason than that the EU has already gone so far in that direction. Our own judgment is that a narrow Europe will not be very successful, but it is now politically impractical to get away from it. Many people want the things that it can try to do, and they are right to try.

There is no reason why those countries that want to be part of a narrow Europe that experiments with more centralization and government control should not do so. But it would be a great advantage if that movement did not have monopoly power over the economic advantages of a European common market. Unfortunately, it is now true that countries that want the benefits of full participation in the common market, and in the only form of "Europe" that exists, have also to accept the momentum toward increased centralization and planning, slowed as it was by Denmark's voters' rejection of the Maastricht amendments to the EU charter and the result of the too-close French referendum. As a result, the reluctant integrators get more integration than they like, and at the same time the enthusiastic integrators are kept from having as much integration as they think they want.

In view of the trap that Europe has put itself in—having gone so deep that it cannot go as broad as it would like—how might it be possible to move toward a more ideal situation? There are both structural and political problems in moving toward having both a "universal" broad Europe, and an optional narrow Europe, but the structural problems can be solved. The real question is whether the institutional changes that could theoretically produce the desired result are politically practical.

The suggestion that there should be both a broad Europe and a narrow Europe would create a dilemma for those Europeans who want to continue the momentum toward integration and technocratic control. Their "ambitious" reaction would be negative. It would mean giving up their ability to limit the advantages of being full members of a large common market to those countries who accept their integration plans. The result would be that some countries would be tempted to drop out of the integrated narrow Europe, because dropping out would not prevent them from staying in the European common market and trade bloc. Brussels would no longer be the only European game.

But the "two Europes" approach would also bring two advantages to Europeanists. It would improve the ability of European countries to compete with the United States in doing business in Eastern Europe, because Eastern Europe would be more firmly part of the European trade bloc. Also, it would make Europe a larger, although poorer, trade bloc. At the same time, it would enable the integrationist efforts of a smaller group of countries to go further and faster because the countries most opposed to doing so would drop out and would no longer provide resistance.

France's traditional interests in Europe might be well served by the "two Europes" solution, with the prospect of France and Germany at the center of a Europe that is small and homogeneous enough not to get out of hand, but big enough to be a superpower. (The agreement to form a Franco-German military unit reflects such an attitude.) And this would be a Europe in which Britain and other countries with "inappropriate sensibilities" would cease to be obstacles. The disadvantage would be that the narrow Europe would not have exclusive claim to being "Europe" and would have less economic weight than a broader grouping, although it could use its weight more effectively.

French reaction to the idea of a "two Europes" arrangement would be dominated by their perception of how Germany would act if there were two Europes. The French would worry that Germany might not choose to stay in the small Europe or would regard it as such a secondary concern that it would lose significance.

Germany might well see the same virtues in small Europe as France. But there would be only minimal economic advantages for either France or Germany from membership in the small Europe. Germany might feel that it was sufficiently "bound" to Europe through its commitment to the big Europe and would not need to participate in small Europe to dispel any residual fear among its neighbors. Germany might also feel that it would have greater influence in the larger Europe than in the smaller one. Big Europe would be where Germany could express and gain support from its traditional eastern interests. Finally, Germany might not like to go so far toward a stronger Brussels as France would probably go if English reluctance were removed.

The "two Europes" approach would probably be attractive to England and some other countries that are uncomfortable about the directions of Brussels and about French inclination to strong integration but that do not want to isolate themselves or be excluded from the European economy and financial markets. The problem would be if Germany became part of this group and decided it did not care about being part of narrow Europe.

The bottom line is that two Europes would make political sense if Britain decided to get out of narrow Europe and Germany decided to stay in and take it seriously. But if Britain stayed in narrow Europe, broad Europe would have so much second-class aura that it might be impossible. And if Germany would not stay involved in small Europe, France would prefer that big Europe not be created.

The United States has conflicting interests concerning the direction of Europe. The creation of a broad Europe would serve American interests in the extension of democracy and economic growth to Eastern Europe. But the United States would be in a weaker position to do business in Eastern Europe if those countries were part of an extended EU. If Europe were not too protectionist, this would be a moderate cost, and in no event could it be a decisive cost because Eastern Europe does not have nearly as much money as Western Europe or Japan or the United States.

Real harm to the United States would come only if making Europe broader increased the chance that it would be protectionist. Although giving Europe more economic weight may slightly increase the danger that Europe will be tempted by protectionism, this danger is probably balanced by the political factors introduced by the broader membership.

Overall, we believe the creation of a broad Europe is in the U.S. national interest, partly for reasons that are discussed in the next chapter. We also believe that the creation of a smaller, more unified Europe—alongside a broader European common market—would be good for the United States. We believe that the Brussels efforts, contrary to their intentions and American fears, will make the narrow Europe less competitive. We do not need the benefit we would get from their mistake, but it would make things a little easier for us. Also the defects of the narrow Europe might partially inoculate the world from making the same mistake on a broader scale. (Of course, if we are wrong, and narrow Europe turns out to be a brilliant success, it can also be a useful lesson for the world.)

C. Two Forms of Subnationalism

In Europe the nation-state has been partly a unifying force, as in the obvious example of the United Kingdom, which brings together England, Scotland, Wales, and Northern Ireland. Originally the price for unification in each country was paid partly because of national security reasons and other feelings and perceptions that will be largely outdated in the current world order. A democratic England and a democratic Scotland no longer need to have a common government to avoid endless wars with each other.

Countries in the zones of peace no longer have to be large to protect themselves against attack. Small countries do not necessarily mean isolated economies. Their businesses can operate in large markets.

Since in much of Europe ethnic groups are mixed together, any territory that gets "self-government" for its majority will also have within it ethnic minorities. The more countries there are, the more some ethnic groups will be divided. Moreover, ethnic groups controlling a sovereign state are more dangerous to the minorities living among them than ethnic groups that are themselves a minority in a larger state. But in a democratic Europe where massacres and oppression are felt to be things of the past, this concern may become less frightening, reducing another barrier to the division of some of the current states.

Under the umbrella of peace, democracy, and a European market, we can expect old "provincial" units and suppressed nationalities to seek greater recognition and possibly autonomy or independence. The disintegrating states will not feel as strongly about preventing their components from going off on their own. Keeping states together always involves some compromise, some dilution, as the price of grandeur. If the peeling away of ancient components does not lead to dangerous military weakness, or make war more likely, there will be growing reluctance to pay this price and more willingness to accommodate separatist feelings.

The possibility of new small states is probably more important in Eastern Europe than in the settled democracies. In Central and Eastern Europe, where the boundaries of empires have been fought over for centuries, a number of substantial ethnic or national groups have not made peace with their minority status. The increased viability of small states may make it easier to find ways of resolving the conflict stemming from such national feelings, particularly if experience brings confidence that there will not be violence.

COMPETITIVE SUBNATIONAL UNITS

This section about a second kind of subnational government, unlike most of this book, does not describe what is happening, but gives an idea about how to make things better. Our proposal for reorganizing governments can be both a conservative way of protecting against trouble and an adventurous way of increasing efficiency and spurring innovation. It can be used to deal with the historic problems in old nations and with the challenge of creating new ones.

We believe the countries that have more than 20 or 30 million people would achieve important benefits if they assigned most of their economic functions to subnational units of government, as the much smaller Switzerland does.

The idea is for countries to transfer responsibility for the economic part of government from their single national government to multiple regional or provincial governmental units. Since most politics follows the money, this transfer would make the politics of the province at least as important as that of the nation. (Although we have to assume that a movement toward this kind of decentralization is not equally appropriate for all political cultures and is not likely in Europe, the overall international order that is coming into existence in Europe will be more hospitable to such a movement if it somehow gets started.)

This idea is not an attack on nationalism. While nationalism has caused much harm, it has also been a creative and valuable force. In any event, people's attachment to their nation is too strong and valuable a force to reject. Building strong subnational units will make nations more capable of dealing with the increasing internationalism of the modern world. And we will describe the ways in which transferring responsibility to subnational units will make the nations better governed.

Our vision of government in the future does not involve sharp changes toward either world government or local government. We do not see continual struggle for supremacy among competing layers of hierarchical structure. Increasingly we think there should and will be a complex, continually and subtly changing web of overlapping governmental units, local, regional, national, and supranational, mostly with specialized functions, each with the suitable source of authority, form of politics, powers, and constituency.[12]

The basic distinction between national and lower levels of government is that there can be only one national government within a nation, but subnational units of governments always have other parallel governments in the same country with which they can be compared. The declining importance of military security issues, first in the zones of peace and democracy and gradually in the zones of turmoil, will make such a change more realistic than it would have been in the past, although the approach can also be used in a country that has severe security problems and needs a strong military force. The Swiss have always had an essential and effective citizen army with a limited central government.

Before talking about the advantages and uses of this idea we should describe how it would work—first in big countries like Japan, the United States, Spain, and Germany. The constitution would be amended so that responsibility and authority for most matters concerning economics and business would be transferred from the national government to the next lower level of government—whether existing units such as states or provinces or new regional units of government. National governments would keep responsibility for defense and foreign policy, national culture and identity, and some environmental protection and essential functions that require a single national policy.

This idea of "competitive subnational governments" is different from many discussions of decentralization. Usually decentralization is thought of as an administrative device, transferring either purely administrative functions or relatively unimportant matters to local levels of governments, but keeping most power at the national level. But the idea discussed here is quite different: It is a constitutional transfer of so much power to the subnational unit that the politics of the province becomes the main politics of the country, or at least equal in importance to that of the national government. This is what will happen if most taxes are raised by the province, and most business and welfare legislation is enacted by the province.

Different countries would assign different functions to their subnational units; the specific allocation between national and subnational units is not critical. The key to the idea is that the subnational units have so much authority that they are more important to most businesses, and to the commercial concerns of most citizens, than is the national government. As long as the taxes imposed by the national government are much lower than the taxes imposed by subnational units, the politics of the subnational unit will not be subsidiary to national politics, which is the object of the proposed constitutional change.

Today, when the economy is bad, Americans are inclined to change their president. The effect of our proposal would be that citizens would normally hold their regional government responsible for economic troubles and judge their national leaders on other grounds.

Competition. The primary reason for assigning most practical responsibilities to subnational units of government is to gain the stimulating and regulatory benefits of competition. As the world gets more complicated, and as governments get bigger, it becomes harder to understand how governments should act to achieve their goals, and politically more difficult to get them to change their ways. To prevent governments from doing a poor job we need to harness the power of competition. Division and competition is also protection against disastrously bad government, perhaps the biggest danger in a rich world.

If most government activity were carried out by subnational units, two forms of competition would operate. First, the citizens and political opposition of a province that perform poorly would be able to point to other provinces that do a better job, to show that improvements are necessary and possible. Second, citizens and businesses could move from a badly governed province to a better governed one.

It is not a light matter to move from one province to another; neither individuals nor businesses would make such a move because of a mild disagreement or unhappiness with the government of their province. But if any province has a government that gets worse and worse, and all efforts at reform have failed, the normal inflow would be reduced and some extra people and businesses will begin to move out. The result would be embarrassment for the government, combined with a loss of revenues. These would strengthen the position of those who want to correct the government's mistakes. Even a small movement of citizens and companies out of a province will likely be a powerful force against unwise policies.

The ability to move to another province is also a safety valve protecting the citizens against the extremes of bad government. Those who are most disturbed by the failures of a provincial government can move. Those who are not bothered enough to be willing to move are hurt less.

The Arrogance of Power. The power and respect that must be commanded by the head of a national government makes it more difficult to protect the government against the human weaknesses of national leaders. The second great advantage of narrowing the scope of national government is reducing the harm done to the character of the individuals who operate governments from the awe and mystery that must attach to the leaders of national governments.

The semisacred character of government attaches primarily to the national government. Its leaders inevitably are touched by the honor and authority of their position. But if their responsibilities are fewer, it is easier to control or limit the harm done by the arrogance of power. Of course, many provincial governments will also be powerful, which will tend to corrupt their leaders too. But their power will be moderated by competition.

Narrowing the national government is a further application of the same principle as separating the office of the ceremonial head of state from the office of the executive head of government. In England and many other countries, the head of state is kept "above politics," representing all the people. Similarly, a narrow national government will avoid many divisive issues and temptations of decay and so be better able to represent the whole people on critical issues.

Government should express the ideals of the people. And idealistic people should work for the government, motivated and controlled in part by the honor of their position. But the supply of idealists is limited. Power tends to produce corruption. If the government is too big, it is easy for corruption to escape exposure. It is much easier to keep a small national government, with narrow responsibilities, clean and idealistic.

Smaller Government. Part of the problem of government is bigness. This is a problem in all kinds of organization, but especially in those where price and profit cannot be used to measure success or efficiency. The problem of bigness is reduced when government is divided among the national government and a number of provinces. This is another fundamental advantage of competitive subnational governments.

Vitality in Politics. Another major advantage of the provincial system is that it helps preserve the democratic vitality of the national government by providing additional sources of political leadership and party and organizational strength.

With a centralized system, a single party can be in power so long that the other parties find it difficult to keep the vitality and experience necessary to provide a genuinely competent alternative to the ruling party. But since a single party is not likely to be in power in all the provinces for a long time, experienced alternative political leadership for the national government will always be available from at least one province.

And in a provincial system there would be a number of governments in which young politicians and administrators could learn, develop, be given responsibility, and be tested and observed so that the nation would be assured of a steady flow of tested governmental leaders to choose among. (But if national and provincial politics are as distinct from each other as they are in Canada, this advantage will be lost.)

WHAT ARE THE NEGATIVES?

What reasons can be given not to transfer most government responsibilities in the big countries to four or a dozen or twenty provinces? Of course, the immediate reason why the idea will not be adopted is that governments are not redesigned every day, and many people have a stake in the existing arrangements. But there must be more to say in defense of the existing system than that it is hard to change.

The first objection is that the new system might represent wasteful duplication of political functions. There would be more legislatures, elections, party leaders, and so on.

Another objection is that political/governmental talent would have to be spread more thinly. It is hard enough to find one first-class head of government; how can a country expect to find five or ten? But when the job is broken up, it becomes easier. So there will be more people capable of being head of government of a province than there are capable of being head of the country's government. And since the national head of government will have an easier job when the national government has a narrower set of responsibilities, more people will be capable of doing the job.

Probably the greatest objection for many people will be the idea that it is very hard to get the government to do the right thing (for example, to overcome inertia and selfish interests), and if the government is divided into many pieces the struggle to get the government to do its job will be much greater. If there is a right way for the government to take care of poor people that the national government can discover, then it would be foolish to turn the power over to half a dozen provinces, forcing each of them to discover the right way for itself. Some of them would almost certainly do an inadequate job. And none would be able to afford the research and study required to find the correct techniques.

But this objection is largely a misunderstanding. It is rare when there is only one right way. Local variations in conditions and values are often important, so what is right in one area is wrong in another. Usually there are a number of more or less equally valid ways to accomplish a government task, and they usually are not found by rational analysis, but by trial and error or by successive stages of approximation. So there is little reason to expect that a national government will have better answers than a dozen smaller governments.

In fact, the opposite is more likely. Small governments are almost certainly better at learning from trial and error, both because small governments will produce more experiments and because they should be faster to move away from mistakes.

Another objection will be that when most government responsibility is in the hands of competitive provinces, business will be too strong because national and international industrial giants will be dealing with "small" governments that they can play off against each other, and because business will have the power to shift assets to those provinces that are "pro-business." But businesses are not completely free to shift assets. They are partly tied to customers and workers. If customers and workers prefer a province that is "pro-people and antibusiness," then business will not be able to stay away. While it is true that the power of giant corporations relative to government will be greater in a provincial system, the power of other groups, especially local ones, will also be greater in the provincial system.

Or it may be argued that passing government responsibility down to competitive provinces will result in people moving to provinces that have low tax rates—or all provinces will be "forced" by competition to have low tax policies. But provinces that have low taxes will not have enough money to provide good services. People will then be able to choose between "high tax-good service" and "low tax-limited service" provinces. And that is a good thing. Why should people have to live in a high-tax regime if they are willing to forego the services that the high taxes provide?

The argument will be made that selfish people will move to low-tax provinces in order to shirk their responsibility to the disadvantaged. This problem is easy to exaggerate. Maybe it is not so nice to live in a province full of selfish people. Few people can be so sure that they, or someone in their family, will never need the services of a "compassionate government" that they will want to move to a "selfish province."

While there are some real choices that governments have to make about tax policy, about the level of services, about the degree and extent to which the government should implement the compassion of the community, many of the arguments against letting people have a choice of governments are really a defense of inefficient government. The world is full of examples of governments that cost a lot in taxes and restrictions but deliver little in effective compassion or service because of corruption, inefficiency, or ideological blindness. If competition forces the province to keep taxes low, it may do even more to force the province to provide high-quality service, including compassionate services that genuinely help the needy, rather than help primarily the government service providers.

It is increasingly important that we find ways to introduce competition into the provision of community services and programs. In a wealthy world a decreasing share of human effort will go to manufacturing and to providing things for individuals and families. An increasing share of our life will be devoted to community services and to other intangibles in which the community is necessarily involved. Many of these services are difficult to measure and evaluate quantitatively. Their economics are so subtle and complex that the cost for the same benefit can be $1 or $100, depending on how cleverly it is done—and great expenses can even produce negative results. Experience in the production of goods is strong evidence that lack of competition often produces enormous inefficiency.

In a newly democratic country, especially one in which there are ethnic or other historic enmities, another set of advantages may accrue to putting most responsibility below the national level, advantages that may be even more important. A strong national government makes politics a winner-takes-all game that no one can afford to let his rival win. When there is only one head of government, one side or the other—North or South, black or white, Catholic or Protestant—is on top and the other is out. If the national government does not matter as much as the regional governments, then it does not matter so much which side controls it. Dividing up power can make learning to live together easier. But if ethnic or regional antagonisms are too strong, even a limited central government may not be sustained (as the U.S. Civil War demonstrated).

Even if there are no long-term fissures in the society, dividing government power geographically makes it easier for a society to learn to live with democracy. In a new democracy the greatest problem is turning the government over to the other party. This is much easier if there are many different governments.

Appendix 6.1
Sample List of Members of UN Democratic Caucus and Possible Allocation of Votes

The 77 other democracies listed in table 6.3 (pp. 138–41) are the United Nations members rated as "free" in the 1995 Freedom House survey of freedom, the top subgroup in the survey's category of "partly free," plus Colombia, the Dominican Republic, Fiji, Nepal, Paraguay, the Philippines, Russia, Ukraine, Zambia, India, Jordan, Pakistan, Thailand, Turkey, and Mexico. The distinction between this group and some of the other "partly free" countries is intended only to be illustrative; there is no clearly appropriate dividing line. Essentially the same result would be achieved if some countries were removed from or added to the list. We would not make much of an argument for the particular illustrative line we have chosen here.

One column of table 6.3 shows the gross domestic product (GDP) per capita of each country, calculated in dollars of equal purchasing power ("purchasing power parity," or PPP dollars). These are standard international estimates. All such calculations are defective, but it is clear that these comparisons come closer to reflecting actual consumption standards than do the standard comparisons based on GDP per capita defined in terms of international exchange rates.

The allocation of votes proposed here is an approximation of what one would get by applying the following formula:

$$\frac{\sqrt{\text{population (in millions)}} \times \sqrt{\text{per capita gross domestic product (in PPP\$)}}}{50}$$

The fourth column gives the rounded results of this formula.

If population and GDP per capita were multiplied without first taking their square roots, the highest number in this column would be more than 20,000 times as big as the lowest number, instead of only 150 times as big. It would seem unfair or unseemly for the United States to have 20,000 votes, although its share of the total would be about the same.

As a practical matter, if countries are positive enough about having a system of weighted voting to begin a practical consideration of what the weights should be, agreement about a mathematical formula will not be necessary. The following would be the key issues that would have to be decided by political negotiation and agreement.

1. Do the members of the EU have separate membership or should they be represented as Europe? If separately, as we assume, will Germany be equal to the United Kingdom, France, and Italy?

2. If, as we assume, the big European democracies will each have the same number of votes, what should the ratio be between each of them and the United States? We assume that there would be resistance to the United States having more than twice as many votes as France, for example—but anything less than twice as many votes would not be reasonable for the United States.

3. Should Japan have more votes than the big European countries, since it has 50 percent more population and at least as much GDP per capita? If so, how many more? Putting Japan halfway between the United States and the European countries seems like the simplest solution. If this is unfair to anyone, it is to the United States. Since Japan stands alone, there are no great consequences to giving it a few more votes than it is "entitled" to. And to the extent that the European big four are really one, they are overweighted compared to Japan—as well as in comparison to the United States. (If Europe were to act as a single unit in the United Nations, the United States and Europe might have 60 votes each in the UNDC and the other countries the same as before.)

4. Which, if any, less developed countries should have as many votes as the big European countries? It seems to us objectionable to exclude all developing countries from the highest category. It is hard to see why it would be harmful for Brazil and India to have as many votes as Germany and France. It certainly would not be acceptable to give them many fewer votes than the European democracies, and no substantive benefit would be gained by insulting them by giving them slightly fewer votes. There are no other democracies that have close to as good a claim as Brazil and India. Brazil and India do not have a good claim to have significantly more votes than the Europeans; specifically, they do not have a serious claim to have as many votes as Japan. (On the other hand, there would be no great harm if Japan had only 20 votes, like the other great powers.) Of course, if population were the main criterion, India would be entitled to many more votes, but the United States and the other advanced democracies would not accept that principle, nor should they.

5. If it is agreed that the ratio of votes among the big countries is 2:3:4, the next question is, What should the ratio be between the big countries and the little ones? How many more votes should the United States have than the smallest country? Forty to one seems like a modest ratio for the United States to have, in relation to countries like Botswana or Bahamas, and certainly in relation to such tiny island members as Vanuatu

and St. Lucia, with populations of fewer than 100,000 people. Compressing the range from 40 to 20 would leave the big powers' fraction of the total nearly the same but it would increase the importance of the smallest countries and decrease that of the medium countries, which seems neither useful nor politically effective.

The answers to these few questions are enough to determine the political shape of the caucus. And once the general principle of weighting to take account of both population and level of development is accepted, it would not seem to be too difficult to agree on a set of answers comparable to those we have chosen.

All the other members would be divided by population size and level of economic development into four groups, which would get 1, 2, 5, or 10 votes respectively. Countries "half as big" as the European democracies would get 10, "one quarter as big" would get 5, and so on. The range of uncertainty about which countries should get 2, 5, or 10 votes would be small enough so that it would not raise any issues of principle or affect anyone except those directly concerned. While there would be a few countries on the borderline, the fact that each level is twice as high as the one below would make most assignments fairly difficult to dispute—particularly if they were all made at the same time.

The final column in the table shows what the distribution of votes would be using a minimal weighting system in which each country gets either 1, 2, or 3 votes. The effect would be almost the same if the big powers got 2, 3, or 4 votes, and all the rest got 1 vote each. Also, there is no substantial change in the share of the votes for the United States or the leading democracies if population is given greater weight, or if level of development is given greater weight.

TABLE 6.3

POSSIBLE MEMBERS OF UNDC

Country	Popula-tion (millions)[a]	GDP per capita (PPP$)[b]	Formula value[c]	Votes	
				Main proposal	Alternative proposal
Leading democracies					
United States	250	$22,000	48	40	3
Japan	125	19,000	31	30	3
Germany	80	20,000	25	20	3
France	60	18,000	20	20	3
Italy	60	17,000	20	20	3
United Kingdom	60	16,000	20	20	3
Rounded subtotal[d]	640			150	18
Australia	20	$17,000	11	10	2
Canada	25	19,000	14	10	2
Netherlands	15	17,000	10	10	2
Spain	40	13,000	14	10	2
Belgium	10	17,000	8	10	2
Sweden	10	17,000	8	10	2
Rounded subtotal	120			60	12
Austria	8	$18,000	7	5	1
Denmark	5	18,000	6	5	1
Finland	5	16,000	6	5	1
Greece	10	8,000	6	5	1
Israel	5	13,000	5	5	1
New Zealand	3	14,000	4	5	1
Norway	4	17,000	5	5	1
Portugal	10	9,000	6	5	1
Czech Republic	10	7,000	5	5	1
Ireland	5	11,000	4	5	1
Rounded subtotal	60			50	10
Total 22 leading democracies	820			260	40

NOTE: Notes appear at the end of the table, pp. 141–42.

TABLE 6.3 — CONTINUED

Country	Population (millions)[a]	GDP per capita (PPP$)[b]	Formula value[c]	Votes Main proposal	Votes Alternative proposal
Other democracies					
India	880	$1,000	20	20	3
Russia	150	7,000	20	20	3
Brazil	150	5,000	18	20	3
Mexico	85	7,000	16	20	3
Rounded subtotal	1,270			80	12
Turkey	60	$5,000	11	10	2
Ukraine	50	6,000	11	10	2
Colombia	35	5,000	8	10	2
Philippines	65	2,000	8	10	2
Republic of Korea	45	8,000	12	10	2
Poland	40	4,000	8	10	2
Argentina	35	5,000	8	10	2
Venezuela	20	8,000	8	10	2
South Africa	40	4,000	8	10	2
Thailand	60	5,000	11	10	2
Rounded subtotal	450			100	20
Bulgaria	10	$5,000	4	5	1
Chile	15	7,000	6	5	1
Hungary	10	6,000	5	5	1
Bangladesh	115	1,000	7	5	1
Ecuador	10	4,000	4	5	1
Peru	20	3,000	5	5	1
Rounded subtotal	160			30	6
Costa Rica	3	$5,000	2.6	2	1
Estonia	2	8,000	2.5	2	1
Latvia	2	8,000	2.5	2	1
Lithuania	2	5,000	2.1	2	1
Trinidad	1	8,000	2.1	2	1
Uruguay	3	7,000	2.8	2	1
Cyprus	1	10,000	1.7	2	1

Continued ...

TABLE 6.3 — CONTINUED

Country	Popula-tion (millions)[a]	GDP per capita (PPP$)[b]	Formula value[c]	Votes	
				Main proposal	Alternative proposal
Other democracies — continued					
Luxembourg	0	$20,000	1.8	2	1
Bolivia	7	2,000	2.5	2	1
Dominican Republic	7	3,000	2.9	2	1
Honduras	5	2,000	1.9	2	1
Jamaica	2	4,000	1.9	2	1
Nepal	20	1,000	3.0	2	1
Papua New Guinea	4	1,500	1.5	2	1
Zambia	8	1,000	1.8	2	1
Botswana	1	5,000	1.5	2	1
Benin	5	1,500	1.7	2	1
Panama	2	5,000	2.2	2	1
El Salvador	5	2,000	2.1	2	1
Paraguay	4	3,000	2.4	2	1
Slovakia	5	4,000	2.9	2	1
Slovenia	2	7,000	1.8	2	1
Congo	2	3,000	1.6	2	1
Jordan	4	3,000	2.1	2	1
Madagascar	12	800	1.9	2	1
Malawi	9	800	1.7	2	1
Rounded subtotal	120			52	26
Bahamas	0	$12,000	1.1	1	1
Barbados	0	9,000	.9	1	1
Iceland	0	17,000	1.3	1	1
Malta	0	8,000	1.1	1	1
Mauritius	1	7,000	1.4	1	1
St. Kitts-Nevis	0	4,000	.8	1	1
Dominica	0	4,000	.4	1	1
Belize	0	3,000	.5	1	1
Cape Verde	0	1,500	.5	1	1
Grenada	1	4,000	1.1	1	1
St. Lucia	0	3,500	.4	1	1
St. Vincent	0	3,700	.5	1	1
São Tomé	0	600	.2	1	1
Solomon Isles	0	2,000	.5	1	1
Vanuatu	0	1,500	.3	1	1

TABLE 6.3 — CONTINUED

Country	Population (millions)[a]	GDP per capita (PPP$)[b]	Formula value[c]	Votes Main proposal	Votes Alternative proposal
Other democracies — continued					
Western Samoa	0	$2,000	.4	1	1
Mongolia	2	2,000	1.3	1	1
Marshall Islands	0	4,000	.4	1	1
Micronesia	0	4,000	.4	1	1
Monaco	0	10,000	.6	1	1
Namibia	1	2,000	1.0	1	1
San Marino	0	10,000	.6	1	1
Eritrea	2	2,000	1.3	1	1
Andorra	0	10,000	.9	1	1
Comoros	1	700	.4	1	1
Liechtenstein	0	14,000	.4	1	1
Fiji	1	5,000	1.2	1	1
Guinea-Bissau	1	750	.5	1	1
Guyana	1	2,000	.8	1	1
Mali	9	500	1.3	1	1
Suriname	0	3,000	.7	1	1
Rounded subtotal	20			31	31
Total 77 other democracies	2,000			293	95
Total 22 leading democracies	800 29%			260 47%	40 30%
Grand total 99 democracies	2,800			553	135

SOURCES: UN Development Program, *Human Development Report, 1994* (New York: Oxford University Press, 1994), for population and real gross domestic product per capita values in PPP$.

NOTES: The UN has 183 members.

a. Population figures have been rounded.

b. Per capita gross domestic product (PPP$) values have been rounded. The value of gross domestic product is usually shown in dollars based on the international exchange rate of currencies. Although this exchange rate reasonably reflects the part of an economy that is influenced by international prices, it does not reflect relative living standards. In recent years, major research efforts have been devoted to estimating values of each country's currency that better reflect purchasing power in that country. Results of this research are the PPP dollars used in this column.

It should be understood that all GDP or GNP numbers, whether expressed in trade dollars or PPP dollars, are abstractions that have no absolute objective referent because they have to be calculated on the basis of index numbers that cannot be consistent from year to year or country to country. These numbers should be understood, therefore, to be accurate only within perhaps 10 or 20 percent.

    c. The formula value was calculated by multiplying the square root of the unrounded population in millions by the square root of the unrounded gross domestic product per capita and dividing the result by 50; that quotient was rounded.

    d. Subtotals and totals as shown cannot be exactly derived by adding the columns because they have been rounded. These approximations were used for two reasons. First, the underlying information does not justify more precise numbers (in fact, in some cases more precision is shown than is justified). Second, the degree of precision shown reflects the intended purpose of the table. The inconsistency in some of the subtotals and totals will remind the reader that these quantities should not be thought of as precise.

Notes

1. This uses the mid-1995 list of UN members (see appendix 6.1, table 6.3). These designations are made for illustrative purposes only—largely on the basis of Freedom House's annual survey of freedom (see chap. 2, note 2), which is widely regarded as the best classification available. They do not claim to be careful or final judgments.

2. This principle could be implemented in either of two ways. Either membership in the caucus could be voluntary, and all countries who agreed to be members obligated to accept the caucus decisions—with provision for special exceptions—or the same effect might be achieved by making membership in the caucus automatic for all democracies, but limiting the obligation to be bound by the decision of the caucus to those democracies that choose to participate in caucus deliberations.

3. Israel, partly because it is uniquely in danger of being destroyed by its enemies, may have reason to fear increased UN power. The momentum of political opinion that has been built up against Israel by the old communist-Arab-Third World alliance creates a risk that a UNDC would jeopardize Israel's security (although only by measures intended to protect Israel). And if misguided UN action resulted in the destruction of Israel, the experience would be so terrible that the harm to the rest of the world from being implicated in that evil would be greater than all the good that came from a stronger United Nations.

4. The assignment of voting weight is roughly related to the square root of population and the square root of the level of economic development, but a full vote is given to each small country, even if its weight under the formula would entitle it to only a fraction of a vote.

5. Russia and China would too, of course, but China would not be an initial member of the caucus, and Russia might well not still be eligible by the time the caucus was formed.

6. Weighted voting has long been used in international financial organizations, such as the World Bank.

7. Stanley Hoffmann, "Delusions of World Order," *New York Review of Books* (9 April 1992), 41.

8. See Daniel Elazar, *Exploring Federalism* (University, Ala.: University of Alabama Press, 1987), for an argument that a "matrix model" is more appropriate than the familiar model of a hierarchical pyramid.

9. The original discussions might also include Brazil and India, and if so the invitation to the formative meeting would be from eight countries (possibly nine if Russia was a democracy at the time).

10. The United States has a different relation to Europe. It is a daughter civilization, now separate and distinct both because of distance and because of the independent size and power of the United States and its cultural creativity. Although no one would fail to understand if the United States—or Australia—were referred to as "European." If there were no United States, Latin America would be seen as part of Europe. It is not part of Europe because of its distance and because the United States gives the Western hemisphere a competing identity.

11. Narrow Europe might have a population of 280 million—assuming the United Kingdom would choose not to be part of it. The current population of the other countries that may eventually be included in the rest of broad Europe, with-

out Russia, is somewhat larger, but those countries have only about half the production of narrow Europe. Russia would add another 150 million people, but only about 10 percent to the production (see table 6.2).

   12. Elazar, *Exploring Federalism.*

CHAPTER 7

POLICY FOR THE ZONES OF
TURMOIL AND DEVELOPMENT

While George Bush was president, the goal of the United States in the zones of turmoil was "stability." As he said several times, "our enemy is unpredictability." What this really meant was that President Bush had no goals for the zones of turmoil—and he was partly right not to. The United States has no geopolitical or strategic interests in those areas that are important enough to dominate our policy.

Traditionally we would have had to construct our policy around assuring that strategic places not fall into enemy hands, preserving various regional and world power balances, and protecting against the expansion of power by long-term enemies. Now strategic locations have too little importance, there are no competing blocs of great powers, and no enemies so powerful that we have to design our policy around them. In the current world order there is no good basis for a long-term political or strategic policy for the United States in the zones of turmoil. Instead our policy—outside of economics—should be to support principles (while avoiding foolish consistency), principles chosen to try to make the international order somewhat more civilized, primarily by developing and enforcing traditional international law. The main exceptions are that for the next decade or two we will probably have to be concerned about the possibility of Chinese aggression, and we have long-term interests in keeping Turkey oriented to Europe and in keeping control of the Persian Gulf oil divided among at least three countries. Another exception is added on pages 171–73 in our discussion of the former Yugoslavia, maintaining that the United States needs to lead the major European democracies in making a commitment to make it possible for multiethnic states to survive in Eastern and Southern Europe.

President Bush also meant that our country wants peace for the zones of turmoil because we generally wish everyone well. But our desire for peace does not say anything about whether victims should resist aggression or whether people should rebel against tyrants. Similarly, the call for stability does not express our position about the use of force by a government to protect its power—as when the Syrian government bombarded the city of Hamas with artillery for ten days to quell and intimidate opposition. Although such an act certainly could be regarded as the preservation of stability, it is not clear that the United States should support stability at such a cost.

The goal of stability suggests that America does not want change, or at least not rapid change, even from poverty to prosperity or from authoritarian government to democracy. But it would be more correct to say that the goal of the United States for the zones of turmoil is *change*, not stability. Our real desire is that the zones of turmoil change into zones of peace and democracy. Since that cannot happen suddenly, we can pursue both goals, stability and change, at the same time. But when we state the two goals together the tone of the goal of stability changes, and the possibility that the two goals can sometimes be in conflict is emphasized.

The goal of stability makes it too easy always to decide to support governments that are resisting change and to favor existing borders. Often the result is that change comes later with more violence and disruption. A more profound definition of stability would sometimes require support for change to prevent some drastic upheavals later. But no one has articulated such a complicated version of the goal of stability.

President Clinton has not articulated an operating vision of a goal beyond stability for the zones of turmoil. And the practical fact is that there will be great changes in the zones of turmoil regardless of our wishes and our policy. Some of the good changes will come peacefully, but others will come suddenly and with violence. Along the way there will also be setbacks and disasters. Unfortunately the United States is likely to have more ability to slow down favorable changes than unfavorable ones. All in all, it is a mistake for us to use stability as the touchstone of our objectives for the zones of turmoil. We cannot defeat unpredictability, and we do not want to prevent change.

For Russia and the former Soviet Union, too, the conventional wisdom has been that the primary goal of democratic policy should be to try to preserve stability—to prevent violent disorder. (The former Soviet Union is not yet thought of as just one of the zones of turmoil.) It is even said that our safety depends on being able to preserve stability in Russia. This seems self-evident to many. How can the United States not try to prevent disorder in a country where there are 30,000 nuclear weapons?

We disagree with this conventional wisdom too. Of course the democracies should prefer stability to anarchy for Russia, especially while there are nuclear weapons there, but that preference should not be the primary objective of our policy, because, however much we try, the United States does not have enough wisdom or power to have much chance of being able to have a positive influence on the survival of stable government in Russia. The forces at work there are too strong. Regardless of U.S. policy, the chance of preserving stability is too low for us to depend on it. Fortunately, while chaos in Russia is not without risk to the United States and other undesirable consequences for the world, it is not a major threat to the United States, certainly not to our survival. Nor will any plausible outcome in Russia produce a dangerous threat to Western Europe. For the reasons described in chapter five, almost all the victims of Russian chaos will be in Russia, and possibly the other parts of the former Soviet Union. We should not be unconcerned about harm to them or to anyone else in the world, but we should distinguish between danger to parts of the zones of turmoil and danger to ourselves or to others in the zones of peace and democracy; the first we cannot eliminate.

The ultimate justification for the conventional commitment to the goal of stability in Russia is the reasonable argument that our policy must have some goal and that stability is certainly better for us than instability (which sounds unobjectionable); therefore we should do what we can to achieve stability—even if the prospects are poor. But this argument seems more reasonable than it is. It assumes that we pay no price for trying to preserve stability, and therefore it doesn't matter if the chances of success are low. But there is no way we can be committed to preserving stability in Russia without paying a heavy price. In fact we have begun paying already. In pursuit of stability in the Soviet Union the United States supported Gorbachev and was negative to Yeltsin. In pursuit of stability first in the Soviet Union and then in Russia, the United States sharply limited its support of the independence of the Baltic states. And in pursuit of stability in the Soviet Union the United States wasted billions of taxpayer dollars, with no benefit to the Russian people. In pursuit of stability in the former Soviet Union, we urged the minor Soviet nuclear republics to send their nuclear weapons to Russia instead of trying to get them to send the weapons out of the former Soviet Union to be dismantled.

Furthermore, when we decide that an unrealistic goal is essential to our national security, it becomes almost impossible for our diplomats to report the truth. They must turn a blind eye on reality to be loyal to their president. For example, when President Nixon said in 1969 that the security of the United States depended on achieving peace between Israel and the Arabs, the State Department had to find a view of Arab politics that would make peace possible—because if the president says that the safety of the United States depends on peace somewhere, no one can say "Sorry,

Boss, it can't be done with present conditions; perhaps in a few years." Everybody has to develop the best idea they can about how to achieve peace right away, even if that means refusing to face the facts and thus making unrealistic attempts that actually hurt the cause of peace. On the other hand, if the president says, "We want stability," or "peace," but also seeks a policy to protect our security in the meantime, diplomats can propose policies that fit the facts as they are.

If our policy continues to be that American national security depends on preserving stability in Russia, we will lose objectivity, credibility, and bargaining power—without significantly increasing the chance of achieving our objective. We should *prefer* stability, and certainly not try to cause instability. But we should assume that instability is reasonably likely and do what we can to protect ourselves against its dangers. We should not sacrifice other objectives, such as getting as many nuclear weapons as possible out of the country or expressing democratic principles, even if pursuing those objectives conflicts with current theories of how to achieve stability. We certainly should not depend on stability in Russia to protect our safety.

Will "the South" Be against "the North"?

People and governments in the zones of turmoil can be expected to be radically ambivalent about the advanced democracies, especially the United States. Regardless of what we do, we will be admired and desired and at the same time despised and rejected, sometimes by the same people. We must be prepared for both reactions since it is inevitable that proud, healthy people who for many years will be in a position of learning from us, receiving benefits from us, seeing us with more luxuries, having to give up their own traditions to become more like us, and being less powerful than we are, will sometimes have intensely negative feelings about us. And we will sometimes give real as well as psychological justification for some of the hostility toward us.

Some argue that the key issue after the cold war will be the conflict between the zones of turmoil and the zones of peace, that is, between poor countries and rich ones. And some offer a vision of an "invasion" of immigrants from the "South" overwhelming the "North." These views are not a realistic picture of how the future will be shaped.

Of course, the current situation cannot last. It cannot stay true forever that one-sixth of the world is very wealthy while at least half the world is so poor that life expectancy is twenty years too low and most people are still working with their backs and not their minds. But the solution will come from increasing productivity and wealth in the currently poor countries. And that solution, although it takes a lot of time, is the only realistic one. The movement of poor people into rich countries will play only a very small part. And virtually none of the solution will come from poor countries taking things from rich countries or forcing rich countries to give things to them.

A large part of the solution will come from the movement of knowledge and influence from the already rich countries to the not-yet-rich countries, and from the benefits that the not-yet-rich countries will get from trade with the rich. A smaller share of the solution will come from resource transfers and other help that the rich countries provide out of altruism. And some of this "altruism" will be partly motivated by a kind of general fear that bad things will happen if the rich do not help the poor. But none of it will happen as a result of threatening actions by poor countries against rich ones.

Consider how unrealistic is the scenario of a poor country taking the wealth of a modern democracy. Suppose Algeria defeated Spain in a war and then occupied Spain—or that Spain surrendered to prevent a nuclear attack. This is unlikely but not impossible. Algeria could then impose a tax on Spain and send the proceeds home. But governments already find that if they try to increase taxes too much, people don't earn as much. How much tax could an occupying power extract? How many of Spain's most productive people would leave rather than work for the benefit of Algeria? How long would occupied Spain keep the ability to earn money by competing in world markets? It is very doubtful that Algeria could extract enough to pay the costs of the force it needed to defeat and occupy Spain—even if the other countries let Algeria get away with it. The same is true for all the poor countries together.

For reasons described in chapter 3, a poor country has little chance to defeat a rich country if the rich country has had time to prepare. The wealthy army has the advantage because it is defending its country, and because the factors that produced wealth can produce fighting power. A poor country could try to use nuclear or other weapons of mass destruction to win a long-distance war, but wealth is also an advantage in a high-technology conflict of advanced long-distance weapons.

But could poor countries irrationally attack rich ones, despite the fact that it would be a poor investment for them even if they won? Certainly it is possible, at least once. But attacking a modern country, especially from the sea or over a distance, is very difficult. There are not many cases where poor countries are next to rich ones. It is almost impossible to give realistic illustrations of the idea of armed hordes from a poor country storming the borders of a rich country.

What about blackmail? How much money do you think a poor country could get by telling the United States or France or Japan, "send money or we will explode bombs in your cities"? Perhaps some, especially if they asked cleverly, but not very much for very long. The rich country would soon build the force it needs to protect itself if the other democracies do not protect it.

One can imagine that there might be a few peculiar scenarios along some such lines, but there is no way that such scenarios can be an important part of history. They will not be the solution to the problem of unequal income distribution. The poor will get wealth the old-fashioned way, they will earn it.

A Clash of Civilizations Is Not the Next Phase of World History

If it were true that the clashes with fascism and communism must be followed by a new, greater conflict at the center of world history, then a clash of civilizations might be the most plausible candidate.[1] But the current phase of world history does not have to be dominated by any great clash —and we think that it will not be.

Although it is true that the current leadership of major elements of the Moslem world are fundamentally opposed to the West, Islamic civilization will not become a major military-political challenge to the West comparable to either Hitler or the Soviet Union. The divisions in the Moslem world are too great and its power is too limited to present a threat that will shape our history.

A number of countries on Islam's fringes are likely to face pressure from Islam for many years, and Islamic terror may be a danger for individuals anywhere in the world for some time. But neither jockeying for territory around the edges of Islam nor even large-scale terror actions can be more than footnotes to the history of the next century.

Many Islamic leaders and thinkers have demonstrated that Islam has within it major streams that do not hold enmity to the West. Its future is more likely to be determined by clashes—peaceful or military—from within rather than by clashes between Islam and other civilizations.

Many Asians also see themselves as part of a society to which the West is alien and at least culturally threatening. (Those who feel this way do not necessarily feel part of the same society.) Asian antagonism to the West may quite possibly become much more of an influence than it is today. But even if it does, the economic and political forces of the modern world mostly work in ways that will prevent such cultural antagonism from creating political-military conflict that could be the center of world politics.

One cannot deny the likelihood that cultures and civilizations will be in conflict with each other in coming years, but the conflict that is inevitable is not a political-military clash, but a collision of ideas, sensitivities, values, and styles. This collision can coexist with economic and political collaboration or, in some cases perhaps, mutual avoidance. There is no reason why such conflict needs to be resolved or to lead to military confrontation, on any broad scale. A clash of civilizations may become a backdrop in the next phase of history, although we think it will be no more than a minor theme, and it certainly will not be the organizing central theme of world affairs.

Emigration Is Not the Answer

Part of the reason we can be confident that emigration will not be an important part of the solution comes from the numbers. If enough people moved North to double the population of the wealthy countries, that would only take care of one-sixth of the people in the poor countries. And their moving out would not increase the average income of those left behind because income comes from people, not from countries (except in a few very small, resource-rich countries).

For perspective, we can remember that immigration to the United States was as high as 1 percent annually for only the peak decade (1901–1910), and it has been less than half that for eighty years. The only country that has ever taken in a high percentage of immigrants is Israel, which tripled its Jewish population in its first four years and has taken close to 10 percent in the last few years. It would be very surprising if altogether the rich countries took as much as half their current population during the next century, and it is virtually impossible that they will take as much as 100 percent. In neither case would emigration to the rich countries begin to match the natural growth of the poor countries—even if all the policy recommendations aimed at curbing population growth were adopted immediately.

For the reasons discussed in chapter 3, the bulk of the currently poor countries can be expected to achieve modern standards of living in the next century or so without substantial emigration. But if the rich countries keep growing at reasonable rates, the poor countries will not catch up with them. They cannot catch up until the rich countries slow their own growth in productivity and wealth, either because of economic mistakes, unexpected difficulties in further growth, or because the people decide that they have enough wealth and prefer to increase leisure or other values that are not traded in the market.[2]

Can immigration destroy the wealthy democracies—reducing differences of income by making the rich poor too? Democracies will not be physically compelled to take in masses of immigrants (refugees) because they will have the power to keep them out by using physical barriers and military force (if necessary to capture and remove most of those who sneak in). The harder question is whether some democracies will lose the will to exclude masses of desperate people at their border and will then be brought down by the result of their lack of ruthlessness. If this happens in some country, other countries are likely to learn from the experience vicariously. Certainly it will not happen to enough countries to change the shape of things.

If millions of people walk or sail to the borders of the democracies to escape poverty and bloodshed in the zones of turmoil, the likely result will be that the democracies will organize some way to take care of those people outside of their borders. One can imagine mass refugee camps or zones outside their borders, paid for by the democracies. Compassion and guilt feelings would lead democracies to spend enough to keep up the quality of life in such refuges. But so long as the refuges were good enough to attract new migrants faster than they could become productive, the cost would keep rising. If the quality of life in the refugee camps becomes bad enough, people will stop coming to them. It would be a nasty race between the democracies' pocketbooks and ingenuity and their compassion.

It is unlikely that all or many democracies will be destroyed by floods of immigrants or refugees or by conflict over the measures necessary to protect against them. However, if such floods came to the borders, they would be a serious challenge to democracy—which means that failure is possible in some countries, even though it is not necessary or likely.

U.S. Self-Interest

The practical side of American policy for the zones of turmoil will be about taking care of our national interests, such as avoiding being bombed and protecting American workers from predatory trade practices. For most people, the more interesting part of our policy will be about trying to improve the international order in these zones.

The evolution of technology and the spread of wealth will mean that more and more countries in the zones of turmoil will have the means to deliver weapons of mass destruction against the cities of the zones of peace.

Antiaircraft and missile defense systems can sharply reduce the danger of such attacks, but they cannot provide complete and reliable protection; and in any event democratic cities will remain vulnerable to weapons smuggled into their harbors and rivers. In every democracy, the first goal of policy concerning the zones of turmoil will be to make sure that its citizens are protected from attack. By and large this primary goal will not require much attention. Few cities will be threatened; most years, the question will not arise. Usually there will be fewer than a dozen nondemocracies with long-range weapons of mass destruction.

The danger to our cities will not come from countries that want to go to war with the United States because they hate us or want our wealth. It will be from countries (or groups) whose aggression or genocide we are trying to stop, and whose message to us will be "stay out of our business or we will hurt you." (But there will also be some danger from groups, such as Moslem extremists, who hate the United States for what we are and because we are the most prominent part of the West.) While there will be many nuances, the fundamental choice democracies will have is between trying to protect themselves by staying away from conflict in the zones of turmoil and trying to protect themselves by some measure of policing those zones. Trying to make things better in the zones of turmoil can be dangerous, but if successful it can reduce our danger.

The more common and prosaic policy issues about the zones of turmoil will involve neither bombing nor justice, but trade and investment. We can confidently expect many portentous news analyses and political pronouncements about the danger of Europe or Germany or Japan maneuvering so that their businesses can dominate the lucrative market in some corner of the world, leaving American business and workers out in the cold. (And other countries will see new generations of the American challenge threatening their business interests overseas.) But these alarms should be understood as journalism's abhorrence of a blank page and not cause too much excitement. The important thing to remember is that the conflict about business in the zones of turmoil will not be truly important. The democracies' major trade and investment will be with one another. The many competitive disputes between democracies in the zones of turmoil will be an economic sideshow that is important to the individuals and companies involved, not to their nations' economies. Markets are measured by spending, not by spenders, and for many years spending will be mostly in the zones of peace, even though most people live in the zones of turmoil.

The more we trade with and invest in the zones of turmoil, the more occasions for conflict we will have, although both sides will benefit from the relationships. And while our government policy may be to help developing countries, business will be done by companies whose concern is to make profit, not to help development. Some companies will certainly over-reach, and others will be accused of exploiting even when they are acting generously. Moreover, few countries will be so poor that they will not have government agencies or businesses that are capable of trying to take improper advantage of rich foreigners. If on balance business relations are reasonably fair, it will only be because hundreds of companies, industry groups, and diplomats are assiduously pursuing and protecting their own interests from others who are doing the same. That is the nature of business and politics, domestic and international. It will not change.

This endless conflict will go on whether the United States is pursuing a liberal or a protectionist trade policy. No matter how open trade is, businesses and industries will try to manipulate government to gain advantage over their competitors both domestic and foreign. Therefore, international relations will involve endless efforts by nations to protect their citizens from being taken advantage of by foreigners—as well as to help them get a little "legitimate" edge themselves. While strategic generosity may be called for, it would be foolish for any country to think that it can afford to be tactically generous without causing its citizens to suffer what to them are substantial and unfair burdens. Decent relations will always depend on all parties working hard to protect themselves from elbowing in the clinches.

In this endless conflict the governments will often be the victims of deception or political domination by the interests they are representing. Every business knows that it has to protect itself from the danger that its country's foreign ministry will be misled into wasting its diplomatic strength on the unfounded concerns of other companies, instead of pursuing its own, much more justified complaint.

We need not consider the ordinary stuff of policy concerned with this bickering. But to deal with other issues it is necessary to recognize this background, which will fill the lives of diplomats and the pages of the newspapers.

Most of what happens in the zones of turmoil will not depend on the policy of the democracies. Even if the democracies were intensely engaged in maintaining order and helping the zones of turmoil, most conflict there would be handled without foreign intervention. And the historically powerful influences on the zones of turmoil will not be conflicts but the long-term development processes described in chapter 3, the pace and success of which are overwhelmingly determined by local considerations.

Even if the democracies multiplied their economic aid by five times, that aid would not be as important to development as the automatic unintentional effects of the democracies' economies and their example or as important as the developing countries' own efforts to change. So the policy of the democracies is not likely to be truly important in shaping the history of the zones of turmoil, although the democracies' existence will be central. The greatest importance of the democracies' policy may be to themselves, as a test and expression of their national characters. Acts of generosity or justice can be more important to the donor than to the beneficiary.

The point of all this is to provide the context for the question of U.S. policy to improve the international order of the zones of turmoil. That policy will be of only secondary importance to most of the life of the zones of turmoil. And for the United States, that policy will have lower priority than its policy concerning the zones of peace, and lower priority than protection of its national interests, including pervasive economic issues. But after we have done what we can to protect our national interest, we will have to deal with questions about what, if anything, we should do to improve the international order in the zones of turmoil. Young people, and idealists of all ages, will be most concerned with this part of our foreign policy. And on these issues our interests will be essentially the same as those of the other democracies, especially the other large democracies.

Altruism

The grandiosity of the idea of improving the quality of the international order should ring alarm bells. When a country gets away from pursuing its national interest, disciplines that normally protect against foolishness are weakened. Special caution and humility are in order when, as we must, we go beyond the protection of our narrow national interest. Our main motivation will be our primarily altruistic sense of obligation, as a good (leading) citizen of the world to show that aggression does not pay and that innocent people cannot be slaughtered without consequences.

The idea of altruistic policy causes so many negative feelings that we need to state some basic facts. For one thing, "altruistic" policy can also be useful to the country undertaking it. This is so, first, because our morale depends in part on our seeing ourself as a responsible and generous member and a leader of the world community. Second, our citizens are better off if they live in a more decent world. So an altruistic policy is not necessarily an irresponsible use of government power by misguided idealists. Neither should we accept the opposite charge, that the United States only uses the pretense of altruism to hide its pursuit of selfish interests.

The tricky problem of disentangling altruism from selfishness has been the subject of a lot of philosophic analysis that is too deep for this book.

But the following points about the behavior of the United States in the past will probably also be true in the future. The foreign policy decisions of the United States or any other democracy are always the result of pressures and decisions from many sources, and therefore always represent mixed motives. Typically, some of the pressures will be based on altruism and some on self-interest—and the self-interest will often be disguised. Sometimes "altruistic" pressures come from leaders who are pursuing their personal self-interest by pretending to represent their constituents' altruism—without necessarily caring whether what they advocate would really help those they claim to care about. Inevitably, all the actions of democracies that claim to be altruistic actually involve a combination of altruistic and selfish motivations. The United States is not as altruistic as we should be, but we probably are at least as altruistic as any other large democracy.

Despite these contradictions, it is neither naïveté nor hypocrisy for us to take seriously the idea that U.S. policy in the zones of turmoil is intended to improve the international order there. By taking seriously the claims of altruism in our analysis of such policy, we do not deny that the application of the policy will often be distorted by those with less altruistic agendas.

Fortunately, we do not need to worry too much about disentangling false altruism from true altruism, because there is little if any relation between how altruistic U.S. policy is and whether it benefits or hurts other countries (partly this is because benefiting other countries is often in the U.S. interest, and partly this is because policies intended to benefit other countries often harm them). For all policies, but especially those that are intended to be altruistic, the test must be the actual results, not the expectations or intentions.

Overall Perspective for Policy

The broad approach to policy that we propose is that in the zones of turmoil basic policy thinking should mostly be about categories and procedures, not about countries; about principles and process, not about politics and strategy.

The starting point must be a vision of the zones as a whole. Although implementation depends on understanding Brazil, Russia, Kenya, Malaysia, and so on, policy should be made about genocide, aggression, protection of democracy, and the like. This approach of emphasizing principles, rather than political commitment, does not imply either an isolationist or an interventionist U.S. policy. It is neither an argument for staying out nor an argument for going in. It is a framework within which people of all points of view can argue about how many or which goals we should pursue and with what commitment.

There are four reasons for responding to the zones of turmoil by principles applied to a population of countries rather than with traditional foreign policy approaches:

1. What happens anywhere in the zones of turmoil will be of secondary importance to the U.S. national interest. The countries in these zones do not have enough wealth or power to threaten our welfare.

2. The politics of these areas are too complex and fast changing for a democratic political and governmental system to understand well enough to manipulate wisely. Perhaps democratic nations could understand one or two such situations, but there will be too many, and even the most important will have low priority for us. In the zones of turmoil, governments and political alliances will come and go in rapid succession. Today's crisis will be tomorrow's irrelevancy. Hence democracies will rarely be able to accomplish much of long-term value by trying to influence political patterns there (although it will frequently seem as if they might).

3. Often the local political forces and feelings will be too strong for the democracies to be able significantly to influence in the long term with the means that they will be willing and able to use.

4. The United States can have more positive effect by following a policy of principle, rather than the traditional political approach of influencing who rules. And pursuit of political goals would be likely to reduce our ability to implement our principles.

An Allegory

Suppose you are the director of a boarding school for 1500 boys aged 10 through 16. Each boy is an individual with a unique history, character, and needs. The life of the school will be a complex pattern of customs and relationships. Each dormitory will have its own character and leaders and rivalries. Among the students there will be cliques and gangs; there will be social and scholastic and athletic competition, and school politics, and other organizing patterns. And there will be another set of relationships among the faculty, and between the faculty and the administration, and between each of these groups and the students.

As director of the school, you need to understand as much of these human and social dynamics as you can. But you would be foolish if you thought you could manipulate these processes in detail, making Joe's group in dorm 5 less cliquish and more like Phil's group in dorm 6. You can influence anything if you focus on it. But you cannot focus on anything for long, and you cannot adjust long-term behavior patterns unless you keep focusing on them for a long time. And there are too many things going on for you to be able to concentrate on any few of them for long.

The basic thing you have to try to do is to shape the institution so that it has as good an overall effect on the body of students as possible. Whatever the school does, they will all change from when they came from their homes as ten-year-olds until they return six years later. Your job is to have as large a good effect on as many students as possible.

Someday when you are walking through the hall you will see an eleventh grader named Herbert chasing a seventh grader named Norman with a baseball bat. To construct a sound policy about Herbert you would need to know about his family background, the groups he associates with at school, his emotional development stage, and many other things, but you are not equipped to learn all those things. What you can do is to have a policy about eleventh graders chasing seventh graders with baseball bats, so you can grab the bat and send Herbert back to his dorm.

Many of the developing countries in the zones of turmoil have great ancient civilizations; they are by no means like children. And it would be wrong for the United States not to treat them with the respect due to peers. But these countries are going through a development process, which means we know that they will soon be different than they are now. Much of their conduct is the result of the pain of change, and of where they are in their own development. It would be foolish not to recognize the extent to which their behavior is the result of being in the middle of a painful transformation that will be completed in the next few generations. The forms of national "adolescence" cannot be predicted or shaped, they must be lived through. And getting through them is easier if we recognize how much they are temporary problems.

Encourage Democracy!

The primary long-term goal of altruistic U.S. policy in the zones of turmoil should be the encouragement of democracy. This goal serves our altruistic purposes of minimizing violence (aggression, war, and government mass murder) and speeding economic development.

Chapter 2 showed why democracy is good for peace. While democracy does not necessarily speed economic growth, actions that would provide an improved base for democracy are the best way to get growth started in countries where economic growth has barely started (or stopped before going very far). The key to economic growth in those countries is for the government to stop doing things that interfere with growth. Therefore, U.S. economic assistance to such countries should concentrate on promoting policies and behavior that are conducive to both economic growth and the development of stable democracy. Intermediate objectives, such as the rule of law, contribute to economic growth as well as to providing the basis for sound democracy.

While the U.S. Agency for International Development (AID) has recognized many of the appropriate intermediate goals—such as holding down the size of the governments of developing countries—it has not given these goals as high a priority as is appropriate and necessary. Therefore it has taught by its actions that those goals were not important. But movement toward those goals would do more for economic development and democracy than the aid programs.

Reasonable economic growth—an average 2 percent per capita per year —is "natural" in most countries today. Foreign-aid professionals who have had years of frustration, despite their great efforts to get economic growth moving in many countries, will greet this statement with disbelief, if not contempt, believing that it is contradicted by a mountain of experience. But the experience of failure to achieve growth with great efforts does not contradict the assertion that growth is "natural" today. That assertion would be contradicted only by pointing to several countries that are doing correctly the basics listed on pages 160–61—which any country can afford—but are still failing to grow. But in fact there is no substantial group of countries who are doing the basics right and nevertheless are not growing at a reasonable rate per capita. Essentially all countries that maintain a stable currency, minimal informal economy and capital flight, protection of property rights, and small government are growing at least 2 percent a year per capita.[3]

Growth almost always depends primarily on getting the basics of government policy right, not on sophisticated economic, social, or political analysis and specialized government or donor programs. In almost all instances where "natural" growth is not being achieved, it is because the local government is doing things that prevent growth. So, the way to get reasonable growth started is to induce the government to stop doing whatever is preventing growth and to do the basic things that a government is needed to do. Paying attention to anything else is a diversion that is likely to harm the recipient country more than it helps.

If a country is failing to achieve reasonable economic growth because it is not taking care of the basics, it is a waste of money, or worse, to do anything to help that country's economy other than try to convince and help it do the basics of economic growth policy right. There is much more gain in eliminating antigrowth policies than in anything else that can be done. And working on anything else makes it less likely that the government will concentrate on the most important changes it needs to make or that it will be pressured to do what needs to be done.

This rule, that the most useful effect we can have on no-growth countries is to concentrate all our effort on getting them to reduce the obstacles to growth created by their government, applies whether we are interested in achieving development, democracy, or almost any specific benefit. It is hard to do more good for a people than the good that comes from reducing governmental interference with freedom to be productive.

Sometimes people think that developing countries need new programs to help them provide essential functions, like credit for small farmers. It is supposed that the locals do not know how to do it or that their businesspeople have not got the idea. But the problem rarely is that people do not know how to perform the necessary function or lack anything that we can provide. Almost always, when basic functions are not being performed, it is because something is preventing them from being done, either the government or someone whose predatory behavior is protected or ignored by the government.

For example, providing agricultural credit is a profitable business. Lots of people know how to do it profitably. The returns are better than many businesses that attract funds in those countries. Lending money to farmers is not a new idea. If it is not happening, the way to make it happen is not to start a program to do it but to find out what is stopping it. It may be that the government does not enforce loan agreements or does not prevent people from interfering with collection measures, so lending is not feasible. Or it may be that local bankers or businesspeople are using strong-arm or improper commercial power to protect their monopoly of credit. But when the credit is missing, the answer is not to provide it but to find out what is preventing it from being provided privately and locally. And there are many other things like credit.

Therefore, the main focus of U.S. efforts to spread economic development—and to encourage democracy—should be on convincing and helping countries whose economies are growing less than 2 percent per year per capita to work on the basics, mostly by reducing government impediments to economic growth that are also impediments to the long-term prospects for democracy.

The basic things that government must provide for economic growth and a solid democracy are

- Protection for the right to own property (e.g., by establishing titles to land)

- The rule of law
- Stable currency
- Low marginal tax rates
- Making political influence of minimal importance to economic success
- Small government
- Frugality and simplicity of government
- Individual private freedoms
- Enforcement of contracts

Economic growth will start or accelerate in any country where the government does not destroy the stability of the currency, excessively interfere with people's opportunity to produce and sell, tax excessively, or make it easier for people to make money by seeking benefits from the government than by producing and marketing—provided that there is peace, protection against violence, and a system that recognizes property rights and enforces contracts. All these things also encourage democracy.

More and Different Foreign Aid

We believe that the United States should spend more on helping the needy outside our country. Thirty years ago, we spent nearly 1 percent of our GNP on such programs (while we were much poorer and were also spending 8 percent of GNP on defense) and that seems like a better expression of the generous character of this country than the small fraction of GNP that we are spending now for foreign aid.[4]

The key problem about economic assistance is how to give it without harming the recipients. If a country's economy is not growing, we will not be able to get it started by providing aid. Where there is no economic growth because government actions stand in the way, economic assistance can enable the government to continue to stand in the way and therefore be worse than useless.

But when governments have created the conditions that allow growth to take place, there are a number of ways that our economic assistance can help people. For example, we can provide transportation and communication infrastructure that will both aid economic growth and perhaps improve the physical base for democratic interactions. We can also provide some of the resources needed to reduce the environmental damage from economic development sooner or better than countries would do for themselves. If wisely used in such ways, our money can improve the lives of the people in nations less fortunate than our own.

But the most important influence on the character of the environment in most of the world will be developing countries' decisions about whether to use trade barriers to prevent their large increase in food needs from being supplied by imports. As much of the world gets richer (and more populous), it will eat more milk and meat products, which will greatly increase the need for grain. If increasingly prosperous countries decide that their own farmers should grow nearly all the food their country eats, even though the needed increase could be imported at lower costs, millions of environmentally fragile acres will have to be converted into farmland, which would have a devastating impact on the world's environment. But if developing countries allow their increased demand for food to be supplied by imports, which would save a great deal of money for the poor, then new food demand could be met without damaging the environment.

Most of our assistance can be used to help refugees and meet other specialized needs in emergencies and other special situations, such as the aftermath of a war or the end of an authoritarian government. In other words, most of our foreign aid should not be used for regular programs to speed economic growth, but in special programs to respond to temporary needs.

Special emergencies—like Somalia or the floods that come to Bangladesh from time to time—often require so much money that we cannot afford to do as much as makes sense to do. In an emergency a great deal of money can be spent usefully without creating dependency and other negative results.

If we were to make a full response to emergencies, the average cost, even though very large emergencies would not come every year, could well be something like half of 1 percent of our gross national product. This suggests that we should not raise our regular foreign aid budget too much above the current modest level, but we should automatically budget an equal or greater amount each year for emergency and special programs. In years without an emergency the money would be accumulated so that in some years we would have even more than 1 percent of our gross national product available to commit to responding fully and generously in genuine emergencies. (It may be politically easier to budget behind rather than ahead of emergencies.) This change in our approach to foreign aid would also mean that the regular foreign-aid organization would be kept small, because temporary special purpose organizations would be created for each large emergency and these organizations would be disbanded when that emergency came to an end.

Charitable giving is easy if you do not care who you hurt—and do not mind wasting money. If you want actually to help people, it takes thoughtful and sensitive work. Internationally it is harder to give money away usefully because the giving must be done by a government agency which is necessarily run by a political process in which the people being helped do not have a voice. And a government agency giving foreign aid naturally prefers to deal with government agencies in the recipient countries. So foreign aid tends to increase the number of government employees in both countries, which makes it harder to keep both governments honest and efficient.

We could try to give our foreign aid through the United Nations or other international agencies. But international organizations usually have the same weaknesses as government agencies and often are worse because they are governed by an even longer chain of political process. Of course, if we give money through an international agency, we could say that we were not to blame for the harm done by that bureaucracy—and our government would not be hurt. But this does not seem like a sound way to fulfill our national need to be generous to the less fortunate. If the fundamental reason for giving the money is our obligation to help, then we should not provide money unless we are ready also to expend the political effort required to make it beneficial.

Difficulties in Supporting Democracy

The measure of our support for democracy is not how much pressure we put on authoritarian governments. In most places we can only encourage democracy, not impose it. While it is important to the United States that other countries become democratic, it is equally important that we do not go too far in pressuring them. The United States should want each country to decide for itself to be democratic. There is a theological analogy to this position about democracy in other countries. Some believers ask, "If God is all-powerful and wants people to be good, why doesn't He make them good?" They answer, "God cannot do more to make people good without compromising their free will, which He wants just as much." Unless the citizens and culture of a country come to believe in the value of democracy, understanding how frustrating and difficult it is, their democracy will be vulnerable.

But if each country has to learn democracy for itself, how can the United States make democracy the center of its policy? What can we do that can make a difference for democracy in other countries? Our greatest support for democracy will come automatically, without any policy decision or program, from the example that we and other democracies give —both of the desirability and feasibility of democracy and of the measures used to make democracy work.

To encourage democracy we need to recognize, understand, and believe in the virtues of democracy and of our system, which is built on a combination of three pillars: democracy, a market economy, and our social and moral values, all three of which are essential.[5]

In this book we have tried to illustrate one of the basic measures to encourage democracy. Some readers have probably been struck—and perhaps troubled—by how much we have talked about applying policies to "the democracies" and have used "nondemocracies" as a policy-relevant category. And some may have had the reaction of asking, "Who can say which country is a democracy? All kinds of countries call themselves democracies." Or, "How can the United States talk about encouraging democracy and discriminating against 'nondemocracies' when we have so much racism and injustice, and our government pays so little attention to what the people believe and want?" But it is not necessary to agree on exactly where to draw the line between democracies and nondemocracies. The United States, United Kingdom, France, and Costa Rica are democracies; and there are many others. China, Syria, Burma, and Uganda are clearly nondemocracies; and there are many others.

Democracy is not sainthood. Saying that a country is a democracy means that popular political processes determine its leadership and basic policy, and that at least most people have reasonable freedom to organize and to debate policy. It does not mean that it is a good country with happy people or that it provides all the civil and political liberties it ought to. Our representatives should have reasonable confidence that the United States is a democracy, that democracy is the political component of the best system of government ever discovered, and that other countries would in the long run benefit by becoming democracies. We should not hesitate to speak and to act on these judgments. We do not need to, and should not, think or say that our democracy is without defects or does not need improvement, or that it is the only or best form of democracy, or that every country has to have democracy right away.

A valuable change in American foreign policy would be to define significant policies as applying to democracies or nondemocracies. Our policy debate has been cast in terms of policy toward "allies" or the "free world" or the "Soviet bloc" or "nonaligned nations" or the "Third World" or "less-developed countries" or geographic categories like "Southeast Asia" or "Sub-Saharan Africa." None of those categories is all democracies or all nondemocracies. ("Allies" usually included only democracies, but it is significant that it was not defined in that way.)

If we define policy in terms of democracies and nondemocracies, there will be a great deal of argument about whether or not some countries are democracies. Good. It is good for the world to have people and diplomats arguing about which countries are democracies. It is good for countries to try to demonstrate that they are democracies. It is good for nondemocracies to be embarrassed about being nondemocracies and to feel discriminated against.

To show that we think that democracy is important we should act as if we do. The first step is to care about which countries are democracies, then to show that we care by having different policies for democracies and nondemocracies. Creating a caucus of democracies at the United Nations, as discussed earlier, would be a powerful use of the distinction between democracies and nondemocracies.

Also we could agree with the other democracies that none of us will sell the most advanced military equipment to a nondemocracy. Such an agreement would not result in any country losing sales to another democracy. And the democracies are the only countries that will have the most advanced equipment to sell. As a group the democracies will not lose too much business by refusing to sell advanced weapons to nondemocracies because the democracies have a major share of what the nondemocracies want to spend their money on. If the nondemocracies do not buy advanced military equipment from the democracies they are likely to buy something else. Therefore agreeing to refuse to sell very advanced weapons to nondemocracies would not require the democracies to make a substantial economic sacrifice, and it may not be as unrealistic in the future—when the distinction between democracies and nondemocracies has become more important—as it seems today, when we do not conduct foreign policy on those terms.

Another way we can encourage democracy is by making our example more widely available and more influential. We can expand programs, such as the National Endowment for Democracy, designed to provide "technical assistance" in democracy to parties, governments, and other groups in other countries. We can do more educational and exchange-of-persons programs, provide more books and videos describing our country and how democracy works in theory and practice.

Most of the materials we now provide to other countries put little stress on the question of democracy. We have not wanted to seem to be promoting our own ideology or arrogantly presuming that our political system is better than that of other countries. We have not wanted to offend countries, such as the Moslem countries and the communist countries, that are not democratic. Basing U.S. policy on the distinction between democracies and nondemocracies was regarded as an implicit attack on the Soviet Union, a "confrontational" approach that only "cold warriors" would use.

In order to live safely with the Soviets and other nondemocracies we generally avoided ideological conflict.

All these attitudes should now change. It is safe now to think of the world in terms of democracies and nondemocracies. While we should respect every sovereign state, we should act as if the United States generally has more positive feelings about democracies and thinks less well of nondemocracies. We are important enough so that our feelings matter to other countries even if we are careful not to impose on them. We should use our influence to support democracy by showing that it is important to us and that we believe in it.

Reducing Violence

When we talk to students and others about horrible violence in the Horn of Africa or Liberia or the former Yugoslavia, they want to do something about it. They think that such things ought not to be allowed to happen in a modern, civilized world. But most of them also feel strongly that the United States should not use military force to intervene in such violent situations. They also think that the United States should not let itself become responsible for running any other country, nor should it do anything that will require it to take in large numbers of refugees. During the time before our long-term policy of encouraging democracy succeeds, can we effectively limit the horrors that we must expect, with the amount and quality of the effort that we are prepared to use?

Recent experience provides examples of the kinds of dilemmas we and other democracies will face as we consider intervening to try to preserve peace, prevent or nullify aggression, protect democracy, and prevent mass murder by governments. The hardest problem in situations like the former Yugoslavia, Somalia, and Iraq is what to do when we have won and it is time to go home. Do the democracies have to be deterred from entering by a judgment that when we leave the basic problem will still be there?

In Somalia the basic problem was that there was no government and that armed gangs found it useful in their struggle with one another to keep food from getting to the people. In 1992 we chose to try to solve this problem temporarily, but how could it have been solved more than temporarily without creating a government that can sustain a monopoly of force?

In Iraq there were three problems, of which we were able to solve one and a half. One problem was the conquest and occupation of Kuwait. A second was that Iraq's power threatened its neighbors and that Iraq was building nuclear weapons. (These two problems had the added danger that Iraq would get control of all of the oil of the Persian Gulf region, a unique asset in the world that up to now has been protected from abusive use by the fact that it has always been divided among a number of rival countries.) Desert Storm took care of the first problem and weakened Iraq and set back its nuclear weapons program, which was a useful way to deal with the second problem, even if Iraq will be able to restore its strength after some years. The third problem was the persecution of Shiites and Kurds by the Iraqi dictatorship, and its dreadful treatment of its own citizens. This we did nothing about.

The Yugoslavian conflict raised not only the standard issue of secession or division but also questions of aggression, massive abuse of civilians, and the protection of democracy. Serbia and the national Yugoslav government were run by an old-fashioned communist dictator who had been the head of the former Yugoslavian regime (although he had used the power of his incumbency to win the first almost-free election the communists had allowed in Serbia, and at the end of 1992 another badly tainted election). Croatia and Bosnia and Slovenia, the breakaway states, which had less dictatorial regimes, had held more genuine elections even though their democratic credentials were not all very strong. Furthermore, a strong case can be made that in the struggle first to decide whether the provinces would be separated from Yugoslavia and then what the borders would be, Serbia was an aggressor, brutally using its control over the national army to ignore the claims of the other provinces and the international community.

The emotional power of the tangled history in places like the former Yugoslavia is apparent in this report to his colleagues by anthropologist Eugene Hammel:[6]

> What may come of this? It will be a blessing if the horror of this civil war will not simply advance the cycle of death in the tradition of Balkan blood feud, leaving us, regardless of the formal political solution, with another Northern Ireland, another Lebanon. It will be a blessing if the costs will quickly become so great that the contestants will stop, and come exhausted to the negotiating table, having advanced their politics and their territory as far as they can. That, I think, has been the EC strategy, and almost surely the strategy of the United States. It has a bitter justice. No externally imposed solution will work; centuries of failed imperialism have proved that. The first mistake was to keep treating Yugoslavia as though it were a functioning entity and to impose sanctions without distinction, even when that same policy identified one side as the primary aggressor. There is a second error intrinsic to the views of those accustomed to well-

ordered polities. That error is the presumption of coherent authority. The West knows how to deal with multiparty constitutional democracies and with dictatorships, but it does not know how to deal with political chaos. Chaos is what it confronts. The justice and the bitterness of the confused Western response are echoed in the line, *Gorak je vijenac pelina*. Nothing in my experience matches the deliberate destruction of symbols of Croatian cultural identity, such as churches and museums, by the Army and the Serb irregulars, no doubt in retaliation for what the *Krajina* Serbs saw as a reduction of their own cultural heritage. Nothing matches the insane butchery that is occurring in Bosnia. . . .

What do we see in this mirror? We see children and the aged driven across minefields as Army trucks loot their homes. We see the psychopaths incited to violence as others plead from their cellars that ethnic differences were unimportant to their lives as neighbors. We see the conflagration of hate aid only those demogogues who have no substantive message but require the adulation of rabid mobs. We are drawn into a pit of medieval violence, from which the only exit seems to be the victory of blood. Is this the solution?

No, the only solution is for the people themselves to see the abyss and turn away, and to do so before the Western policy of letting them starve in their tiny economic barnyards pushes them even deeper into the misery of the Third World. How they can avoid national suicide with the politicians they have escapes my imagination. If they had The Bomb or the Black Gold, the West would be paying more attention. But the West, and especially the United States, are not blessed in their politicians either, and their populations will soon become infuriated with the costs to them induced by the comic opera antics of politicians and the savagery of bandit warlords in countries whose names they cannot even pronounce. Other demands weigh heavy on potential heroes—the needs of the former GDR, of the CIS, the cities and the underclass in the United States. Shall our sons again die in fires lit by those who play with ethnic matches? No, my old friend, just as it has been only the Serbs who can destroy Serbia, so also it is only the Serbs who can save her, and perhaps also the rest of us, as they did on the front at Salonika, but it will take even greater courage than it did then, in a simpler time.

This is an old story. Help is likely to continue to be as scarce as Hammel says it will be. Today there is one difference. Hammel reports getting a thousand lines a day from electronic networks in the former Yugoslavia. There is observation and communication. A modest difference by itself, to be sure, but one that may make a large difference over time if we and other of the world's democracies stand ready, and build the necessary institutions and practices, to assist and welcome those who wish to build democracy on the ruins of despair.

In the former Yugoslavia, where the basic problem is that ethnic groups[7] with a tradition of hatred and massacres (as well as of friendly living together) are intermixed, and dictators and politicians stimulate ethnic enmities to increase their power, the long-term answer can only be either that the peoples of the Balkans learn to live peacefully with each other, and/or there is an almost unimaginable movement of peoples and borders from where they have been for centuries, until each nation has its own state and the states decide not to fight each other. Outside democracies can step in to stop a war or egregious massacres, but such intervention is not likely to achieve either of the two kinds of long-term solution.

The narrower the goal of an intervention, the more likely it will be achieved, but the less good it will do. For example, if the democracies had intervened just to get the Serbs to stop using artillery to kill civilians in Sarajevo and other cities, the Serbs would probably have learned that it was a mistake to use artillery to kill civilians, and stopped doing so—if only to get the interveners to go home. But they would probably have continued to kill civilians with pistols or knives. This would be a useful gain —and a useful precedent—but we might not find it a very satisfying result.

Unfortunately the basic problem of the Balkans exists in many parts of the world—although in most places it is not quite so intense. The success of our democracy—and the ruthlessness of totalitarian suppression of dissent and conflict—have led many of us to forget how much of the world has not yet solved the basic problem of government—domestic peace. Internal peace is the first requirement for a country. Without it there can be neither safety nor justice nor democracy nor economic growth.

It is both discouraging and encouraging to remember all the things that prevented internal peace in the democracies in the past: religious wars, factional or family wars (such as the Wars of the Roses), ideological wars, wars about slavery or secession, wars between ethnic groups, and conflict between people simply fighting for personal power. The rest of the world will not have internal peace until each country develops institutions and commitments that are strong enough to prevent fighting for any reason, because there are always excuses for fighting. Domestic peace will only come to each country when enough people in that country have become so committed to peaceful ways of dealing with disputes that those people who want to fight will not have enough support to defeat the government's monopoly of legal force. Against great obstacles eventually we were able to do it, so maybe others can too. And our example must make it easier. (Modern technology and economics make it both easier and harder.)

Until internal peace is achieved throughout the world the dilemma the democracies will face many times, in many forms, is whether there is anything immediate that can be done to alleviate particular horrors of war and oppression, even though there is no way for outsiders to bring long-term internal peace without installing and protecting a government. (The historian Paul Johnson has suggested that this is what the democracies need to find a way to do.) There are good theories about how intervention can advance the process of learning to live in peace, and there are good theories about how outside intervention will set back that process. Sometimes intervention is helpful, sometimes its long-term effect is harmful, and sometimes the effect of intervention depends on exactly how it is done. But we cannot reasonably hope to get the right answer every time. (Neither about whether to intervene nor how to intervene.) The decision in each case will have to be made on the basis of agreement among the governments of a number of countries, each with their own political complications. Therefore part of the price of intervening is being ready to accept the pain of finding that some of our interventions have done more harm than good. (Sometimes the good will be short-term and the harm long-term, and sometimes the opposite, but there will be no intervention that everyone agrees did more good than harm.)

The best we can do is gradually—by trying to find the best way to deal with particular problems and learning from experience—to develop principles and procedures that are the closest approximation we can reach to sound policy. This approach will work best if, each time intervention seems to be called for, the democracies respond mostly on the basis of principles that they expect to follow in similar cases in the future, consider both long-run and short-run effects of intervention, and pay as much attention to the procedures for reaching decisions as to the decisions themselves.

Our experience provides basis for both pessimism and optimism about the prospects for peace in the zones of turmoil. The fact that the democracies have been able to achieve internal peace after many centuries of internal fighting is ground for optimism. On the other hand, our experience with how many kinds of conflict there were that we had to put behind us, and how long it took, is ground for pessimism about rapid achievement of internal peace in some parts of the world.

The democracies could not have stayed out of the original dispute about the independence of Slovenia and the rest because the key issue was whether the components of Yugoslavia would be recognized by the democracies as sovereign independent nations. Refusal to accept the credentials of Slovenia and the others was support for a Serbian-controlled Yugoslavia; recognition was support for the new states. As is often true, the democracies would have preferred a third alternative: honorable negotiation between Yugoslavia and the component republics to agree on the future arrangement between them. But in the end there was no third alternative; the only choice was between supporting the Serbian-dominated Yugoslav government or recognizing Slovenia and the other new states.

When we try to improve things in the zones of turmoil we will often find that the only real alternatives available to us will be to support one or the other of two sides, neither of which we would prefer. That is, it will turn out that whatever we do, even if we are trying to achieve some third result, such as negotiation and compromise, the main practical effect of our action will be to support one side or the other. If we are to be effective, we have to do better than we have done in the past at recognizing when our efforts to promote a third alternative will just have the effect of helping the worse of the two alternatives that we do not want to choose between.

And we can easily be misled by coming into the middle of an old situation. For example, Serbian aggression in former Yugoslavia was partly the result of the fact that the internal accommodation designed by Tito had left Serbia with less than its "fair" share of territory, but the opportunity to gain control of the army.

The breakup of Yugoslavia also illustrates how difficult it can be for us to be neutral or to do nothing. One of the earliest decisions we had to make was whether or not to give diplomatic recognition to the Republics that seceded from Yugoslavia. Was recognizing them inaction, or would refusing to recognize them have been inaction? Neutral-seeming action, like forbidding the delivery of weapons to the area, often really favors one side, as in Yugoslavia where the arms embargo hurt the newly separate states and helped Serbia, when it was able to gain control of the former Yugoslav national weapons.

Making It Possible for Multiethnic States to Survive in Eastern and Southern Europe

In the second half of 1995 NATO, led by the United States, finally used substantial military force in former Yugoslavia and then pushed the parties into an agreement intended to end the war in Bosnia. Because this action came so late, many more horrors were added to the war, and the conflict was much more difficult to resolve. Even worse, the peace that the United

States put together seems to have been designed more to produce temporary quiet than to deal effectively with the political realities of the Balkans, and it is likely not to last more than a year or so at best.

One of the main reasons why the United States and the European great democracies were so slow in summoning the will to act, and so half-hearted when they did act, to limit the tragedy in the former Yugoslavia is that no one has yet formulated a goal that seems achievable and worth substantial cost in lives and political capital. We think there is such a goal and that it is important enough to make us willing to violate both of the general rules we suggest for the future—that is, it justifies a "political policy" and strong leadership by the United States like that exercised during the cold war.

The goal is to make it possible for multiethnic states[8] to survive in Eastern and Southern Europe—not necessarily *all* multiethnic states. If there is to be a general understanding that multiethnic states are untenable and cannot be sustained when they come under pressure, then the former Yugoslavia will be only the first in a series of tragedies in Eastern and Southern Europe. The populations and histories are so mixed in much of that part of the world that there will be slaughter after slaughter if people come to believe that every ethnic group or most such groups are entitled to their own state, and that the only way to achieve peace is by separating peoples. It will become too dangerous for people to remain as ethnic minorities, and country after country will be in danger of falling apart.

The reason why the multiethnic states' survival in Eastern Europe is a major national interest of the great democracies is that their collapse would produce a series of wars in that area which would put great pressure on the survival of democracy in Western Europe.

The dangers to Western Europe are not that war will spread to their own countries from Eastern Europe, nor the heavy influx of refugees, nor severe economic losses; the primary danger is that if Western European countries are unable to do anything to prevent or limit a series of tragedies like those in Bosnia in their own region and culture, the continued helplessness in confronting nearby evil will likely undermine morale and faith in their own governments. And this danger will be compounded by the stress of dealing with European refugees, whether they are admitted or excluded.

If democracy in any of the "big six" fails, the current world order would be changed, reducing the national security of the United States. *It is of fundamental national interest that the United States assist in preventing the destruction of all Eastern European multiethnic states.* We can afford to see some of them collapse; we cannot afford the assumption that they are all doomed and that there must be a complete separation of peoples in that area, because that is a process that has no end and will bring too much blood to the doorsteps of democratic Europe. (Of course we have an altruistic as well as a selfish interest in preventing these tragedies.)

There is much that the great democracies can do to preserve multiethnic states in Eastern Europe simply by exercising their political influence. The key is for all the great democracies to come to understand their common national interest in the survival of those states, so that they can begin to use their power and influence toward that end. But it is likely that in at least a few cases some of the democracies will need to use force or the specific threat of force. We believe that if the democracies' national interest in making it possible for multiethnic states to survive comes to be appreciated and becomes a major goal, they will have the political will to use as much force as necessary, although quite possibly strong United States leadership and participation will be required.

This train of thought does not necessarily imply any specific outcome for the former Yugoslavia. It implies that the question each of the great democracies must ask is, How can we make sure that the outcome in the former Yugoslavia does not make it less possible for other multiethnic states in the region to survive? and that the answer justifies a major national effort.

It may be too late for the former Yugoslavia. But even if there is complete failure there, the democracies can demonstrate that they have learned a lesson and that in the next crisis they will act early to prevent other multiethnic states from destroying themselves.

We do not say that it *is* too late. When the democracies achieve the will to act they can cause the creation of a Balkan confederation (including Albania and Bulgaria), for example, which might make it possible for the fraction of each national population that favors peace and accommodation to work together to preserve a regime established with the help of the democracies. This would add to the equation positive local forces that now have no influence because they are divided among small national states.

The most disastrous outcome would be if the great democracies justify failure to act in Yugoslavia by telling themselves—and everyone else—that the destruction of Yugoslavia was inevitable and that no answer was possible except the separation of peoples. It is in our power to prevent that outcome. If we are not wise enough to prevent it, the current world order and our fundamental security may be jeopardized.

The Need to Distinguish among Nationalists

Nationalism has long had a bad name as being primitive, parochial, divisive, and in conflict with universal values like socialism, peace, or democracy. Nevertheless, on occasion the values of self-determination, and freedom from imperialism, communism, and colonialism have led to sympathy for nationalism. Realists have argued that whether or not nationalism is desirable, it is so strong that it is unwise to try to resist it.

Unfortunately, it is not possible to have a sensible policy that is either for or against nationalism in general. And because nationalism will continue to be such a powerful force, it will be even less possible to ignore it. Sound policy requires making subtle distinctions among nationalisms and among nationalists, favoring some and opposing others.

The subject is too complex to deal with satisfactorily here. One obvious distinction is between integrative nationalism, such as Yugoslav or British, and divisive nationalism, such as Serb or Scots, although even this distinction can depend on context.

Nationalism forces us to have a complex view of democracy, because nationalism's popularity means that a nationalist government can sometimes be genuinely representative of the national will without being genuinely democratic. And nationalists can often use democratic procedures, like elections, to achieve power. But democracy is more than elections and the reflection of the majority's will; it includes respect and protection for minorities and the process by which national decisions are made.

It may be that the key distinction to be made is the difficult one between aggressive and defensive nationalists, or between exclusionary and pluralist nationalists, or warlike and peace-seeking nationalists. One practical distinction is between politicians who increase national (ethnic) conflict to gain or maintain their personal power, and politicians who have other claims on public support, who could win in times of ethnic peace, and who try to reduce ethnic conflict.

It is especially important that we resist the fallacy that only extreme nationalists are legitimate. It is not true that "moderate nationalist" is always an oxymoron that describes an "Uncle Tom" who is not truly nationalist, nor it it always true that working with moderate nationalists is doomed to failure because they will inevitably be replaced by "genuine nationalists" who are more extreme.

While we may prefer political leaders who put democracy or some social ideology first, sometimes ethnic or national groups will only accept leaders who are known for their commitment to their people. When that is true, we need to support those ethnic leaders who have the greater commitment to peace and democracy, rather than leaders we are inclined to prefer because of their careers as advocates of peace or democracy if they are not accepted as "nationalists."

Supporting Democracy

President Alberto Fujimori's actions against the legislature and courts in Peru in 1992 are an example of the problems of supporting democracy from outside. Fujimori was a freely elected and popular president. He claimed that Peru's legislature and courts were corruptly standing in the way of the reforms desired by the majority (an entirely reasonable claim), and he therefore rejected the constitutional authority of those institutions. There was no doubt that Peruvian democracy was weak; the question was whether Fujimori's illegal actions—which he claimed were temporary measures needed to preserve real democracy and were undoubtedly broadly popular at the time—really were necessary to preserve Peruvian democracy or whether restoring the constitutional powers of the Peruvian legislature and courts would preserve Peruvian democracy.

Even if Fujimori was truly committed to democracy and was doing the best that could be done for democracy in Peru in the circumstances, one could argue that to protect democracy in other countries, Fujimori's actions had to be reversed in order to support the principle of abiding by constitutional requirements and systems of checks and balances.

There are many different ways that democracy can fail. Peru might have been an example of the kind of failure that occurs when democratic procedures prevent a democratically chosen leader from implementing his program or fighting effectively against an enemy of democracy, after which conditions worsen until democratic government does not have enough support to stand against an authoritarian regime. Or Peru might have been an example of the kind of failure that occurs when a democratically chosen leader resorts to undemocratic measures and gradually loses his popular support and retains power by becoming an authoritarian. A third kind of failure occurs when democratically chosen leaders and representatives keep choosing policies that have such bad results that democracy is rejected by the population. (Authoritarians are at least as likely to make the mistake of choosing harmful policies, but when they do, it is not a failure of democracy.)

What defines democracy is not some list of required rights and procedures. The essential feature of democracy is that leaders and policies be reasonably freely chosen by the general population. (This implies protection of critical rights of political minorities.) No particular procedure, not even the rule of law, is always appropriate. No democratic norm is as important as the protection of democracy as a living whole. However fair a democratic procedure—say, *habeas corpus*—may seem, a country becomes less democratic, not more, if it insists on that procedure when it has the effect of preventing democracy from working or from protecting itself.

Whether a procedure is democratic is not a matter of theoretical fairness; it is a matter of how it works in that place and time.

The idea that a democracy can fail by being "too democratic" is self-contradictory. Nothing that would cause the failure of a democracy is "democratic" for that country at that time, however good for democracy it is in most situations. Any rule that makes a democracy fail is "*un*democratic" at that place and time, however much the rule is usually essential to democracy. Survival is the first requirement of democratic government. The ultimate test of whether a country, that is trying to be a democracy and struggling to survive, really is a democracy is whether the leadership submits often enough to a genuine test of popular support, and whether movement toward full democracy starts again. Democracy is not about just one election.

We do not know who was right in Peru, but we believe that the fundamental principle of democracy is more important than particular rules and that sometimes new democracies have to violate democratic norms to succeed well enough to move toward full and stable democracy (but maybe not in Peru in 1992). Moreover, we believe that democracy in the world is hurt more by seeing a democracy fail than by seeing a democracy temporarily violate democratic rules in order to deal with its problems and ultimately survive as a democracy (but maybe Fujimori could not restore democracy).

New democracies will face many forms of the dilemma of whether it is more important to stick to democratic procedures or to do what has to be done. Almost always the temptation not to follow democratic procedures should be resisted—but there are exceptions. There is no set of rules that can give the right answer to such dilemmas. Outsiders should lean much further toward accepting whatever choice has been made locally than they would if they were making the choice for themselves, but whichever way we lean we will be wrong some of the time. (In 1995 Fujimori was re-elected and given a majority vote in the legislature, although the Peruvian democracy is still an open question.)

There is only one thing we can be sure of when we try to improve the international order in the zones of turmoil. However modest the goal we decide to pursue, it will be difficult for us to know which of the practical choices that face us will help achieve our goal and which will be harmful. But this is a counsel of caution, not of passivity.

Notes

1. This is the hypothesis offered by Samuel P. Huntington. See "Clash of Civilizations," in *Foreign Affairs* 72, no. 3 (Summer 1993): 22–49.

2. There is no reason to think that growth has to stop soon in the very wealthy countries. Nobody understands what the economics of our societies would be if we became four times wealthier than we are now because such wealthy societies have never existed and they might well be so different that our experience would be misleading. (If "traditional" rates of growth were continued, we would become four times as wealthy per capita as we are now in less than eighty years.) But we can say something about the fundamental questions. The key point is that already in 1992 most of our economy is essentially arrangements in which we buy each other's time. Even when we buy a car most of the money goes to pay for people's time—mostly white-collar people.

Increasing wealth does not necessarily mean producing more physical goods. Increasing wealth means that people's time becomes more valuable, and generally it means that increasing shares of income are spent on more and more specialized human skills and services—whether they are musicians and painters, psychiatrists, basketball players, or chefs and masseurs. As the population becomes wealthier they bid up the price of special human talents and the total income of the society can keep rising. Because of this process there is no inherent reason why the per capita income of the United States cannot increase to $50,000 a year or $100,000 a year without harming the environment and without people becoming mere collectors of ever more silly gadgets. Such incomes would not be just the result of inflation—although comparative prices would be hard to measure. The test is whether the prices we are willing to pay for each others' work are genuine, which is determined by whether some people in other countries are also willing to pay those prices.

If we keep growing at anything like the traditional rate, the currently poor countries will not catch up for centuries even if they grow substantially faster than we do.

3. Capital flight and a large informal economy are signs that the government is interfering with the economy too much.

4. Opinion polls indicate that while most American believe we should spend less that we do on foreign aid, they think we are spending much more than 1 percent of the GNP. Therefore, public opinion is not necessarily a bar on increased foreign aid.

5. Michael Novak, *The Spirit of Democratic Capitalism* (Lanham, Md.: Madison Books, 1991).

6. Eugene Hammel, *The Yugoslav Labyrinth* (Berkeley: University of California Center for Slavic and East European Studies, May 1992), 11, 13.

7. "Multiethnic" is used here to stand for a variety of divisions between people, only some of which are literally "ethnic." For example, while Serbs, Croats, and Bosnians are the same ethnic group, and the defining difference between them is religious affiliation, their conflict is not about religion. Their different religions are essentially group badges. The same may be true in Ireland today.

8. See the prior note.

CHAPTER 8

SHAPING U.S. POLICY ON INTERVENTION

U.S. policy about when to intervene to improve the international order in the zones of turmoil must have two branches. One branch answers the question, "For what purposes will we intervene?" The other branch tells us how we should decide about particular cases, which really means, "Which countries or international institutions have to agree with us before we are satisfied that intervention is necessary?"

On the first branch it is easy to decide what we want—peace, justice, democracy; it is much harder to decide what narrower practical goals we should commit ourselves to. The problem with the obvious ambitious goals is that we cannot accomplish them. The serious part of policy is recognizing that we cannot get all we want and asking "What will we *make sure* happens (or does not happen) even if making sure requires major efforts and possibly the use of force?"

It is easy for us to tell countries or governments what they should not do—things like "ethnic cleansing" (although if we do say that we will not allow "ethnic cleansing" we will find that it is not as easy to define as it seems). It is hard to decide what we will take military action, if necessary, to prevent. But the decision about what we will use our forces to prevent is in some ways the key element of our policy about intervention in the zones of turmoil, even if we rarely actually use military force.

The democracies can do a lot of good by example and by moral suasion and economic leverage. But, as we have recently been reminded in the former Yugoslavia and Iraq, there are some evils that the democracies cannot avert unless political leaders in the zones of turmoil believe that democracies might step in with military force and that, when they do, they will win and make decisive decisions.

If the democracies want to have an altruistic influence on the events that will be determined by force calculations, they need to understand three ancient truths about how to exercise power where there is no law enforcement. The first rule is not to let those you are trying to influence believe that you are unwilling or incapable of using force. The second is, when you use force, be sure to succeed and make whoever forced you to fight regret his action. (Being an influence for good requires being willing sometimes to go too far—to overreact—recognizing that innocent people will be killed.) The third is, do not often request something strongly and allow the request to be ignored, and practically never demand something and allow the demand to be rejected.

If these rules are followed, we can do a great deal without having to use force. But if we act as if we will not use force, or if we regularly call on countries to stop doing things that violate our principles and then do nothing effective when they fail to stop, we will have little ability to stop anybody from doing anything, except by using military force.

These rules lead to our seemingly warlike insistence that the key area of policy starts by deciding which objectives we are potentially willing to use military force to achieve. It is not that war is the main part of policy. But when it comes to things like preventing aggression or genocide, it is imprudent to announce policies that are broader than our potential willingness to use military force.

Although we cannot have ambitious *objectives* without being willing to fight, we can have ambitious *principles*. No country has a responsibility to fight to force the rest of the world to follow its principles. So we can stand for more than we are willing to fight for. But we must make clear the distinction between what we believe in and what we are determined to make happen or to prevent.

The principle of being clear about what we are willing to fight for is an easy principle to violate. For example, if dramatic TV stories create a public demand that some dictator be stopped from oppressing a neighbor, although there is no popular support for using our own army to prevent him, the president will be tempted to try to solve his political problem by making requests/demands on the dictator, accompanied by hints that we might use force if necessary, in hopes that the dictator will feel that he has to comply. This is called bluffing; it is cheap and sometimes it works. That is why it is a temptation; but it is a temptation that should usually be resisted.

The ability of the democracies to stop future Yugoslavias depends not only on whether they can agree and are willing to provide forces. There will be few horrors stopped if each intervention requires a hundred thousand troops and yields thousands of casualties; civilized behavior is much more likely to be imposed if it can be done with air power or with only tens of thousands of troops and scores or hundreds of casualties. But the number of troops and casualties required depends on the skill with which the force is used and the ruthlessness of the tactics. The most efficient use of force—which may require cleverness and creativity combined with an intimate knowledge of the practical details and political facts—may take only a tenth or a hundredth as much as the standard calculation produced by conservative military staffs. Since decisions are made on the basis of predicted military requirements, the democracies' ability to act depends on the quality of judgments made by military staffs. Those people who are eager for the democracies to prevent future Yugoslavias need a keen interest in developing and supporting brilliant generals and ruthless tacticians and in making realistic assessments of military risks. There are real costs to both overestimating and underestimating risks.

We have seen in Somalia that even intervention to prevent famine and the carnage of anarchy, where the intervention is not opposed by a military force, requires troops to provide security against criminals, gangs, and small groups of soldiers. All use of military force is messy and confused, and the use of military force to maintain order can be especially difficult. People are bound to be killed from errors of judgment and implementation in any intervention, including some of our own and allied forces who are killed by friendly fire. No major military action can expect to escape casualties from friendly fire. Therefore our ability to exert leadership depends in part on the quality of followership at home and among the other democracies. The more irresponsible and unrealistic criticism, and the less intellectual and political support against such criticism, the less likely that American or other democratic political leaders will be willing to pay the prices and take the risks of leadership.

Democratic political leaders who will face demands for action in the zones of turmoil have a real interest in the education of democratic publics in both sides of the reality of the zones of turmoil: that not every problem has a solution, but every solution creates a multitude of problems, costs, and embarrassments. If democratic publics have no tolerance for error, there will be no intervention and no outside help for victims in the zones of turmoil. Every effort should be made to inform the public that negative aspects of intervention cannot be avoided.

To appreciate the problem of justifying the bad results of even a successful intervention, consider the following thought experiment. Imagine that Britain and France had intervened against the German occupation of the Rhineland in 1938, and as a result the Hitler government had fallen and Germany had stayed in disorder for years. Everybody would have blamed Germany's troubles on the "precipitate intervention" of England and France—their failure to rely on diplomatic measures. No one would have been able to explain that the German troubles were insignificant because they had prevented World War II and the Holocaust. (This is a point first made to us by Herman Kahn, to whom this book is dedicated). Since no one can make disasters that are prevented believable, the most successful interventions can look the worst.

In the former Yugoslavia, for example, it would not be difficult for the democracies to defeat the Serbian army; the problem would more likely come afterwards if the democracies feel that they must guarantee borders and protect against guerrilla attacks. If, however, the democracies wanted only to hit Serbia hard enough to shift the balance of force so that Bosnia and Croatia could defend themselves effectively, the costs of intervention would be much less, perhaps low enough to be politically feasible. But after such a limited democratic intervention was over there would almost certainly be extended fighting and atrocities on both sides. Some of the atrocities would be committed by those whom the democracies had armed or helped. The "sensitivity" to be troubled by such responsibility is admirable and comfortable, but it reduces the likelihood that democracies will prevent or ameliorate many of the future Yugoslavias.

In the summer of 1992 we simultaneously watched large numbers of people dying and being killed in Afghanistan, Somalia, and Bosnia (and less intense violence in and around Israel, Ireland, Cambodia, Sudan, Mauritania, and other places). Probably it will be unusual to have so much violent conflict at the same time. But the conflicts are typical of what can be expected throughout the zones of turmoil, maybe at an average rate of two or more a year through the next generation, maybe more or less frequently depending mostly on what scale of violence is noticed. If the democracies are going to deal with most of these outbreaks of violence, we are going to have to develop standards and practices for making prudent decisions and operating efficiently and for sharing the load as well as the decisions. The United States cannot for long carry too greatly disproportionate a share either of the decisions or of the human costs. If we do develop such standards and practices the need to intervene may decline somewhat as nations learn what they will not be allowed to do, and begin to avoid actions that the democracies will not tolerate. But, even if such a lesson is learned, and many atrocities are deterred, it is a lesson that is likely to have to be retaught fairly frequently because the pressures for violence will be intense and rational calculations will have limited influence.

We do not want to leave this subject with a sense of hopelessness. The democracies do not always have to sit idly by, telling each other about all the dangers and complexities, when the conscience of civilization is offended by slaughter or injustice. Action often produces unexpected support and solutions as well as problems and criticism. We have immense power and creativity if we can harness it. There are sometimes quite good measures that could be taken in situations that seem to the newspaper reader or casual observer to be hopeless. (Many guerrilla wars that would seem hopeless by normal calculations have been won quite quickly by regular forces that found the guerrillas' special vulnerability—sometimes after years of failure.) If our objectives are reasonably modest and we accept appropriate standards of judgment, bold leadership can enable us to do a lot of good. If we demand perfect solutions, we will be able to do nothing. And if we try to do too much, we will lose the opportunity to deal with the problems that could be handled.

A Peacetime Army for the United States

While history has not come to an end, the age of heroism in American foreign policy is thankfully over. Individuals will have opportunities to be heroes serving the national interest or in pursuit of altruism, but nowhere in sight is there an occasion for an American to die defending the freedom or survival of the United States. This happy change will have profound implications for all parts of the American military establishment.

A "peacetime army" does not mean an unnecessary army or one that will never see battle. It means only—but very importantly—a military whose personal motivations and political support cannot be based on potential need to defend the survival or freedom of the homeland. What do we need to do to construct an American military establishment suitable for the current world order? The fundamental requirement is a political consensus about the need for a serious and competent military force.

The obvious reason for needing a political consensus is to get Congress to provide the necessary money, but in the long run this is likely to be the least important part of the problem. The primary dangers to the effectiveness of a U.S. peacetime army are comfort seeking in the military leadership and political diversion by the Congress. The danger is less that we will not spend enough money on the military than that the military will have only a fraction of the effectiveness that could be achieved for the amount of money it is given.

By the nature of things, it is very difficult to keep a fighting edge on a military force that does not fight much. In addition to various prosaic problems, it is difficult because the force cannot be kept sharp unless military commanders are willing to embarrass one another, to put pressure on one another, to make short or awkward career paths, to avoid using political compromise to settle disagreements between the services. When the real world does not provide tests for the quality of your work, it is much easier for the top people to have a live-and-let-live attitude toward one another. The natural evolution of unchallenged organizations is to find a way so that everyone is as comfortable as possible, and no one makes waves. (This may not be too destructive for an organization that does not have to face an enemy looking to use its weak points to defeat it.) If the military force is to be effective, it will have to find a way to avoid this strong organizational drive to prefer comfort over effectiveness.

The second problem reinforces the first; it is the tendency of politicians, especially when there is no threat to their country's safety, to see military funds as political opportunities. If the country is not in danger, why should not Congress use the military to solve social problems or to try out important new ideas about human relations? And why should not powerful legislators make sure that military funds are spent in ways that help their own constituents?

On the one hand, if Congress is diverting military funds for its own purposes, without regard to whether fighting effectiveness is compromised, why should military commanders make their own personal relationships difficult by upsetting long-standing practices, just because they are not as militarily effective as they ought to be? On the other hand, if the military leadership is operating the Defense Department as a mutual protection society in which everyone scratches everyone else's back and no one gets in trouble for failing to be militarily sharp, why should the Congress not make good political use of all that taxpayer money? There has to be a political and motivational consensus that keeps both the Congress and the military leadership serious about the fighting effectiveness of the peacetime military or else, however much is spent, most of it will be wasted.

Roughly speaking, our military will need three kinds of effectiveness. First, it needs to be as effective as possible in providing protection against missile (or airplane) attacks using nuclear, chemical, or biological weapons against American cities. Second, it needs to have capable forces available when there is a democratic decision to intervene in a zone of turmoil. Third, it needs to be ready to mobilize to deal with a (very unlikely) change in the world that produces a major threat to the country.

In addition, our military has to provide a nuclear deterrent force as long as there continues to be a nuclear world. But since we have already gone farther in this direction than we will need to go in the future, this is a smaller challenge.

We do not want to get into a debate about exactly how big a military force the United States will need or how much it should cost. It is clear that it does not have to be as big as the force we had when we had a substantial worldwide enemy. But we will let others debate whether it should be one-third as big or two-thirds as big, or some other fraction, and how costly it needs to be.

The critical requirement is that the United States have a force that can intervene quickly and decisively against all but the biggest and best non-democratic military forces in the world. We do not need a very large force to be able to be militarily decisive anywhere in Latin America, Africa, the Middle East, and parts of Asia. We do need to have a force that takes advantage of our technical and social strength so that it can be counted on to defeat a force several times as large as itself. (We cannot afford a force big enough to be able to intervene decisively against some of the large forces that exist in Asia.)

Getting the military force we need is less a matter of money than it is determination to use that money to buy real fighting effectiveness. This requires at least the following: developing and selecting the right advanced military technology and buying or producing it in sufficient quantities; disciplining and training the force so that it can fight well; organizing so that unity of command is not sacrificed for interservice peace; developing generals (and admirals) who are good at commanding in battle, whether or not they are good at other things; and planning for the kinds of missions we will face.

The result should be a force that can quickly deliver military power anywhere in the world with intimidating and overwhelming effectiveness. While technology makes this possible, it is a formidable challenge to make the capability real and ready.

It may be that part of our force should be internationalized. For example, all or part of a missile defense system defending most of the world could be international. Or perhaps it may become appropriate to assign the task of providing a residual nuclear deterrent in a nonnuclear world—against hidden nuclear weapons or weapons secretly developed after the agreement—to an international force of some kind. We do not say that either of these possibilities would be a good idea. In some circumstances they would; in others, not. There are many possible forms of international forces. A UN force is one possibility, but so is a force composed of units contributed by the large democracies, or some of them. Or there could be a new specialized agency created to operate such a force and governed by a group of countries. As we pointed out in chapter 4, such an international force, even with a nuclear monopoly, does not have to be a political threat.

Whether or not the nuclear deterrence and/or the strategic defense parts of our force are internationalized, our force should intervene abroad only in self-defense or in cooperation with other democracies. We should not be the judge, jury, and executioner of the world, even if we believe that we could save millions of lives by doing so.

The Only Political-Military Superpower (Unfortunately)

In economics there are three superpowers: the United States, Europe, and Japan. Nothing we do can either increase or decrease the number of economic superpowers. In culture the United States is the only superpower, and this can be touched by policy only slightly. But in this section we are not talking about economics or culture.

The United States is the only military superpower, even if we ignore nuclear weapons. In 1990 the United States did not really need any other country's military forces or money to throw Iraq out of Kuwait. We could have done essentially what we did using only our own forces, and no other country could have done so. The nature of the fighting between the coalition and Iraq showed that a force one-third or less the size of the actual coalition force could have defeated the Iraqi army, just as completely, with great confidence, and with fewer or the same number of casualties. This was apparent in advance to sound military analysts, and a number of them said so at the time. That capability is what made us the only superpower. If we now cut our military forces in half, there will be fewer situations where we will have enough military power to be decisive by ourselves, but we will still be the only superpower, because there will be no world crisis where there is another country that is the only foreign power that has enough strength to come in and be the dominant force. (Although there will be more situations where neither the United States nor any foreign power has enough force to do that.)

There is no single answer to the question, Should the United States try to continue to be the only political-military superpower? We should *not* try to prevent a democratic Europe from deciding to unite part or all of its foreign policy and thus to become a second superpower. But we should do whatever we can to prevent some authoritarian state from building up its forces enough to become a second (or a third) superpower. The brief controversy early in 1992 in connection with a leaked draft of a Defense Department memo that suggested that the United States should work to "prevent the re-emergence of a new rival," shows the sensitivity of the "sole superpower" issue and the tendency to view it in shallow terms. On serious examination, the issue has an entirely different character.

If Japan becomes authoritarian (although this seems very unlikely), we should certainly be against its becoming more heavily armed, and we should probably increase our forces enough to stay comfortably ahead so that Japan would not be an equal superpower. On the other hand, if a democratic Japan wants to have the political position of a world superpower, without substantially increasing its level of military expenditures, this would be fine, whether or not Europe is a superpower. That is, we think the United States should welcome a democratic Japan as either a second or a third superpower, if Japan is willing to fulfill the responsibilities of that role.

Some will argue that if Japan becomes a superpower—and is armed accordingly—it will force the South Asian countries to arm to protect themselves, and therefore we should be against Japan becoming a super-power. Perhaps; it certainly would be a costly result if it happened, even if the danger were only in the minds of the South Asian nations and Japan's intentions concerning them were wholly innocent. But this possibility should not lead the United States to oppose a Japanese decision to become a world superpower.

Nothing we have said about democracies not fighting each other implies that a democratic Japan cannot become a threat to nondemocracies in South Asia. While a democratic Japan is unlikely to adopt a policy of using threats of force to dominate South Asian countries, one can easily imagine conflict growing out of different perspectives and interests. So diplomacy still has important tasks ahead. However, it is not unreasonable to hope that the United States and the other great democracies could find ways to step between a democratic Japan and those countries that were afraid of it, well before serious threats of war.

Nations cannot be relied on to be rational, but the fact that Japan has little to gain and much to lose by throwing its weight around in South Asia gives room for hope that she can be headed off if she starts to go in that direction. This is an example of a classical balance of power situation which seems to require less than the traditional degree of paranoia in the current world order—which is not to say that it is free from peril.

Some would argue that we should resist Japan becoming an equal superpower, not beholden to the United States for protection of its security, because then the United States would no longer be able to protect itself against unfair Japanese trade practices (or prevent untoward behavior in South Asia). There may be some truth in such a concern, but we would reject it for two reasons. First, it is not at all clear that we know how to use Japanese dependency to protect our economic interests, or that we could not use our economic strengths to protect ourselves just as well. Our main economic problems with Japan are to a large extent the result of (a) the differences in the ways our economies work, (b) the Japanese government's political inability to do some of the things we tried to convince them to do, and (c) our failure to understand business realities or what negotiating goals and techniques would help us.

Second, Japanese security dependency on the United States will probably decline sharply in coming years whether or not Japan decides to be, and is accepted, as a second or third superpower (although perhaps not before the end of the decade). Already the Soviet/Russian threat is disappearing. China may well become less a threat to Japan. There is quite a reasonable chance that a united Korea will be democratic, and not so heavily armed that Japan needs protection from it.

In any event, Japanese security dependency is more a matter of the level of their military force than of whether it chooses to be, and is accepted as, a superpower. We should be willing to accept Japan as a superpower even if it does not increase its military force. Contrariwise, Japan might choose to increase its military force to avoid dependence, but not choose to act as a worldwide superpower.

The United States does not need to have any country dependent on it for security in order to be able to protect its legitimate business and trade interests. And it may turn out that U.S.-Japanese negotiations will go better if we negotiate as equals—although it is also quite possible that we will have a tougher time with a Japan that sees itself as a superpower.

If a democratic Japan were to decide to increase its armed forces enough to make Japan militarily more or less equal to Europe and the United States, which is quite unlikely at present, the United States probably should be quietly unhappy, but not do anything to influence the Japanese decision or substantially increase our military force to stay ahead of Japan. One way of preventing such a Japanese decision is to give Japan equal superpower status (including a permanent seat on the UN Security Council) if it wants it, even if it does not increase its military force levels. A reasonable way to think of the current situation is that Japan is so respected that it is given credit for having the large modern military force it could build, although perhaps eight years would be needed before the unbuilt force would be equipped and ready to fight. Contrary to conventional wisdom, what should matter to the U.S. force planners is not the size of the Japanese military but whether Japan stays democratic.

Europe, China, and possibly Japan are the only imaginable other political-military superpowers for the next generation or two. To be a hostile superpower a country or tight alliance has to have military expenditures at least half as great as those of the United States. There are no likely prospects for any other country or group of countries to have such a defense expenditure, even if the United States cuts its defense program by half. If we say that a GNP half as large as that of the United States is required to be a superpower, there are no potential candidates before 2020 besides Japan and China. What nation might have a GNP one-quarter as large as that of the United States by 2020? Maybe Germany, no others. There is nothing we have to do to prevent any other superpower from coming into existence; and we could not create one if we wanted to.

In previous world orders the possibility of the great European nations combining forces and becoming a single political-military power would have been unthinkable. National security was the fundamental issue for each country. Nations felt that they could not put their military forces into a combined force and turn over responsibility for their safety to an international group and still be independent nations. But in the international order described in chapter 1 the great European democracies can turn their responsibility for the zones of turmoil over to a European military institution without jeopardizing their independence, and they may well find it convenient to do so. Of course, such a European institution would not be able to take military action that produced substantial numbers of casualties among troops from any country without political support in that country. (An international volunteer military force would be easier to use, although politically more difficult to put together.)

Whether or not Europe becomes a second superpower outside the area of economics will be influenced by how Europe resolves the conflict discussed in chapter 6 between becoming "deeper" and becoming "wider," and whether there is one Europe or two. But any outcome of those choices is compatible with Europe becoming a political-military superpower. Europe could decide to become a political-military superpower—or decide not to—whatever institutional form it takes. Either a small Europe or a large Europe could eventually become our equal partner in dealing with the zones of turmoil.

Unfortunately, despite the honor, there are grave disadvantages to being the only political-military superpower. Of course, the U.S. Department of Defense is correct that it needs to plan to prevent, if possible, the development of a new authoritarian superpower. One of the DoD's major assignments must be to keep alert for the potential development of an authoritarian superpower and to conduct active research and development and mobilization programs to be prepared to be militarily predominant over any such superpower if it arises. Fortunately, this will probably be a long-range assignment. For a long time it will be unlikely that there are any authoritarian countries within ten years of becoming a military match for the United States.

Superior power is always resented. As long as the United States is the only superpower, a feeling of antagonism against the United States is virtually certain to be at least a major current in national thinking in most major countries, even though the United States will be recognized as being basically friendly and as playing a positive role in the world. Any country that thinks in balance-of-power terms is likely to try to balance U.S. power. (We cannot be part of a bloc because there will be no country too big for us to match without being part of a bloc.)

We will be a superpower that other countries will never respect out of fear in the way that countries have feared and respected Japan or Germany or the Soviet Union or the Ottoman Empire in the past, although smaller countries will correctly fear that we might do them great harm by mistake or out of misunderstanding. (It is easy to be hurt by even a very well-meaning elephant.) Also, just as it is true that other countries can sometimes succeed in manipulating our system to their advantage, it is sometimes true that our system can lead us to be unreasonably overbearing to other countries.

Almost all countries will usually have some negative feelings about the only superpower. Most countries will have a sense of common cause with other countries against the superpower—not to destroy or challenge it, but to resist it and prevent it from automatically exercising power. Even when countries and individuals clearly understand that their most fundamental national interests are served by the U.S. superpower role, they would on most day-to-day matters feel antagonism toward the United States, regardless of how well we behave.

Our unique power does not mean that we will get our way in everything, or even most things. In fact, it usually means the opposite. That is, we will have to let others have their way, and even exploit us, on many smaller things, just because we are so powerful. Of course, there will also be many small matters on which others excessively defer to us because of our power.

There are worse problems resulting from being the only superpower than having to be generous and deferential. Suppose, for example, that a new genocide began in Uganda or Cambodia and the United States was concerned about stopping it. If, as the only superpower, we approached other nations seeking their support to do something about the genocide, their response would be likely to be determined not by their views of the alleged genocide but by their policy toward the United States. They would be likely to care more about their relation to the United States than about the genocide.

The result will be that countries that have been complaining about U.S. arrogance will deny that there is any genocide and resist U.S. effort to organize a coalition against it. In contrast, governments that have been trying to improve their relationship with the United States will support our effort against the genocide. (And their domestic opposition parties will attack them by denying the genocide and claiming that their government is toadying to the United States.)

The discussion and politics of responding to genocide will turn into a discussion and politics dominated by reactions to the United States. Every country will know that the United States can handle the genocide problem without its help. Why should any government let its actions be influenced by worrying about the latest faraway genocide, rather than respond to the crisis in whatever way serves its own national or political interest best? No country has any more reason than any other country to care about the genocide rather than about its own political advantage. So why should any of them subordinate that advantage to an altruistic concern about stopping a genocide for which their help is not necessary—and for which the United States, as the sole superpower, has a unique responsibility? Undoubtedly some countries will respond less selfishly, but history suggests that they are likely to be relatively rare.

If Europe decided to act as a second political-military superpower (rather than as separate countries), the situation would be very different. Europe and the United States would have many disagreements but would each accept the other as an equal superpower, especially in relation to the zones of turmoil. Neither would need to try to match the other's military force. We would not be competing to be "more of a superpower," nor would we be concerned about the possibility of fighting each other. If we accepted each other as equals, there would be no reason for either of us to use a possible intervention in the zones of turmoil to make points about the relative status of the United States and Europe.

In the case of the hypothetical genocide in Cambodia or Uganda, both the United States and Europe would be in the same situation. Either would have the power to intervene, and each would have an equal degree of obligation. Neither would have any greater responsibility to do so than the other. If Europe and the United States agreed to take action to stop the genocide, it would be an agreement between equals, not the submission of one to the other. There would be no reason why either should contribute more of the necessary resources than the other, nor any general reason why either should or should not accept the views of the other. In discussing what to do, both parties, the United States and Europe, would understand at a fundamental level that their long-term relationship with each other requires that each act to the other as a responsible equal, ready to carry its share of the load.

Of course, in dealing with any crisis in the zones of turmoil, both Europe and the United States would be influenced by domestic politics—and

European politics would be somewhat different from American politics. And whenever a crisis arose, Europe and the United States would be engaged in a variety of complicated economic conflicts with each other and with others. So there is no guarantee that either or both superpowers would deal with the genocide crisis on the merits in a responsible and altruistic way. But the great advantage would be that there would be only two equal parties that would need to discuss the problem and reach agreement.

Once Europe and the United States decided what to do about the genocide, they could either do it themselves or together raise whatever support they decided they needed from other countries. Once there was agreement between Europe and the United States every country would know what the outcome of the international discussion would be (and might as well commit to the winning side). The United States and Europe could not be prevented from carrying out their decision. They would not have to fear that other countries would try to punish them for their action.

The fact that the decision of only two powers is enough to be decisive may seem unfair, unjust, undemocratic, and undesirable to some, but it is the way in which the world works. It is not the result of conspiracy or power grabbing. It is caused by the fact that European and U.S. societies have been able to organize themselves to be so much more peaceful, united, and productive than other societies in the world.

While there is no guarantee that Europe and the United States together will do the right thing about genocide in Uganda or Cambodia, or about any other challenge to the altruism of the democracies, it is more likely that those two democratic governments will agree to do the right thing than that any other group of nations will agree to do so. It is meaningless to say that the United Nations should decide; the United Nations is just the nations sitting together (with a particular voting system and institutional filter). The United Nations does not decide anything except that which its member governments have already decided. If there is a democratic caucus with weighted voting at the United Nations, almost any decision the United States and Europe agree on will become a UN decision.

If the European countries act separately, the United States will have the sole-superpower problem in the United Nations as well as outside it. So our interest in having Europe become a second superpower would be just as great if we have a policy of being committed to the United Nations. If Europe decides to act as a unit on all foreign policy, and if there is a UNDC, then it would probably be appropriate for Europe to be a single participant in the UNDC, with the same number of votes as the United States. Then the European nations would either not participate in the caucus separately or perhaps have one separate vote each.

While some will argue that Europe is less likely to be willing to intervene altruistically to prevent horrors in the zones of turmoil than the United States, it is not realistic to think that the United States would intervene against the resistance of Europe, whether or not Europe is acting together as a great power. While there is some chance that the United States might act by itself if it were the only superpower, this is less likely than Europe as a superpower either acting with the United States or specifically agreeing that the United States should act by itself.

If Europe becomes a superpower, it will be in almost exactly the same relationship to the zones of turmoil as the United States. We will both be very rich democracies, too powerful to be endangered by any outcome of conflict in the zones of turmoil, and with the responsibility that power brings. It is more likely that we will find ourselves in agreement with superpower Europe than with any group of governments.

In trying to make sure that we are not stuck with the whole bill for international altruism, it is even more important to us that Europe come to be accepted as an equal superpower. If the United States and Europe are both superpowers, it will be obvious that each will pay the same as the other and that together we will pay about half the cost. (The U.S. standard share of the UN budget is about 25 percent.) Together we can try to get others to pay a share of the costs, and it will be much easier to induce other countries to contribute if we are asking together. Neither of us would be merely trying to relieve our own burden, and no country could avoid its share of the burden by playing one of us off against the other.

There will be a question of Japan's role in relation to the two superpowers. But for the purposes of this discussion it does not matter what the answer turns out to be. Japan may be content to be the greatest of the non-superpowers. Or Japan may want to be treated as a third equal superpower, paying an equal share of the cost in return for having an equal voice in the decision. The question whether there is a third superpower is much less important than whether there is a second. If Europe did not come together, Japan might be the second superpower. But it would be harder for Japan to decide to be a second superpower than to be the third, and, except in Asia, agreement between the United States and Japan would not be as decisive as agreement between the United States and Europe.

It is impossible to say whether decisions about international altruism would be better made by Europe and the United States or by Europe, the United States, and Japan. Obviously the dynamics of a relationship of three is different from the dynamics of a relationship of two. Sometimes two would work better and sometimes three would. Two can get locked in disagreement, and sometimes the third can break the jam. Sometimes three become paralyzed by maneuvering to avoid being the "odd one." But almost always it would be easier for the United States to deal with either one or two equals than with many nonequals.

Intervention in Specific Cases

The two branches of our policy—objectives and procedures—come together in decisions about whether to intervene in a particular conflict in the zones of turmoil. The second basic branch of U.S. policy to improve the international order of the zones of turmoil is the question, "With whom shall we act?" When something terrible is happening, and other countries are not willing to do anything, or disagree about what is right, will we act alone to do what we think is right, or will we act only with partners or with international authority? And if so, which ones?

There is no basis on which the United States could claim the right to decide unilaterally what should be done on these issues, since they do not affect our major national interests. (Why should the United States decide that Mauritania's massacre of its citizens must be stopped, if the United States has no special interest in Mauritania?) By ourselves, we have no obvious right to enforce our principles, or our diagnosis of a particular conflict, on the rest of the world. If no other country agrees with us about a supposedly altruistic intervention, we probably should reexamine our thinking. So our question will be, If we are not to be the judge, who is? With what institution or group of nations should we decide what must be done to maintain a minimum degree of "order"? Should we let the United Nations decide? Should the great powers follow their own consensus? Should we be concerned primarily with the judgments of the democracies? or the large democracies? Should the decision about what we do to maintain order be reached through ad hoc discussions or through an institutional procedure?

We will have to reject actions that are not agreed to by other countries not just because of doubts about our right to act; generally there will not be domestic political support for risking American soldiers for missions of good citizenship where there are no other good citizens. Some international agreement will be necessary to gain support from the U.S. public.

Americans would accept at least hundreds of casualties to prevent Yugoslavias, even if the other democracies do not do their share, provided the president gives the reasons and says he believes the country should do it, and the use of force is competent and successful. And a president who leads a clearly successful solo intervention will gain politically. But the decisive fact is that a president who decides to intervene without support from other democracies will be taking a huge risk that he will be politically destroyed if things go wrong. And, while he will usually be able to protect against the intervention becoming a disaster, it rarely will be possible to be confident that success will be recognized, even if the intervention is successful by suitably modest standards. (Which is not to say that sometimes presidents will not be able to make even a failure seem to be a success.) There is much less political risk to the president from participating in an intervention for which there has been a truly joint decision of the great democracies and where the United States provides no more than its proportionate share of the troops.

The way the two branches of U.S. policy can be connected is to make a commitment to use military force in support of our principles whenever a specified group of nations or international organization has decided that it is necessary to do so. For example, we might decide to act militarily in any case where we have agreement and help from either the five or nine leading democracies, the United Nations, or all the democracies in the region of the dispute. Such a commitment meets the need for clarity about which of our principles we are willing to use force to achieve and provides a source of decision for applying the general rule to the particular case.

When we combine the two branches of policy this way, we can espouse broad principles without committing ourselves to fight for them. At the same time, we would be providing deterrent power to the international group whose decisions we decide to accept. The group could take care not to warn without acting. The United States by itself would only speak of preferences and would eschew independent action.

What Kind of Multilateralism?

It would be a mistake for the United States to use the United Nations as it currently operates as the essential source of moral authority for action to enforce standards of international order in the zones of turmoil. As a matter of principle, we should not continue to accept that democracies and nondemocracies have equal moral standing. Also, we should not accept the moral claims of an organization that has as little integrity to its own rules and principles as the United Nations has so far displayed (despite recent improvements).

This does not mean that the United States should reject the United Nations or that we should fail to live up to our legal obligations to it. But it does mean that when millions of lives are at stake somewhere in the world, we should be more concerned about the judgments of democratic governments than about the outcome of the UN's vote-trading processes.

The UN's decision in 1991 to retract its statement that "zionism is racism" was not a victory for Israel; rather, the retraction was a limited victory for the United Nations. Zionism was never racism. The United Nations' saying that it was did not make it so, nor did the statement obligate anyone to act as if it were. All the original UN declaration did was to provide a convenient example of the UN's shamelessness. It proved that the United Nations could not be relied on to tell the truth and that it was willing to be a force for evil. The retraction, resulting from a reasonably close vote influenced by a strong U.S. lobbying effort, proved only that a majority of UN members decided that the United Nations should not tell this particular untruth any longer. The Arab countries (except Egypt) all voted to continue the "zionism is racism" resolution, and they did not seem to lose credibility by doing so.

Fortunately, the retraction of "zionism is racism" was also evidence of the shift in the balance of influence in the United Nations that resulted from communism's downfall, a shift that probably will result in reducing the UN's irresponsibility. How much it is reduced depends on how the democracies act in the United Nations.

One of the major choices facing the United States and other democracies is about how much effort to make to improve the United Nations. The ending of the international order dominated by the conflict with communism requires that we rethink our approach to the United Nations. After the postcolonial expansion of the United Nations, and the dominance of the communist–Arab–Third World coalition that followed, the United States generally gave up hope of trying to influence the United Nations to become a responsible organization with integrity.

During the period that Jeane Kirkpatrick was U.S. ambassador to the United Nations, the United States did pay some attention to the character of the UN debate, but the concern was limited, and it largely ended when Kirkpatrick's tour ended. (Earlier Ambassador Daniel Patrick Moynihan had also expressed similar concerns during his time at the United Nations.) Our policy was not to worry about what the United Nations said, except on a few issues where we were able to get the votes we needed by trading and twisting arms. This was the only practical policy for us as long as there was a danger in the world that threatened us and that we had a responsibility to fight even if no one agreed with us. Now that this threat is gone, we have to decide what our future attitude to the United Nations will be.

Roughly, we have three choices. We can try to fix the United Nations and rely on it. Or we can not worry too much about the United Nations and rely on some new organization of democracies or on ad hoc groupings for each crisis. Or we can continue to rely on the United Nations as it is, and in each crisis do what we have to do to get the votes we need to handle the crisis as we think necessary.

This description of the actual alternatives is a reminder that the United Nations is not some independent decision maker that we can turn to for guidance. Nor is it a reflection of world opinion, or even of the opinion of governments. (Mostly governments say what is useful to say rather than give their real opinion. In fact they often do not have the time to develop a real opinion because they are busy figuring out what will be useful to say.) The United Nations is a forum where countries conduct a political process that produces resolutions. While the United States has only one vote in the General Assembly, and one of five essential votes in the Security Council, we have great potential ability to influence UN decisions.

A U.S. policy of "relying on the United Nations," while the United Nations is in its present condition, does not mean going to the United Nations as an independent source of guidance; it means committing ourselves to getting UN support before we do what we think is right. The United States has such a large ability to determine what the United Nations will do that as a practical matter it always has two decisions to make: What should be done? And how much effort should the United States make to get the necessary votes in the United Nations? To get those votes, the United States must decide how much it is willing to reward or pressure small nations. We saw the results of such suasion in the UN's response to the Iraqi invasion of Kuwait.

Of course, it is also true that the amount of effort needed to get UN agreement partly depends on the extent to which other countries share our views and values or can be convinced that they are correct. But it is always hard to tell whether a problem in getting votes is genuine disagreement or opportunistic bargaining. Why should a government admit that it agrees with us if, by pretending to disagree, it can, for example, get a promise of additional economic aid in return for changing its vote—or some additional jobs in the UN Secretariat, or an invitation to the White House, or whatever else it can extract for its vote?

Deciding to rely on the United Nations in its present condition only pretends to answer the question of whose judgment we will rely on in deciding whether to intervene altruistically in the zones of turmoil, because, as the United Nations now is, we often have the power to get whatever UN decision we want. UN support does not tell us that we are right or that a majority of anything agrees with us, it just tells us that we cared enough to buy the votes. Lack of UN support does not tell us that "world opinion" is against us, it just says that someone else cared more than we about winning that particular UN vote.

The idea of a binding caucus of democratic members of the United

Nations discussed in chapter 6 is a combination of two of our three alternatives. It is an effort to change the United Nations so that it would become an appropriate institution to rely on. And it would also create an alternative institution (the caucus itself, the UNDC) that we could also rely on until the United Nations had changed sufficiently.

Apart from an increase in the integrity of UN processes, the effect of weighted voting in the caucus would be to reduce the importance of votes that can be bought cheaply. The votes of the major powers that would have most of the weighted votes are so expensive to buy that the outcome of a weighted vote will represent a closer approximation of a genuine collective judgment by a group of nations. (This is a cynical way of expressing a more complex reality. Larger powers, such as Spain or Britain, are likely to participate realistically in an international decision-making process because they will be concerned about their reputations and relationships with the other major democracies. Therefore they will rarely be so unconcerned about broad international interests, and so impervious to argument on the merits, that they will deliver their vote to the highest bidder.)

Whatever happens at the United Nations, domestic politics is likely to lead the United States in the direction that we think it ought to go: avoiding unilateral decisions about intervening in the zones of turmoil. The real question will not be whether we "multilateralize" our policy but what kind of multilateral process we use; some are much better than others.

The decision about with whom the United States will make decisions about improving the international order in the zones of turmoil depends on what happens in Europe (and Japan) and what we do about the United Nations.

If Europe (and perhaps democratic Japan) are superpowers, we should act in the zones of turmoil on the basis of agreement with the other democratic superpowers, although we probably should implement our decision through the United Nations. If the United Nations becomes a responsible international organization that acts with integrity and is dominated by its democratic members, then we should probably intervene only on the basis of a genuine UNDC process as well as authority from the United Nations.

If there is neither a reformed United Nations nor one or two democratic superpowers with whom the United States can work, it will be much more difficult for the United States to intervene to improve the international order in the zones of turmoil. We believe that the best alternative for the United States in that event would be to make each decision on the basis of consultation with a small group of democracies—some combination of the largest democracies and those most connected to the particular conflict that needs to be dealt with (and not always the same group).

Our conclusion that U.S. policy will and ought to be multilateralized does not mean that the United States is freed from a unique leadership responsibility in the world. We are stuck with the need to do what we can to resist the temptations and character attrition that go with leadership. Our democracy is poorly adapted to our responsibility; we should not confuse the lack of a better alternative to our leadership with any great wisdom or charm on our part. But our qualities also provide some justification for U.S. leadership. (Our democracy is more a license than a justification. Other countries are as democratic as we; and democracy is in many ways a handicap to sound foreign policy.) Despite our spotty record the American people and government, more than those of most countries, have had a largeness and generosity of spirit, and a willingness to pay the price of shouldering responsibility, which are important qualifications for leadership. While isolationism has deep roots in our country, a global perspective is also a strong element of our tradition and current frame of mind. If one asks which of the great nations is most often likely to be a force for good in the world, it is hard to think of any which can be more counted on than the United States.

U.S. Leadership: Sooner and Later

Generally this book focuses on the way the world will be for most of the next generation or more, and its emphases would be different if we were to focus on the question of what we should do for the next few years. To take the most important example, it is clear that twenty years from now Europe will not feel that it needs U.S. troops there to protect them from Russia or from each other. We think it is also clear that U.S. military presence in Europe or U.S. presence in the internal councils of Europe based on our having forces there, will not still be necessary in twenty years to enable European countries to be more comfortable with each other or to hold the European Union together.

Similarly, even if it is true that Europe's failure to respond to Serbian aggression and "ethnic cleansing" demonstrates European democracies' unreadiness to take a responsible role in even their own corner of the world in 1995 and leaves the United States today with a unique responsibility to act to uphold the standards of civilization, it is hard to believe that twenty years from now the United States will still have to make up for the weakness of the other great democracies. In the long run, if at least some of the other great democracies are not going to be responsible actors in relation to the zones of turmoil, the zones of turmoil will have to get along without democratic intervention.

But these firm judgments about the future do not determine how we should act today. Strong expectations of U.S. leadership have been built over the last fifty years. It is only recently that the Soviet threat has been lifted from Europe—and the nuclear remnants of that threat still remain and Russia has not yet become as visibly weak as it will. The European countries' dependence on the United States for protection of their basic safety ended too recently for their politics and psychology to have fully adjusted to the current and future conditions. The realization that their countries' basic safety does not depend on a delicate balance of military power is only beginning to be felt. Therefore today we in the United States may have to act differently than we should in the future.

One of the major transitional issues is U.S. military presence in Europe. Today it is not needed for the defense of Europe, but it may well still be very useful for the political stability of Europe. Furthermore, Europe today may still rely on a kind of leadership from the United States that will not be appropriate twenty years from now—or perhaps even three years from now. And these two issues are partly—but not entirely—tied together.

The question of a possible need for U.S. leadership in the world may go beyond the transition period during which the great European democracies become used to their new position and Japan comes to think of itself as a responsible world power. Even after the transition has been completed, the United States will be a unique power. We will have two to four times the population, and a higher ratio of wealth and influence, compared to any other great democracy. They will be a group of more or less equals, we will be unique. Any one of them can duck an issue without dooming the world to lack of leadership. If we duck, it will be very hard to get consensus for action.

Our dilemma will be how to exercise leadership and at the same time follow a policy of intervening only with the agreement of the other great democracies. Although there is no formula that can reconcile the conflict between exerting leadership and genuinely taking into account the opinion of the other great democracies, the two actions are not incompatible. A key part of U.S. policy will lie in resolving the tension between these two approaches.

What makes the practical dilemma difficult is that leadership does not mean just putting forward a proposal. Every country has conflicting political currents. To exercise leadership the United States will have to put pressure on reluctant governments, thereby helping them to overcome the natural temptation to ignore problems. If we make only gentle suggestions other governments will have less basis for standing up to their internal opposition, and our pronouncements will be taken as mere posturing.

Despite these difficulties we share the view that, particularly during the current transition, but perhaps even when the current world order has become established, there may be an important need for the United States to take leadership responsibility in the world. However, we believe that our country is much more likely to be a useful and effective leader if it sharply limits the number of times in which it tries to act as the leader of the world. We need policies that enable other countries to make our leadership unnecessary. And we need to resist the temptation to exert leadership where it is not essential to do so.

A Willing but Careful Interventionist

We have devoted more space to the question of what the United States can do to prevent massive killing and other evil in the zones of turmoil than to any other issue. Objectively, this is one of the least important policy issues for the United States, but our experience is that it will be the issue our readers are most concerned about and the area that will get the most questions, especially from young people.

We are grateful for the luxury of needing to pay so much attention to the question whether the United States can be more than just a reluctant witness to a series of ugly dramas in the zones of turmoil. Our answer is that we cannot prevent all of them, but we do not always have to stand idly by; we can and should act to reduce or prevent some horrors.

Two classic lines of objection are made to our acting to prevent horrors in the zones of turmoil. The first is simply that the United States has no obligation to prevent Ruritanians from killing Zampetans or themselves, and therefore American lives and tax money should not be used to do so. This is a reasonable argument, but despite our respect for honest selfishness, we do not accept it.

The second objection is that if the United States follows an interventionist policy, on balance our intervention will do more harm than good to those we are trying to help. The power to reduce the horror is also the power to increase it. Good intentions will not be enough to ensure that interventions will have good effects.

The argument that U.S. intervention will do more harm than good is made by two groups of thinkers. One group rejects the premise that the United States can be a force for good in the world, arguing that the United States will inevitably cause harm because it is concerned only with expanding its power and increasing its wealth, because U.S. policy is controlled by rich white men who are racist, or by ideological imperialists representing business interests and the military-industrial complex. Although we have many criticisms of U.S. policy, we absolutely reject any such position.

The other group argues that, although American motivation is usually benign, there are two other reasons why our intervention will often be harmful, and therefore we should usually refrain from intervening. First, it is difficult for even a well-motivated democracy to know how to intervene to do more good than harm. The conflicts are always more complicated than they seem from a distance, and democratic politics are not designed for making sophisticated decisions about what will improve things in a foreign country. Democracy's great strength is the way it integrates the competing interests and views of its own citizens about their own lives.

Second, some of the harm that we might prevent by intervening may be necessary to enable the countries involved to learn how to make the changes they need to make. Political development, and the hardest part of economic development, are things that countries have to learn by themselves from experience. Just as individuals grow up and learn by making mistakes, and outsiders find it hard to understand and find effective ways to encourage development, so countries may have to pay a large tuition of suffering to learn the difficult wisdom of democracy, mutual respect, and law.

Our conclusion is that the United States ought to be prepared to intervene in the zones of turmoil to protect democracy, preserve peace, defeat aggression, and prevent or stop governments from killing large numbers of their citizens—cautiously and on the basis of consultation with other democracies. The hard question of how to resist the tendency to try to fix things that we cannot fix must be answered case by case. There will be plenty of room for reasonable disagreement.

The provisions of our policy about supporting democracy or preventing genocide will have to be worked out as specific occasions arise. The definition of such policies is less important at this stage than the question of what procedures we should use to decide each case, how we should work with other nations to decide. The two principles we would follow are these: (1) to be patient and pay attention to the possibility of the indirect harm we can do by intervening; and (2) genuinely to counsel with other democracies when we seek agreement from whatever international group we have decided to rely on. We should not merely look for support but should let ourselves be influenced by other democracies' perceptions of what ought to be done.

CHAPTER 9

AMERICAN FOREIGN POLICY FOR THE REAL WORLD ORDER

Seeing tragedy in so many places in the zones of turmoil, it is easy to think that the whole world is a mess. But that conclusion misses the profound good news that for the first time in history a major part of the world, which contains nearly all the great powers, faces no danger of military conquest or destruction. The zones of peace and democracy are something new in the world: great powers that do not have to organize into competing political-military power blocs to protect themselves and whose relationship with each other does not depend on their relative military strength.

The nations of the zones of peace continue to face national security threats and still need to maintain high-quality armed forces. But when we make the critical distinction between ordinary troubles and life-or-death threats to the nation, we can see the decisive change in the zones of peace. Focusing on current problems means overlooking the fact that for the first time in history these nations are no longer facing any military threats to their survival—one "small" change that makes all the difference.

Most of the tragic history of the last two centuries concerned wars among England, France, Germany, Italy, Japan, and the United States. Now these countries will have no concern about the possibility of a war with each other. They will not be divided into competing military alliances. Their actions in the rest of the world will not be shadowed by fear that the balance of power will change against them.

The current world order begins with only 15 percent of the world's population in zones of peace and democracy, but because these zones—in which we live—have most of the world's wealth and power, their demonstration that democracy is possible, and that it goes with wealth and peace, will have a radiating influence throughout the world. The good news about the current world order does not end with the zones of peace and democracy. While Americans have the power to prevent only some of the violence and suffering as the rest of the world goes through the kinds of tragedy that we went through before we achieved wealth and democracy and peace, the future of the zones of turmoil is not at all hopeless.

Stepping back from a snapshot of the world's ills at this moment to look with the perspective of generations makes it clear that a powerful process is under way that is transforming human life all over the world. After 40,000 years of human history, only two centuries ago we began to learn how to steadily increase the productivity of work. The result, to repeat, will be that by the end of the next century most people will live long enough to know their grandchildren, will have at least a high school education, will work with their minds or their fingers, and will have moved from the restrictions of traditional villages to the challenges of modern cities.

The immense pain and difficulty of the part of this transformation that still lies ahead should not blind us to the realization that the question is not "Whether?" but "How fast?" In the not too distant future the world's biggest problems will have changed from the problems of poverty, faced throughout human history, to the new problems of wealth—which may be an even greater challenge.

For the United States there is a special excitement to a vision of this world order because democracy will be at the center. Not that democracy will come quickly or be free from bad news in the years ahead. But it is not just chance that there has never been a war between two democracies (except civil war). Democracy is a main reason why the zones of peace will not see war. And as the zones of democracy expand, the area of peace will expand. While each nation has to learn to make itself democratic in its own way, with our example as well as our efforts we can help to make this learning process go at least a little more quickly.

Fashionable Pessimism

The current pessimism over international affairs stems in part from the feeling of being cast adrift, of losing the familiar signs and moorings of the cold war, and being caught in conflict between the cold-war training to take preventive action and the current world order's lack of a strategic imperative that gives coherence to policy thinking. The rest of the angst comes from too-exclusive focus on the zones of turmoil and development without the distinction that makes it possible to contrast these zones with the zones of peace. And it comes from not being able to reconcile the delight that U.S. power is adequate to assure our safety and the disappointment that that power is not enough to impose a more benevolent future on the rest of the world that so plainly seems to need it.

This common ambivalence is well reflected in an essay by a distinguished political scientist, Stanley Hoffmann of Harvard University. In referring to the "depressed mood"[1] that he perceived after the Persian Gulf war, Hoffmann writes that "the problem of order has become even more complex than before."[2] (The word "complex," of course, is supposed to convey foreboding, although complexity is not necessarily the enemy of the good or even of the predictable; it is only the enemy of those who live for simple analysis.) The main reason why "the problem of order" so worries Hoffmann is that he sets very high standards for order—standards never attained in human history. "A policy of world order would require that the many sources of global or regional turbulences be dealt with in ways that would minimize violent conflict among states, reduce injustice among and within states, and prevent dangerous violations of rights within them."[3] Hoffmann's conclusion that "the obstacles to such a policy are formidable"[4] may be the mother of all understatements.

Of course he is right—in most of the world, traditional evils have not come to an end; we have no way of making the whole world orderly. But who could think otherwise? This is not news. The news is that in a fraction of the world—our fraction, the fraction that includes almost all the great powers—these problems no longer appear. Further news is that the feature of the world that produced the most harm in the past—great-power totalitarianism—looks as if it may be gone for some time (except in China, where it is a good bet not to last another generation). The other news is that while we do not have in hand the means to solve problems that have never been solved before, processes are under way that have a fair prospect of removing these historic evils, if we have the patience to wait another century or so.

But Hoffmann does not give us this news. Correctly seeing traditional troubles in most of the world, Hoffmann does not note that there is a part of the world from which these troubles seem to have been eliminated. Correctly seeing great evils, Hoffmann does not note that much greater evils have recently disappeared. Correctly seeing the absence of planned solutions to problems, Hoffmann does not note unplanned processes that can gradually end the problems. The result is that someone so informed and thoughtful lets the stale bad news prevent him from seeing the fresh good news.

Bringing Realism Up to Date

There are more serious reactions to the end of the cold war, which do not come from low-morale pessimism, but which also fail to recognize how fundamentally things have changed. Eugene Rostow, one of the wisest and most experienced diplomats of our time, and our estimable colleague at the Hudson Institute, William Odom, are good examples of that school of thought, which might be called traditional prudent internationalist.[5]

We call the group "traditional" because they continue to see the whole world in terms of more or less traditional balance-of-power considerations —not distinguishing between the zones of peace and the zones of turmoil. They give relatively scant attention to the distinction between democracies and nondemocracies. They merge questions of economic rivalries and conflict with the pattern of military alliances and power balances. They are inclined to think that our allies' transition from dependence on the United States in the cold war to traditional independence and self-responsibility should be very gradual. They assume that the U.S. military will continue to need to be ready to fight a modern great power through the next generation.

We share the attitudes underlying these views. We too believe in caution and skepticism about alleged changes in the way nations deal with one another. We also would emphasize the need for prudence and reassurance, as well as a very long view, where national security is at stake, and would prefer to overspend rather than underspend on defense (but not too much). We too believe that important challenges can be dealt with only on the basis of real military capabilities. We too think that for idealism in foreign policy to be serious it must be based on a realistic understanding of how nations act. And, most important, we too reject isolationism; we share the view that the United States should be active in international affairs where our participation can protect our country or contribute to the well-being of the world, and that there is much we can do without becoming "the world's policeperson." But these shared attitudes do not lead us to the same conclusions.

Partly our difference with the traditional prudent internationalists is a matter of timing. We are focusing on the shape of international relations over the next generation; they are focusing on the next few years. Although much of our description of the world is already true, some of the factors we emphasize are still partly or entirely in the future or have not yet been fully taken into account in diplomatic and political understanding. Nevertheless, while some of our differences with the traditional prudent internationalists are more nuance than disagreement, we do have significant disagreement with what they have been writing so far.

First, we do not think that the traditionalists have fully absorbed how much of a change in the world will be made by the new reality of no war among the democratic great powers. Relations among these countries will not be determined by the need for military allies. Nor will they be concerned with the balance of military power among groups of democracies. Economic conflict among them will not have the character of national security conflict; it is likely to be much more a matter of bickering over a thousand details than confrontations of national power (although some non-military confrontations are likely).

These traditionalists disagree that democracy is important.[6] They do not believe that democracy is a basis for peace among the great powers (China and Russia temporarily excepted) or that the spread of democracy is a basic long-term hope for achieving general peace.[7]

In addition the traditionalists often fail to recognize how weak and unimportant Russia will become. They do not agree that Russia will be weak for so long that we cannot now base policy on the potential effects of a Russia that is as powerful as Germany. Therefore they argue that American foreign policy must be at least as active and expansive as it has been over the last half century; that is, that the world is about as dangerous to us as it had been. While we are willing to have an active foreign policy, we do not think that it can be justified by fear for our peace and safety, as it has in the past. This difference will affect a lot of things, and probably weaken our policy making for many years, but it must be faced.

We cannot base our commitment to an effective military on exaggerated threats. We must adapt to the political perception that our military forces are not essential to our country's life or independence and that the function of our military will be primarily to protect secondary interests, to discharge our responsibility to protect others, and to respond if the world changes or if it is more dangerous than we think.

Another difference between us and the traditionalists is that we are much more inclined to bet that things will turn out better when countries and regions are forced to work things out without much U.S. involvement. This is not because we are isolationist or because we think the United States is evil. It is because we put greater emphasis on countries' (and individuals') ability to rise to the occasion and to gain from having to take responsibility. Also since we emphasize the improbability of war among the great powers, we think that the price that may have to be paid for failure, if countries are forced to take responsibility for themselves when they may not be fully ready, will not be too high.

The prudent internationalists, like most analysts, do not pay much attention to the critical distinction between a threat that can harm a country or kill some of its citizens and a threat to a country's basic safety. A danger that a country could get into a major war to defend itself in which it could be defeated, or that because of military weakness it could lose its independence, is a threat to a country's basic safety. Such threats are qualitatively different from lesser threats to a country's safety or interests. This difference between basic safety and other threats to "national security" or national interests is so decisive that in the great democracies the feelings about military power and about relationships among themselves will be profoundly changed.

The final difference that we have with the traditional prudent internationalists is less clear-cut, but it may be fundamental. They do not accept the idea that the nature of modern productive economies, the sources and effects of modern wealth, have any fundamental influence on international relations. For example, Rostow says, "the glittering prospect of hegemony will be especially tempting in a world where political and geographic barriers to hegemony are no longer available"[8] (because of the power of long-range missiles). But hegemony is *not* economically attractive to a modern country, and to a modern democracy hegemony is not likely to be enough of a "glittering prospect" to justify war. (Of course, there may be other causes of war, even among modern countries.)

All these differences come together in disagreement about the basic thesis of this book, that the world is now divided into zones of peace and zones of turmoil and that the peace and safety of the great democracies does not depend on preventing war and anarchy in the zones of turmoil. Traditional prudent internationalists believe that peace is indivisible;[9] we disagree.

The dispute is not about what the United States should do about conflict in the zones of turmoil; it is about the justification for its action. We and the traditionalists disagree about whether the United States, and the other great democracies, *must* get involved in conflict in the zones of turmoil in order to protect our own nations—as we needed to resist Soviet communism and German fascism to protect ourselves. The question of the justification for our involvement is important for two reasons. First, it is the difference between getting public support for foreign policy by telling Americans that their country is in danger and by saying to them that the United States has a responsibility as leading citizen of the world. While the former is a stronger argument, we think it is untrue and therefore will backfire. The second argument is true and strong enough.

The other reason it matters that the great powers' safety is not affected by what happens in the zones of turmoil is that if it were affected, then disagreements among the democracies about conflict in the zones of turmoil might lead to dangerous conflict among the democracies in the zones of peace. The traditionalists argue that to preserve peace in our zone we need to preserve peace in the zones of turmoil. If they were correct, the zones would not really be separate. Peace would be indivisible, as it was in the past.

Our conclusion that peace in the zones of democracy is compatible with war in the zones of turmoil rests on our other differences with the traditional prudent internationalists. The modern democracies will not be organized in competing military power blocs. Modern economics has reduced the economic importance to the great democracies of the outcome of conflicts in the zones of turmoil. Our prosperity depends on our productivity, not on what happens in the zones of turmoil. So much of the world's money is in the zones of peace that it is not worth fighting over what is in the zones of turmoil, especially since we can produce our own wealth even if we do not get "our share" of their trade or investment. (And any dispute will involve only a fraction of the zones of turmoil, which will never all be organized to exclude any great democracy.) But the most fundamental point is the great reluctance of modern democracies to go to war with another democracy. The world has changed so that it is no longer true that "peace is indivisible." The fundamental safety of the zones of peace is not significantly threatened by war or anarchy in the zones of turmoil. (Of course, this does not imply that we should not be concerned about war or anarchy there.) The divisibility of peace is one of the fundamental advantages of the current world order.

Policy Suggestions Reviewed

Significant challenges lie ahead for American foreign policy, and we would like to end our book by reviewing some of the suggestions we have made. The first is not to forget the good news that we will achieve our essential foreign policy goals—the long-term protection of American freedom and peace—without doing anything, as long as the most powerful nations continue to be democracies. Therefore, foreign policy will not have the same kind of importance to the United States in the current world order as it has had in the past, unless an unexpected threat arises to democracy in the zones of peace.

The second suggestion concerns the main part of the foreign policy agenda, economic cooperation and conflict, primarily with Europe and Japan, our principal rivals, but also with the countries of the zones of turmoil. Our twin goals must be to try to keep international trade as open as possible and to protect ourselves against other countries' efforts to give their citizens special advantages at the expense of our citizens. These goals may last forever. If we want to do a good job on them, the key is not maximizing our power, it is organizing the different pieces of our government and political system so that we can choose and implement sensible negotiating tactics and strategies that reflect our genuine national and political interests. This is a daunting challenge to our domestic politics. It is much more likely that domestic politics and poor diplomacy will lead us to waste our national power than that we will not be powerful enough. If we do not bargain as well as we could, the result will be that more American businesses and workers will be hurt than necessary, and our economy will be slightly less prosperous.

Third, we suggest that the United States should participate with the other democracies in efforts to limit violence and encourage democracy in the zones of turmoil. This policy is not based on the protection of narrow U.S. national interests, and it does not involve any political or military strategy. As leading democratic citizens in the world, we have an obligation to join with other leading citizens to try to make the world a little more civilized. The United States should provide practical support to the principles of limiting aggression, war, and mass murder. While currently we are the only political-military superpower, rather than just one of the leading powers, the policy recommended here is not based on our unique position. In fact, it would be easier for us to discharge our citizenship obligations if there were one or two other superpowers we could work with as essential equals.

The United States should be in favor of a decision by the European nations to act together as a single political-military superpower in relations with the zones of turmoil, and we should accept Europe as an equal superpower and not try to be ahead of Europe or to have any preferred position. And the United States and Europe should stand ready to accept Japan as a third equal superpower if Japan decides that it wants the responsibilities of that role; and we should not require that Japan increase its military forces to be accepted as an equal. If Europe, or Europe and Japan, decide to act as democratic superpowers, then we should be prepared to intervene with force against violence in the zones of turmoil only by agreement with these other democratic superpower(s).

Two problems about intervention in the zones of turmoil are "too much" and "too little." "Too little" can be a failure of responsibility and cause us to feel guilty, leave the world a worse place in which to live, and make it harder to achieve our principles in the future. But failure to intervene will not endanger us or jeopardize our national safety. One of the major challenges we face is that it will be so easy to do too little. And in every case where we are needed there will be reasons not to intervene—cost and danger, the difficulty of reaching international agreement, domestic political objections, and so forth.

Unfortunately we cannot make sure to intervene when we should by becoming enthusiastic interventionists because it is as easy to intervene too much as too little. Intervention can cost too many American lives and dollars and lead to too much entanglement for the good that it does. When stepping into ancient quarrels, it is easy to do more harm than good. Intervention can fail in a way that makes it harder to intervene later when there is more need to do so. We propose to protect against too much intervention by a policy of only using force on the basis of a joint decision by the major democracies—perhaps implemented through NATO or the United Nations.

The question of how we decide to intervene—which countries and institutions we will rely on—will be more important than guidelines about when to intervene. Since each case will be as complex and controversial as our recent experiences in Iraq, Somalia, and Cambodia, it will be hard to know what to do even if we agree about principles and guidelines. As a practical matter, *who decides* will be more important than what the rule is. So the heart of our policy about intervention will be a long-term effort to construct institutions and practices for making decisions with other democracies. (In other words, our view about what should be done in Rwanda, et cetera, is not very important because we think the main thing is to make the decision with the other leading democracies. What we should do depends on what there is agreement about.) The other part of our policy will be gradually building up an international set of principles about when to intervene based on experience.

If Europe or Japan or both become political-military superpowers, we should make our decisions by agreement with the one or two other democratic superpowers—the results of which can be expressed through the United Nations. We should not seek judgment or moral authority from the United Nations as it currently operates (although we may operate under its auspices). But we should attempt to build the integrity of the United Nations, and to increase the influence in it of the experience and values of the major democracies. If we succeed, we can use the United Nations as the institution whose decision will determine when to intervene.

Our policy about the use of force should be reliable and predictable: "never" without international agreement, "always" when the great democracies decide that it is necessary. And we should use our vote and voice to try to influence the great democracies not to make threats or demands that we and they are not ready to back up with all the force needed. The worst evils will come from people like Saddam Hussein and Slobodan Milosevic, who will only stop if forced to or if they are convinced that decisive force will be used against them.

Unless we are able to be serious about our foreign policy, the practical result is likely to be that the press will determine when there will be intervention. When the public in the great democracies has a steady diet of pictures of victims, the democratic political systems will be moved to find agreement about how to intervene. When evils are not easily visible, and when the press is not interested or cannot get pictures (as of the slaughter of Black Muslims in Mauritania or Black Christians in Sudan), the democracies will only be able to overcome the difficulties of reaching agreement to take action with strong leadership. We would hope for a better system, one that permits less "selective morality," but we doubt that it can be produced soon.

We suggest that our overall goal should be the advance of stable democracy so that the zones of peace will be extended as soon as possible. We propose that the United States should pursue this goal in five ways: by making a clear distinction in our policy between democracies and nondemocracies; by minimizing trade barriers; by providing economic aid and advice; by providing an example and a market; and by working with other democracies to preserve peace and improve the international order, even if military intervention is required. But we should not have a policy of forcing democracy on authoritarian countries.

Undoubtedly our greatest contribution to the world comes from our example and the openness of our markets. And we have plenty to do to improve on both of these. Just as we serve ourselves as well as the world when we reduce barriers to international trade, when we act to improve relations among races and groups, or to relieve poverty and injustice at home, we will be serving the world as well as ourselves.

One major idea for implementing our support for the spread of democracy is to make the distinction between democracies and nondemocracies central to our foreign policy. For example, while we should give great respect to the interests and views of all countries involved in any conflict, whether or not they are democracies, the major democracies are the only countries we should pay attention to in connection with all conflicts, wherever they are. Another way to make the distinction between democracies and nondemocracies important would be for the democracies to agree with one another not to sell the most advanced military equipment to nondemocracies (as discussed in chapter 7).

The heart of American policy to reduce violence in the zones of turmoil should be a long-term systematic effort to improve and support international institutions, including not only the United Nations but also informal institutions. We should support the United Nations because it is the only organization that represents all our global neighbors. We did not choose our neighbors, but we have to live with whoever is on this planet; and we want to live together as peacefully and cooperatively as we can. As the original democracy and the richest country, we have a special responsibility to encourage and support our community institution, the United Nations. But this does not mean ignoring its defects and limitations.

While the United Nations is the institution that embodies the world community's effort to act like a community, to preserve peace, and to solve problems together, neither we nor anyone else has chosen to make the United Nations our government. Our government is the United States; the world as a whole has no government. Whether or not that is a bad thing, we cannot act as if the United Nations were the world's government today. Our neighbors are too different from us for us to be ready to join a common government with them. Most of them are not democracies. Nor do they all share our basic moral values or the essential elements of our culture. They are organized into sovereignties, some of which have only a thousandth as many citizens as the United States does, some of which have more than four times as many. And in the United Nations each of these sovereignties has exactly one vote (except in the Security Council).

It is not clear whether it would be possible to make a world government or whether on balance it would be a good idea; or, if so, how it could be done in current conditions. In the meantime, we need to support the United Nations and help make it more effective. We should even be willing to sacrifice some of our immediate national interest for the welfare of the United Nations, but we should not defer to the United Nations as we would to a world government.

Furthermore, while the United Nations as the organization of the world community should be accorded significant moral authority, we need to think clearly about just how much moral authority we should give it. There are three reasons why we should not accept the United Nations as it is today as our principal external moral compass or our highest moral authority: the quality of behavior of the United Nations and of its members, the fact that about half of the members are not democracies, and the lack of weighted voting.

Until the United Nations has improved further, the highest external moral authority for the United States is the other great democracies. Although there is no institution that expresses this moral authority, a formal institution is not necessary and may not have more advantages than disadvantages. When we seek external moral authority in order to make our decisions about whether to intervene with force in the zones of turmoil, we can counsel with the five other great democracies (and perhaps another four to seven major democracies[10]) through normal diplomatic channels or through special meetings.

The governments of the leading democracies, like our government, speak with the moral authority of having been democratically chosen by the citizens of a large country whose citizens share many experiences, interests, and values with us. Since the people of these countries have many basic values in common with us and are in more or less the same kind of a position as we are, and have the same responsibility and kind of experience as we do, why should their opinions not be as valid as ours? Who better can we go to to check our own judgments? Why should we commit ourselves to defer to the preferences of governments that were not democratically chosen? What moral authority do they have? Why should we defer to democratic governments that do not have serious experience in the world, whose countries have not been able to organize themselves productively for a long enough time—or are too small—to have acquired substantial influence in the world? If we agree with the five or nine democratic countries that together with us represent 600 million or 700 million people, why would we need to check with the many smaller democracies which together have fewer than another 100 million people? (The question of whether we also need agreement from Brazil and India, and perhaps a few other large but less democratic counties, raises other issues.)

The United States will need to have a substantial military force that is capable of fighting effectively. Therefore we will have to make creative efforts to find a political basis for maintaining an effective military force. This force should be ready and capable of using our technological and social advantages to defeat much larger second-class military forces in the zones of turmoil. We also need to spend perhaps $5 to $8 billion a year for active defenses against potential missile attacks against our cities, especially missiles armed with chemical or nuclear warheads. Our missile-defense system should also make it possible, or at least make it easier, to provide defense against missile attacks on cities besides our own.

The United States needs to increase its efforts to prevent Soviet-built nuclear weapons from getting to countries and groups that do not have nuclear weapons. Also, if there is an opportunity to put the nuclear genie back in the bottle (or at least a big part of him), we should pursue it and not think that our freedom to use our own nuclear weapons is more important to us than a chance to reduce the future role of nuclear weapons in world affairs. (We should avoid deriving positive benefits from our nuclear weapons, even if it is possible to achieve such benefits.)

We should increase the share of our GNP we spend on helping people and countries outside the United States back toward the 1 percent level we used thirty years ago, taking care not to let our foreign aid harm the countries to whom we give it and not to waste the money, as discussed in chapter 7.

The American government should tell itself and its people that it is not a miracle maker, that intervention does harm as well as good, that it must be circumspect, in part by multilateralizing much of its participation in the zones of turmoil. At the same time, the United States should seek to reward those nations that respect the rule of law and that make sound efforts to improve the condition of their people.

The Implications of Optimism

Our picture of the future has emphasized the spread of wealth, democracy, and peace, which we think have a good chance to cover most of the people of the world by the end of the next century. This does not mean that we see the world becoming free from problems. Wealth, democracy, and peace can be seen as the base from which people can begin working on the permanent problems of making life better. Wealth provides the resources needed to live a human life. Democracy provides freedom from tyranny and a setting that allows everybody to participate in community decisions, and thus to preserve peace. Peace provides freedom from war and from the vast diversion of human effort and emotion required by military preparations.

Wealth, peace, and democracy eliminate what have been the biggest killers: poverty, disease, war, and government murder. With these interferences with human life out of the way, most people will be able to focus on fundamental human problems and die of old age after living the full human life span.

But we are not there yet. Most of the world is not yet wealthy, democratic, or peaceful. How fast the rest of the world joins the zones of peace and democracy depends primarily on the people in the zones of turmoil, but our help can make a difference.

Our optimistic conclusion that the modern democracies have worked their way onto a better course does not tell us that we should pat ourselves on the back and be disdainful of those who have not yet learned about democracy and markets; it obliges the democracies to help others find their own right course.

The view of the world that is most truthful and most useful is to see the democracies' responsibility for improving the world as coming not from guilt and the need to mend our ways, nor from fear for our safety, but from our success and our painfully acquired virtue, and to see our task as long and difficult but with good prospects for ultimate success if we proceed prudently.

The United States must be engaged in the effort to improve the international order in the zones of turmoil, partly for our own sake. We accept Judge Learned Hand's argument:

Even in our own interest we must have an eye to the interests of others; a nation which lives only to itself will in the end perish; false to the faith, it will shrivel and pass to that oblivion which is its proper receptacle. We may not stop until we have done our part to fashion a world in which there shall be some share of fellowship; which shall be better than a den of thieves.[11]

But it would be a terrible crime if, to satisfy our own psychological needs, we meddle in ways that make things worse. As Judge Hand continued,

Let us not disguise the difficulties; and, above all, let us not content ourselves with noble aspirations, counsels of perfection, and self-righteous advice to others. We shall need the wisdom of the serpent; we shall have to be content with short steps; we shall be obliged to give and take; we shall face the strongest passions of mankind—our own not the least; and in the end we shall have fabricated an imperfect instrument.[12]

Notes

1. Stanley Hoffmann, "Delusions of World Order," *New York Review of Books,* 9 April 1992, 42.

2. Ibid., 37.

3. Ibid.

4. Ibid.

5. William E. Odom, *Trial After Triumph; East Asia After the Cold War* (Indianapolis, Ind.: Hudson Institute, 1992); Eugene Rostow, "United States Foreign Policy after the Soviet Collapse," *SAIS Review,* Spring 1992.

6. Eugene Rostow does not mention democracy in "United States Foreign Policy after the Soviet Collapse" (see note 5 above). He speaks of "great powers," of "allies," of "the Western world," of "the integrated capitalist economy and polity" which is the "finest achievement of Allied foreign policy since World War II." He does speak of "aspirants for dominion," but implicitly he assumes that such threats to peace may be either democracies or authoritarian regimes.

7. Rostow argues that the first principle of American national security policy should be to prevent Russia and Eastern Europe combining with the European Union because it is against America's interest now, as it was in Jefferson's time, for all Europe to be "united under one monarch." We believe that the European Union cannot be a threat to American national security because its members are democracies. An organization of democracies cannot be "under one monarch," and we believe that difference is crucial. If the members of the EU ever cease to be democracies, there will be threats to our security—regardless of whether Russia and Eastern Europe are attached to the EU. We should be concerned about the fall of democracy, not about a link between Eastern and Western Europe. Ibid.

8. Ibid.

9. Eugene V. Rostow, *Toward Managed Peace* (New Haven: Yale University Press, 1993), 364.

10. The major democracies are Spain, Canada, Australia, and the Netherlands, possibly India and Brazil, and possibly Belgium, which has two-thirds the population of the Netherlands. Others are some combination of smaller, less democratic, or less advanced.

11. "I Am an American" Day address, Central Park, New York, 20 May 1945, in *The Spirit of Liberty, Papers and Addresses of Learned Hand,* edited by Irving Dilliard (New York: Knopf, 1952; Vintage Books edition 1969).

12. Ibid.

INDEX

Adolescence, national, 157–58
Afghanistan, 181
Africa, 44, 70
Agency for International Development (AID), 159
Air force: vs. army at rest, 44; in zones of turmoil, 43–44
Airline safety, 118
Air superiority, 43–44
Albania, 173
Algeria, 149
Allies, defined, 164
Altruism, 149; vs. self-interest, 155–56
Anarchy: as dangerous, 117; international, 117
Antipodes, 35
Arabs, vs. Israel, 72
Area, defined, 35
Argentina, 70
Armored force: capability of first-rate, 42; qualifications of good, 42–43
Army: appraisal of various countries', 43–44, 44–46; peacetime, for U.S., 182–85
Asia, antagonism of, to West, 150–51
Asian Nuclear Force, 78
Authoritarian governments: Islam and, 54; politics of, 22; resurgence of, in zones of turmoil, 39–40; and use of democratic forms, 58–59

Balkan states: confederation of, 173; U.S. and, 147
Banking system, need for, in Russia, 92
Barbados, 110
Barter, 92
Belarus, 97; elimination of nuclear

force of, 77; nuclear weapons of, 75, 76, 101; and Russia, 84, 85, 97
Belgium: vs. France, 30; separatism in, 26
Bluffing, 179
Bosnia, 167, 171, 181
Brazil: army of, 44; nuclear program of, 70
Brilliant Pebbles defense, 68
Britain, and two Europes approach, 123, 125–26. *See also* England; Great Britain; United Kingdom
Brown, Harold, 67
Brussels efforts, 124, 125, 126
Bulgaria, 173
Bureaucrats, need for productive work from Russian, 89
Burma: as nondemocracy, 164; and nuclear weapons, 71
Bush, George, 145

Cambodia: intervention in, 190–91; violence in, 181
Capital: growth of real, 51; and increased production, 50–51; "soft" increases in, 51
Central Intelligence Agency, 98
Change, as goal for zones of turmoil, 146
China and Chinese: air force of, 44; army of, 44, 45; communism in, 57; elimination of nuclear weapons of, 76; in Korea, 43; as nondemocracy, 164; nuclear capability of, 63, 70, 76; relations of with U.S., 76–78; vs. Russia's nuclear weapons, 75; in South Korea, 40

217